MOYLIS

Successful Contract Negotiation

Successful Contract Negotiation

Tim Boyce

Published by Hawksmere Ltd
12–18 Grosvenor Gardens
London SW1W 0DH
Tel: 071-824 8257

A CIP catalogue record for this book is available from the British Library.

ISBN 1 85418 021 5

Design and production in association with
Book Production Consultants, Cambridge

Typeset by KeyStar, St Ives, Cambs

Printed by The Alden Press, Oxford

This book is dedicated to my mother.

About the author

Tim Boyce is Commercial Manager at a major electronics company. He is a member of the Chartered Institute of Purchasing and Supply and a member of the Institute's National Contract Management Committee. He studied electrical and electronic engineering at London University before joining the Procurement Executive of the Ministry of Defence in 1974. The majority of his six years with MOD were spent in contracts and contracts policy branches.

Since 1980 he has held a number of positions within the aerospace and electronics industry and has been responsible for the negotiation and administration of many multi-million pound contracts and subcontracts. These responsibilities continue in his present position.

Since 1986 he has also been a regular and acclaimed speaker at a number of Hawksmere seminars both in the UK and overseas. His published works include books published by Hawksmere *The Commercial Engineer* and *Successful Contract Administration*, and he is also a joint author of *Government Procurement and Contracts*. He has appeared in the Sunday Times Business Skills video series.

Contents

Foreword

Why write a book about contract negotiation?

The answer is in two parts. First, while there are several good books available on the general topic of negotiation skills, the specific subject of negotiation of a business contract is one that warrants special examination. After all, many billions of pounds of trade in goods is carried on each year between tens of thousands of companies. Such trade is enacted through countless numbers of commercial contracts – is it then not apposite that the activity of negotiating those contracts should be subject to detailed analysis? Second, many works concentrate mainly upon the negotiation meeting, to the exclusion of an examination of the many important events that precede and succeed the meeting. At the heart of successful contract negotiation is the need for good customer/supplier relationships to be fostered and maintained. This cannot be achieved unless proper regard is paid to the whole process rather than just to the meeting.

In focusing on contract negotiation, this book aims to provide guidance in both depth and breadth.

For drafting ease the book refers to the negotiator in the masculine. However, experience shows that men and women are equally competent in the role.

CHAPTER 1

Introduction

Books on negotiation generally have five main limitations.

First, they tend to focus on the eyeball-to-eyeball negotiation meeting, during which the negotiator is supposed to utilise the 243 techniques and tricks which are recommended in the book as the guarantee to overpowering the opposition intellectually. Undoubtedly such techniques and tricks do work and I would not wish to denigrate for a second the benefit of carrying a mental armoury of devices for defeating the other side. It is my experience over twenty years that the negotiator so equipped is likely to have a real advantage over the 'amateur'. However, in these twenty years it has struck me that too often the negotiation is seen as the start of a process which will lead to a conclusion – whether successfully or not – and a resolution of whatever was the issue that precipitated the need for the negotiation. This seems to me to be fundamentally wrong. I see the negotiation not as a start but as the end of a process, or at least as the beginning of the end of a process.

The need for a negotiation comes as a result of a series of events which may have lasted weeks, months or even years. Therefore it is necessary to be aware that day-to-day activities and events may lead to a negotiation and therefore the intention is to manipulate and plan events so that when the time to negotiate arrives, there are no surprises and a platform has been built from which to launch a successful negotiation. And so the first limitation is exposed. That is, the emphasis on the meeting itself is at the expense of treating all prior events (together with the meeting) as a whole process.

The second limitation is similar in character to the first. Other works tend to concentrate on the handling of the meeting, as though the reader is being invited to peer down a microscope to examine in detail the activity of the negotiators on either side as they battle out their arguments across the proverbial table. In practice each negotiator is carrying out his task within a framework established by his company. He may have unlimited authority, he may have some flexibility or he may have been told to charge in the manner of the Light Brigade into an impossible situation with no room to manoeuvre. He may be an ace negotiator or he may be thrown in at the deep end. His corporate organisation may be geared to negotiation or it may not. Before he ever gets to the negotiating table his biggest hurdle may have been to negotiate his boss's agreement to his negotiation plan for tackling the opposition! Inevitably, then, the negotiation is to be carried out within the confines of internal organisational and political constraints. It seems to me wrong to ignore this aspect if the subject of contract negotiation is to be analysed thoroughly.

A successful negotiation is only really successful if events succeeding the negotiation represent the implementation of the parties' agreement in such a way that each party realises the benefit he intended to get from that agreement. In this can be seen the third limitation in conventional books on negotiation. Looking at the negotiation without looking at its consequences, and without looking at implementation of the agreement, is like choosing from the restaurant menu and then not bothering to stay for the meal.

My fourth criticism of much teaching and written material on negotiating is that it is written for purchasing managers and their buyers. There is of course nothing wrong with that in itself. However, there is room for a work which considers negotiation from the seller's perspective, and while advice can be gleaned by both buyer and seller from any book on negotiation, the emphasis here will be towards the seller. The text addresses itself to the 'contract negotiator' who is employed by a company to negotiate contracts with customers. Where organisational and other general matters are discussed the text addresses itself to the 'company'. Generally the text refers to the company and its customers, although where the context admits, the terminology is seller and buyer.

My final criticism is that other books cover the process and not the content of negotiation. This book aims to do both. While it would be impossible to cover the content of a specific negotiation, the field of contract negotiation can be sufficiently bounded so as to permit analysis of the content as well as the process.

In summary, the intention is to examine the negotiation of a contract from both a broad and a deep perspective rather than just from the angle of the meeting itself. The meeting is covered as well, together with the tricks of the trade.

Before moving on there are just two further introductory comments which I should make. In the opening paragraphs of this chapter I referred to the 'opposition' and the 'other side'. In some people's minds these expressions imply an adversarial and aggressive attitude which can be seen as unhelpful in dealing with customers with whom there may be, or may potentially be, a long-term relationship. It is valid to remind ourselves of the positive attitude expressed in the 'win-win' concept but nevertheless it is my experience that when one meets the party with whom the negotiation will be conducted, human nature forces us into this adversarial posture. In my view, without this element of competitiveness there will be a reduced probability of success and certainly little fun. The objective should be to allow this natural reaction but to control and manage it positively. Suffice it to say that I refrained from referring to the opposition as the 'enemy'!

The *Oxford English Dictionary* defines negotiation as 'confer with a view to compromise'. This is an unhappy definition in so far as it smacks of the English disease of compromise. It is true that any negotiator must set out with the aim of winning everything, conceding nothing and still leave the opposition feeling good about it but, while this ideal is sometimes achievable, realism tells us that in the majority of cases an agreement will require some give and some take. With this in mind I can live with the *OED* definition.

The ultimate aim of this book is to deal with contract negotiation in a comprehensive way. Because it has been written from my twenty years of personal experience I have allowed myself to use the first person in this introductory chapter. As a good 'contracts man' I shall henceforth refrain and use the impersonal form.

CHAPTER 2

Legal foundation for negotiation

1 Introduction

In this book the emphasis is very much upon the word 'negotiation'. The word 'contract' is used to set the scene. Many would say that all negotiations are the same, that there is no difference between negotiations for a contract, negotiations over a trade union dispute or negotiations to release hostages. While some of the techniques are common, particularly those at the fundamental level of human interaction, contract negotiation within the genus is nevertheless a specialist field of negotiation.

It is assumed that the reader has a reasonable understanding of the law of contract including the rules of proper formation and the duties of the parties.[1] This being the case, the reader will have an appreciation of the legal depth and complexity of matters contractual. However, the events leading up to the formation of a contract are also influenced by the law.

It is stressed that this work is aimed at business people negotiating commercial contracts. It is not intended to assist the consumer in negotiating contracts with retailers or other forms of consumer transactions.

2 Freedom to negotiate

The first tenet to state is that commercial parties have complete freedom to negotiate their contracts. Provided that the results

[1] If not, the following are recommended: *Contract Law* by Ewan McKendrick (Macmillan, 1990), and *An Introduction to Contract Law* by P S Atiyah (Oxford University Press, 1989).

satisfy the rules of law relating to contract, the parties are free to make whatever agreement they care to choose. This outrageous simplification requires some explanation. Broadly, the rules of contract law and related legal doctrine are very extensive, and the intention in referring to the rules of law is to capture everything from proper formation to anti-competitive practices. With the net cast thus wide, principles such as misrepresentation are automatically caught, and to the extent that these are exceptions to the broad simplification given above, then they are given attention in this chapter.

The point is that there is no law of negotiation. No rules exist 'per se' to describe how the process of negotiation is to be conducted. The law proscribes coercion and (under the Unfair Contract Terms Act) various so-called exclusion clauses, and anti-trust law seeks to prevent commercial arrangements which are intended to operate against the public interest. The contract negotiator needs to be aware of these restrictions. Thus the freedom of the parties to negotiate is not absolute, but nevertheless such restrictions do not go as far as fixing a framework for negotiation nor do they say that each party is not at liberty to use its bargaining power and negotiation strength to its best advantage.

3 Agreement of the parties

The overriding objective of negotiation is to reach an agreement. In contract negotiation the aim is to arrive at an agreed contract. Although the rules of offer and acceptance are relatively accessible it is frequently the case in commercial dealings that there is never a point at which a clear offer can be seen to be followed by a clear, communicated and unqualified acceptance.

Although Lord Denning made attempts (see McKendrick) to improve the sometimes unsatisfactory nature of this rule, the law continues to expect the clinicalness of a simple offer and acceptance. Indeed the classic so-called 'battle of the forms' principle established in *Butler* v. *Ex-Cell-O Corporation (England) Ltd* [1979] shows the absurdity of a rule which in theory requires a complete offer and acceptance before a contract can be formed, but in practice can allow something so commercially important as the contract conditions to be determined by events as they transpired.

To reiterate, this is not the place for an examination of the complexities of contract law. The intention is to provide practical guidance for the contract negotiator. So how can anyone be certain that agreement has been reached in sufficient substance for the purposes of the law? Let it first be assumed that, as negotiations proceed and the parties have a common understanding and intent with regard to their agreements, then the test is as it was stated in 1871 in the judgment of *Smith* v. *Hughes* LR6 QB 597:

> If, whatever a man's real intention may be, he so conducts himself that a reasonable man would believe that he was assenting to the terms proposed by the other party, and that other party upon that belief enters into the contract with him, the man thus conducting himself would be equally bound as if he had intended to agree to the other party's terms.

Thus the test is ostensibly an objective one but depends upon the notorious and fictitious 'reasonable man'. Ideally such an independent test should be unnecessary as the parties' perceptions of the progress towards a complete agreement should converge at the same rate (Figure 2.1).

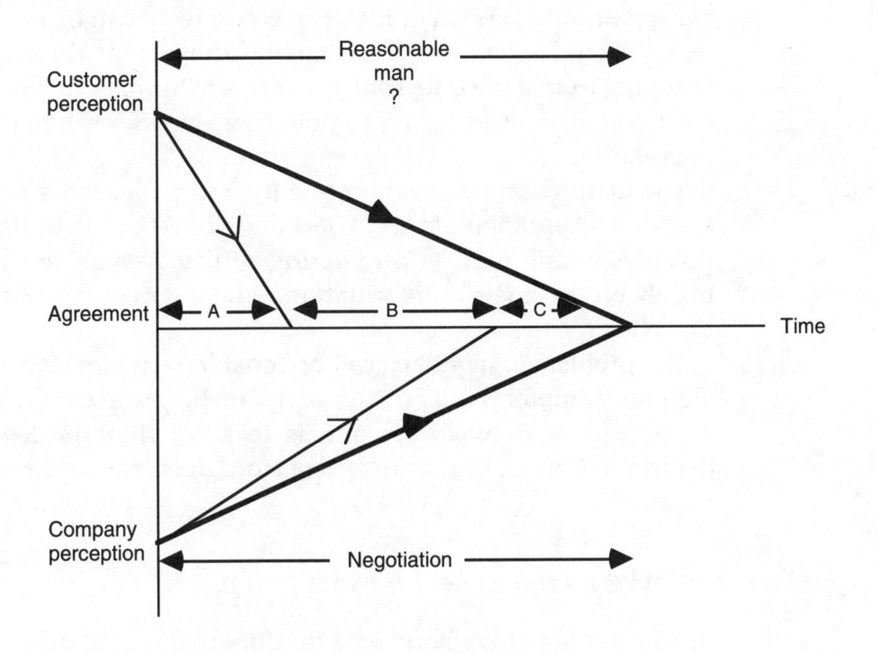

Figure 2.1: Converging perceptions of agreement

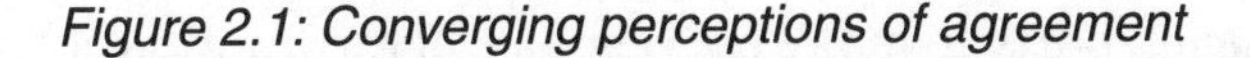

In Figure 2.1 the bold lines show the theoretical convergence of the parties' perceptions, reaching a firm agreement at the end of the negotiation. In practice there is often misunderstanding and each party can at various times wrongly believe (as shown by the thinner lines) that agreement has been reached on a particular point. In phase A neither side believes there is an agreement. At the start of phase B the customer thinks an agreement has been made. The error is realised and the negotiation continues until the company thinks agreement has been reached. This too is an error and once it is realised, the negotiation continues in phase C until eventually a proper agreement is made. If such errors are not realised, at what point could the reasonable man say fairly that agreement has been reached?

In fact, case law provides for more than just the objective test of the detached, reasonable man in assessing whether or not an agreement has been reached. It is possible that a decision could be made on the basis of the reasonable man's independent view of how a reasonable man would have interpreted an offer from the offeree's viewpoint. Finally, but less preferred, is the basis of the reasonable man's interpretation of an offer from the offerer's viewpoint. Any version of these objective tests can be displaced by a subjective test where the offeree knows that the offerer is suffering from a mistake as to the terms of his offer or where the offeree is at fault in failing to note that the offerer has made a mistake.

The distinction between objectivity and subjectivity in these tests is a little difficult to see. The difference is that, in the former, the reasonable man is attempting to discover an agreement purely on the basis of information. Where a mistake exists the search is for the true intent.

The problem of mistakes will be considered again later in this chapter. Chapter 8 will provide advice on how to avoid uncertain agreements. For now, the aim is to show that the legalistic determination of the existence of an agreement is a complex matter.

4 Duty to disclose information

In English law there is no general duty to disclose information which may be of benefit to the other side in the negotiation. It is up to each party to make the best use of the information it holds.

The principles of freedom of contract and freedom of negotiation rely on the idea that each side will enter the negotiation game with a particular set of cards and will play its hand to its best advantage. However, although there is no doctrine as such of integrity or honesty, the law expects what might loosely be referred to as fair play. Thus there are some qualifications to this general no-duty-of-disclosure rule:

1. Taking advantage of a mistake.
2. Representations.
3. 'Uberrimae fidei' and fiduciary relationships.
4. Tort.
5. Contractual duties.

If, for example, in the first case a seller knows that the buyer has made a mistake in relation to the terms of the seller's offer, the seller has a duty to bring the mistake to the attention of the buyer.

A representation is a statement as to fact. Neither party is obliged to bring facts to the attention of the other side but if a party chooses to do so, then the facts as stated must be true. A misrepresentation is a statement of fact which is untrue, is made to induce the other party to enter into a contract, is of some importance and is relied upon by the other party. Misrepresentations can be fraudulent, negligent or innocent. Fraudulent misrepresentation is a statement made with knowledge that it is untrue, or without believing it to be true, or recklessly, careless whether it be true or false. Negligent misrepresentation is a statement made in the belief that it is true but without reasonable grounds for that belief. An innocent misrepresentation is a statement made in the belief that it is true and with reasonable grounds for that belief. Misrepresentation of any sort may allow the party misled to rescind the contract and sue for damages.

So the contract negotiator must always be careful to ensure that anything he says that purports to be a fact is correct or that otherwise he makes it clear that it is not intended to be a representation in the legal sense. Furthermore the negotiator has a duty to disclose information that emerges before the contract is made which has the effect of falsifying an earlier representation. Representations can also be inferred from the actions or inactions of the parties. A true fact which is used so as to mislead is also a misrepresentation.

'Uberrimae fidei' (of the utmost good faith) contracts (eg insurance contracts where the insured has a specific duty to disclose all material facts) and fiduciary relationships (between trustee and beneficiary) are exceptions to the general rule. Similarly there are situations where one side may under a duty of care (in tort) have an obligation to disclose certain information – for example, where a bank should bring to the attention of its customer the nature of a document which the customer is to sign. These exceptions are outside the scope of this book and are touched upon for completeness only.

So far the question of duty to disclose information has been addressed in the sense of pre-contract negotiations. A recurrent theme of this book is that the contract negotiator is needed to negotiate the contract in the first place, but also to negotiate issues as and when they might arise following agreement of the contract. In this situation the contract itself may impose duties to disclose information relevant to the negotiation of such issues. For example, negotiation of revisions to the contract in respect of variations (see Chapter 10) affecting price, performance and time may take place under enabling provisions of the contract which demand the revelation of cost data, construction methods and other relevant details. Needless to say, failure to comply with such provisions is breach of contract and to comply falsely is to make misrepresentations.

5 Representations, promises and puffery

As has been said, a representation is a statement of alleged fact intended to induce the other side into making a contract. In itself it promises nothing other than the accuracy of the fact. On the other hand the contract (which at its most simplistic can be described as an exchange of promises) is a set of promises which implies that each side will do something to the benefit of the other. There is a grey area in between representations and promises called promissory representations. A statement made by the seller intending only to convey a fact might be construed by the buyer as a further promise. Depending upon the circumstances, such promissory representations can be imported into the contract, leaving the seller with an additional obligation for which he made no allowance in the price.

For this reason there is distinct advantage in the contract negotiator ensuring that the final contract document includes a 'complete agreement' or 'entire agreement' clause expressly to describe precisely what makes up the contract and to exclude anything else said or done during the period of negotiations. This is particularly important in major tenders where the pre-contract stage may be lengthy and embrace many voluminous activities including formal negotiations, tender clarifications, presentations and interviews.

Statements of law, of intention or of opinion are not representations although the wary negotiator must avoid holding himself or the company up as expert in a particular field, as the other side may establish a legal basis for relying upon such purported expertise.

Sales talk and other such 'puffery' is not representation but again the negotiator and the company should be at pains to ensure that puffery is understood to be such before any contract is concluded with the customer.

6 Duress and undue influence

The nature of duress is one of threat. The threat may be of physical violence to the person or of damage to property. The threat may be an economic one or it may simply be the threat of breach of contract. The harm may be merely threatened or it may be carried out.

A party induced into contract under duress may at his option avoid the contract since he has not given his genuine consent to its terms. This right also extends to the party making a contract under the undue influence of another.

In general, undue influence exists where the parties are supposed to enjoy a relationship of trust and confidence but where the weaker party did not exercise free judgement in making the contract and the contract is manifestly to the disadvantage of that party and to the benefit of the other. Such relationships are, for example, that between guardian and ward or trustee and beneficiary. Thus it is duress rather than undue influence which could possibly arise in a conventional arms-length business transaction.The contract negotiator should not put himself in a position where his words or deeds could be construed as attempting to subject the other side to duress.

7 Exclusion clauses

Even in business transactions the parties are not entirely free to write their own contract clauses. While for example they do have the right (provided it is expressly done) to exclude the Sale of Goods Act implied undertakings of merchantable quality and fitness for purpose, the parties are forbidden (or if they try it, the clause is void) from excluding or restricting liability for negligence causing death or personal injury. If one party deals on the other's standard terms the latter cannot exclude or restrict his liability for his own breach nor can he claim a right to render no or substantially different contract performance unless these exclusions or restrictions can be shown to be reasonable. These provisions are set down in the Unfair Contract Terms Act.

8 Unfair contracts

The law provides no doctrine of unfair contracts or of contracts of unconscionability. Within the restrictions mentioned above the parties are free to wield their bargaining power to best effect.

9 Agency

If one task of the contract negotiator is to negotiate contracts for his company, then the question must be asked as to the formal capacity within which an individual undertakes this task. The answer is that the negotiator is an implied agent of the company. Agents tend to be thought of as people who are appointed as such and to whom are given formal agency agreements. However, even if the contract negotiator has only a standard employment contract, the actions of employer and employee imply an agreement of agency between them. The negotiator may have specific delegated authority to negotiate contracts of a particular type or value, or such authority may arise through custom and practice or by virtue of a 'job specification' identifying the negotiator's responsibilities. These actions or documents, although not using the word 'agent' or 'agency', nevertheless imply this type of relationship.

As an agent the negotiator owes to his employer (as his principal) duties of care and skill, of personal (ie not sub-delegated) performance, of accountability, of avoiding conflicts of interest and of keeping his employer's information confidential. If the negotiator as agent is rewarded for his services these duties fall to him whether or not they are expressed in any contract of employment or contract of agency with his employer. In the normal course of events the company employee engaged as a contract negotiator will not personally handle payments from the customer and hence the final primary duty of an agent, which is to hand any benefits over to the principal, does not arise.

The actual authority which the contract negotiator can exercise on behalf of his employer can be a combination of express authority (such as an internal memorandum delegating to him financial levels of authority) and implied authority (such as the doing of those things which are reasonably consequent upon the express authority). The agent cannot himself argue that his implied authority overrides or extends his express authority but third parties are entitled to rely upon the ostensible authority that he appears to possess, unless they know to the contrary.

So from a practical point of view the negotiator should recognise that his function is that of agent; he should be sure that he has the express authority of his employer and that his employer understands and endorses the type of activity which he undertakes on the basis of implied authority. He should ensure that the customers with whom he deals understand that he is acting as agent for his company and not in his own private capacity. Simple things such as always ensuring that correspondence is made on headed paper and signed for the company help to reinforce this position.

10 Mistake and mistakes

A distinction should be made between the legal doctrine of mistake and the making of mistakes in the sense of errors or misjudgements. In the former case it has already been suggested that if one side can see that the other side has made a mistake with respect to the first side's offer, then he should call attention to the mistake. If he proceeds to contract without doing so, then the side in error will be entitled to have the contract set aside. If both sides have made a common mistake of a fundamental nature and relating to a circumstance pre-dating the contract, then the contract can be void at law. The mistake must be utterly fundamental. Trivial matters do not count. For example, the parties may have been mistaken as to the very existence of the subject matter of the contract or they may have mistakenly believed (at the time of making the contract) that the contract was physically capable of performance when in fact it was not.

The contract negotiator should always be sure of purported

facts before signing the contract. His aim is to make valid contracts, not ones which are void on grounds of mistake.

Turning to the question of non-fundamental errors and miscalculations or misjudgements, it must be stressed that there is no entitlement to relief from or to either side. The law does not exist to repair or improve bad bargains. If mistakes of this sort are made the only remedy is goodwill. In long-term business relationships the old adage 'do as you would be done by' is axiomatic. A favour done is a favour earned and it is a very clever negotiator who never makes a mistake. The facility to correct an error after the deal has been done rests solely on the ability to exploit in a positive sense the personal relationship with the negotiator on the other side.

11 Uncertainty

This chapter has attempted to outline the legal minefield which the contract negotiator must cross in order to arrive at a concluded agreement. One further pitfall that may prevent the realisation of this aim is the degree of uncertainty which may exist in the agreement.

From time to time it may be necessary in urgent circumstances to record the contract in a summary form. Sometimes referred to as 'instructions to proceed', these limited-form contracts appearing as letters or telexes can leave a lot of detail to be sorted out later. Sometimes the contract itself provides for agreement on price, quantity and delivery to be worked out later. If such agreements are too vague or incomplete then they can be void for uncertainty. A court would look objectively or perhaps subjectively for the intent but it is not usual for the courts to invent terms merely to complete an uncertain and vague agreement.

The contract negotiator should always strive for the utmost certainty and completeness as well as accuracy in making his contract agreements.

12 Framework

The points so far covered in this chapter can be summarised into a framework (Figure 2.2) of principles, restrictions and pitfalls for the contract negotiator.

Principles	*Restrictions*	*Pitfalls*
Freedom to negotiate	Misrepresentation	Mistake
No duty to disclose	Unfair Contract Terms Act	Uncertainty
Freedom to exploit bargaining power	Anti-trust law	Agent duties
		Tort duties
		Contract duties

Figure 2.2: Contract negotiation framework

Perhaps the most indicative aspect of Figure 2.2 is that contract negotiation is not a free-for-all. It is rightly the domain of the imaginative, quick-witted entrepreneur, but the uninformed, the jack-the-lad or the Mr Fixit character can be a commercial danger for the company as he blunders around fixing up deals with no thought as to the possible interpretation or consequences of his words and deeds.

13 Legal assistance

If the process of negotiating contracts is such a legal minefield then, logically, the task ought to be handled by lawyers. And yet in the UK the vast majority of commercial transactions are handled by staff with little or no legal training. The case law which provides so much of the foundation of the law relating to contract matters is perversely based upon the few exceptions to the general practice that business people prefer to settle their differences in private and by negotiation rather than by legal process.

Legal advice or assistance is generally not called upon for reasons of cost, time, value or pragmatism. The cost of seeking professional help is an additional financial burden for companies to bear. Frequently time does not permit the independent review of draft documents or negotiation plans, and the value of such help can be debatable. Business people often feel that the advice they get is either unhelpful or impractical and bordering upon the irrelevant. The advice is unhelpful in the sense that the business person is looking for a positive guide to help in coming to a decision. What he gets is a variety of different views on what a court may or may not say. The lawyers would say that this is exactly what their advice is supposed to be. The business person would say that it is all very interesting but of no practical benefit. Furthermore the independent legal adviser has no intimate knowledge of the particular company, its products, its contracts and its customers and therefore advice given in isolation of such intimacy is bound to have a flavour of generality or theory.

Even the larger companies who run intramural, corporate legal departments will find that the people in the operating divisions of the business avoid using the corporate lawyers for the same reasons of lack of pragmatism. All of this is most unfair to those lawyers who are pragmatic and practical and who seek to help rather than bewilder.

Here lies the message for the contract negotiator who decides to call upon expert assistance. He should go to great lengths to find someone of the right commercial approach to negotiation and business matters. This is someone who understands the validity of negotiation as a principal business process, rather than someone who can only conceptualise a problem or a dispute in terms of how it would be argued in court.

The question then naturally follows as to the circumstances (Figure 2.3) in which the negotiator should consider seeking professional legal advice before proceeding.

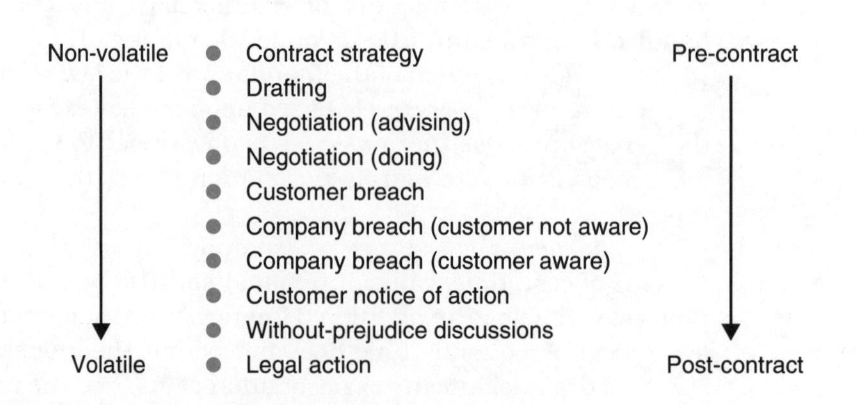

Figure 2.3: Seeking legal advice

At the non-volatile end of the spectrum are the non-contentious aspects. The contract negotiator might consider advice on whether an element of the contract strategy offends any anti-trust legislation. If the contract is unusual in nature or complexity or is of particularly high value or risk, he may wish to have a legal review of the paperwork.

The lawyers can provide a useful drafting service to help put into formal language a commercial concept which has been agreed. While this does off-load a task, the negotiator should nevertheless be fully cognisant of what has been written so that he is both content with it and confident in his ability to argue it face to face with the customer. It is never a good idea to let the lawyers on both sides go into a corner to do their own thing. Constant oversight and pressure is needed to maintain the commercial thrust of the dealings.

If the negotiations are conducted over a period of days, weeks or longer, this permits the opportunity to talk over progress with the lawyers. An option to consider is bringing the lawyers into the actual negotiation. Clearly a judgement is needed as to whether this will facilitate or inhibit progress. A lot may depend upon the attitude and representation of the other side.

Once the contract negotiations have been concluded with an effective agreement and the work is under way, then the level of volatility in matters arising potentially increases. If the company should breach or anticipate breaching the contract in any serious way, it is as well to seek advice as to possible courses of action to take or avoid before the customer becomes aware of the situation. Once the customer is aware then the need to tread carefully becomes paramount. Similarly if the customer should chance to be in breach, then again formal advice can enhance the company information base from which a decision on a course of action can be taken.

If there are serious difficulties with the contract, the company should be on the lookout for unintentional (or perhaps intentional) signals from the customer that the relationship and position are stiffening. The model of international diplomacy has a lot to teach in terms of sending and reading signals in times of tension. If there is a formal notice from the customer regarding breach or an intention on his part to take some action or to invoke an alleged remedy, then legal advice should be taken quickly. Naturally any shrewd business person will admit nothing, deny liability and blame somebody else but in the more serious situations these gut reactions may not suffice!

When things go wrong the aim is nevertheless usually to negotiate a resolution. However, it is crucial that attempts at this are handled in such a way so as not to prejudice the company's position in the event that the attempts prove futile. Legal advice is helpful here. Indeed in such fraught circumstances it would be bordering upon negligence for the contract negotiator to fail in mustering all arguments and defences, including legal ones. Legalistic argument can produce a negative effect in negotiation if used as a blunt weapon of intellectual superiority, or if used to address only hypothetical situations. Used as an additional layer of argument to underpin the company's commercial position, it can add significantly to the strength of the company's negotiating position.

Finally, if legal action (by which is meant action through the courts or through some contractually prescribed method of arbitration – not just a legal-sounding letter) is threatened or taken, then the need for formal advice and assistance is obvious.

CHAPTER 3

Internal factors

1 Introduction

What possible purpose could there be to devoting a chapter in a book about contract negotiation to the subject of internal factors? What are internal factors?

Put simply, the negotiation is being conducted on behalf of the company and therefore it is necessary to take into account the factors internal to the company which influence the freedom, role and performance of the negotiator. The aim always is for the negotiator to represent the company as a whole, to give the appearance of being relaxed, in control and free to negotiate, as shown in Figure 3.1.

In reality life is rarely as simple as this. The negotiator is subject to commercial pressure to secure the deal, personal pressure to be seen to do well, and political pressure to avoid being criticised by other departments. At the same time he is constrained by organisational limitations and restrictions on his negotiation flexibility, and no doubt he has a limited amount of time to devote to a particular negotiation as pressure of other priorities mounts. The real situation is therefore somewhat different (Figure 3.2).

It is one of the tasks of the negotiator to resolve these conflicting and sometimes mutually exclusive factors to achieve a balanced and timely result. The other party has similar difficulties and yet between them they must arrive at a handshake.

Figure 3.1: The negotiator and the other party are single entities pulling against each other

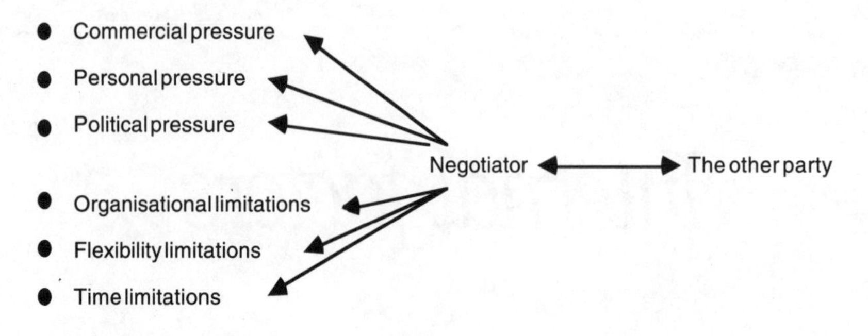

Figure 3.2: The negotiator is really pulled in several directions

The purpose in this chapter is to identify these internal factors and to propose methods of dealing with them so as to minimise their effect.

2 Organisational issues

The fundamental question is one of understanding and deciding where the negotiator best fits into the organisation. Closely related to this is the decision as to whether the negotiator is to have any involvement with the management, administration and implementation of the contract once it has been secured.

Imagine a company whose business is to design and manufacture products or systems where individual contracts can take several months or longer to secure, are several years in duration and are of several tens of millions of pounds in value. The gestation and performance of the contract will occur in several stages (Figure 3.3).

The tracking phase is the phase at the start of which the company has identified a market opportunity. This is the time to establish initial contact with the potential customer and to use all the traditional marketing methods to influence the customer in his choice of product, procurement method and supplier. As the market is being developed, activity will go on against the backdrop of approved market or business development plans and product development plans. Traditionally the contract negotiator is excluded from the tracking phase and yet, to the extent that all routes lead eventually, one hopes, to the negotiating table, perhaps it is an unwise company that ignores at this stage the contribution that could be made by the contract negotiator.

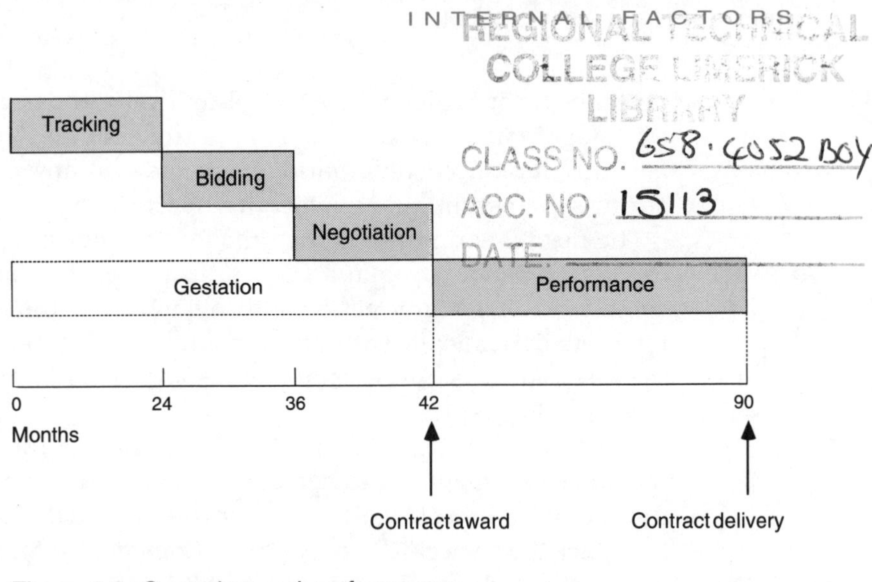

Figure 3.3: Gestation and performance

The contribution which could be made by the contract negotiator during the tracking phase is mainly in two parts. First, he can assist in the formulation of outline proposals or strategy from which the customer may develop his procurement approach. Such assistance may be born not only of knowledge of the type of approach that would best realise the company's commercial objectives, but also of previous experience of negotiating an actual contract with this or similar customers. Second, there is a potential contribution which should be in place at the earliest possible time. This is the relationship which needs to be developed with the potential customer and from which a successful outcome can best be derived. It is very rarely the case that the negotiator can get the best deal if his first encounter with his opposite number is during the pleasantries that precede the meeting by five minutes or so.

In short, there is benefit to be had from finding a way to involve the contract negotiator in the tracking phase.

The bidding phase commences with the receipt of an invitation to tender (ITT), request for quotation (RFQ), request for proposals (RFP) or invitation for bids (IFB). At this point the emphasis switches from pure marketing effort to bid preparation and proposal management. The role of the contract negotiator is to be fully involved in bid preparation, formulating strategy and tactics, and making sure that the bid is formulated on a practical basis (with regard to the impending negotiation) rather than an idealistic or hypothetical basis. Not to involve the negotiator at this stage would be madness. Familiarity with the detail of the bid, the thinking behind various aspects and any policy constraints are essential to an effective negotiation.

The negotiation phase is the time for the smooth and smiley marketing people to take a back seat and let the hard-nosed commercial negotiator get on with his job. How the negotiator interacts dynamically with his company and colleagues during the negotiation is a topic that will be addressed in more detail later in this chapter.

Once the negotiation is concluded and the contract secured, the question arises of whether the negotiator should drop out of the picture completely. Here, organisational aspects begin to influence the answer to that question. Consider the following two organisation charts (Figures 3.4 and 3.5).

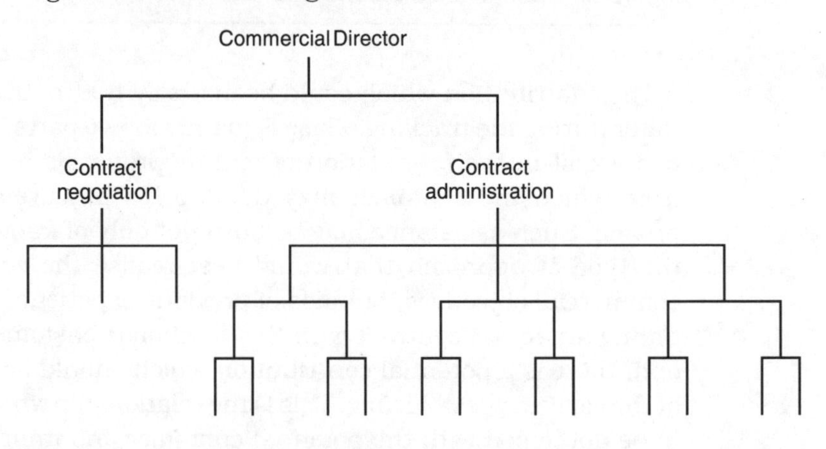

Figure 3.4: Star team organisation

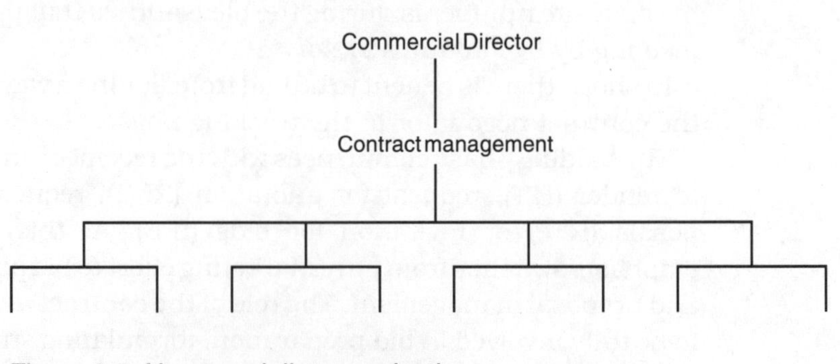

Figure 3.5: Non-specialist organisation

In Figure 3.4 can be seen what might be termed a 'star' team organisation where the negotiators are a small, separate but elite team of people. This has a lot of merit to it. The negotiators are not weighed down by the burden of post-award contract administration, but are free agents, able to travel conceptually and physically from one customer to another in order to get the deal done. Typically such organisations subdivide across the product, customer and territorial lines (Figures 3.6, 3.7 and 3.8).

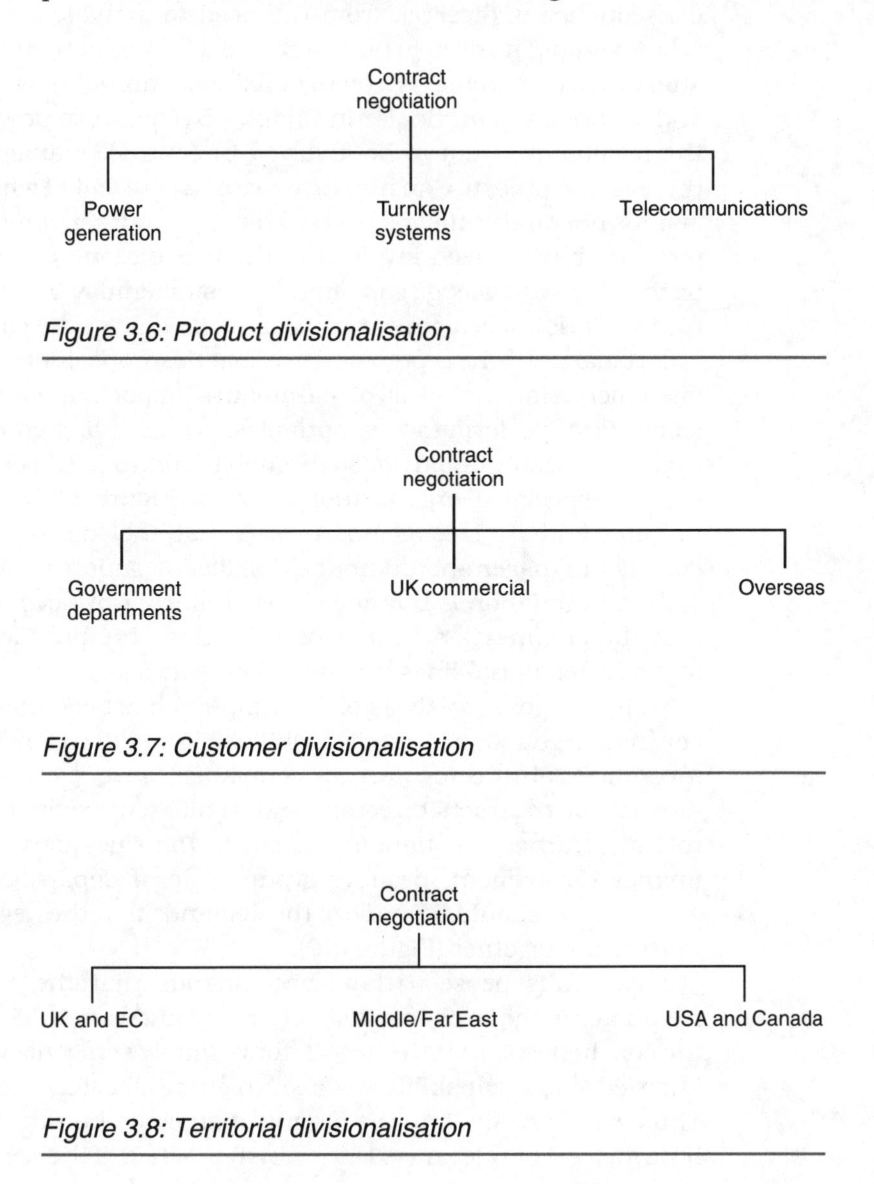

Figure 3.6: Product divisionalisation

Figure 3.7: Customer divisionalisation

Figure 3.8: Territorial divisionalisation

In such star team organisations the individual negotiator becomes more and more of a specialist, provided that the company has enough business to be able to afford to employ more than one negotiator.

However, the star team approach has the disadvantage that the negotiator, because he has no responsibility for the contract or towards the customer once the contract is awarded, is divorced from the problems of managing the contract and as a consequence is divorced from the need to manage an overall relationship. The need to build a sound and productive relationship with the customer is a recurrent theme throughout the book and is covered in particular in Chapter 5 (The whole process). If the negotiator is not to be involved in contract management, there is less pressure on him to arrive at a contract of which the 'modus operandi' must be practicable; the contract administrators, not having been involved in the negotiation, start with a tremendous knowledge gap, and the customer may be less than pleased if new faces appear as soon as he has let the contract.

On balance, if one is prepared to adopt the proposition that the customer relationship is of paramount importance and that commercial performance is optimised by achieving continuity from the tracking or bid phase through to contract delivery, then the 'non-specialist' organisation shown in Figure 3.5 has much to commend it. This is not to say that the 'non-specialist' contract manager should not be a skilled negotiator, only that skill in negotiation is but one of his abilities. Nor does it mean that the organisation cannot be split along the product, customer or territorial lines mentioned earlier.

In the foregoing analysis an assumption has been made that contract negotiation is a responsibility falling within the remit of a commercial director. Not all companies have a commercial director (or contracts director), and in different companies the role of contract negotiation can fall to the sales department, finance department, product group or legal department. An examination should be made of the demands that the negotiator must bring together (Figure 3.9).

It can thus be seen that the demands that the contract negotiator is required to satisfy are many and varied. Therefore the conclusion is that the negotiator is simply someone with the knowledge and capability to effect this multifaceted approach. Thus, where he fits into the organisation could be said to be of little interest or relevance. However, in practice, if the negotiator

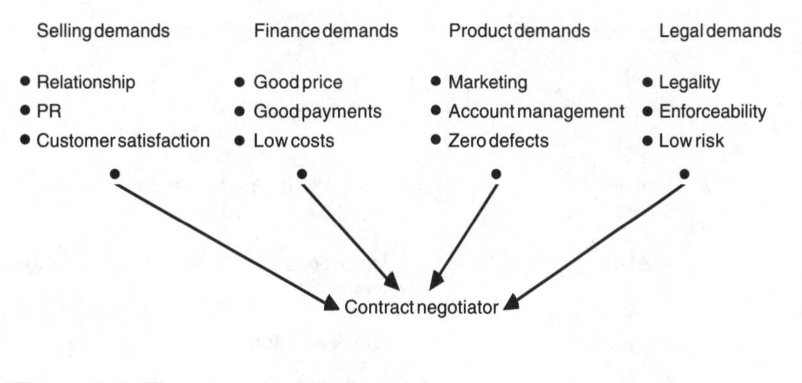

Figure 3.9: The strands pulled together

is in a department other than one (ie the commercial department) whose *raison d'être* is to negotiate contracts, then 'functional loyalty' will mean that the pulling together of the various strands is biased in one particular direction. For example, the salesman negotiating a contract will do so with the 'customer feel-good' considerations uppermost in his mind, and therefore at the expense of the legality of the contract. The lawyers would focus on the certainty and enforceability of the contract rather than the potential profitability. Inevitably one is drawn to the conclusion that contract negotiation belongs in a separate commercial department whose principal (but not sole) responsibility is to negotiate contracts. Other functions which, by logical extrapolation and good sense, belong in the commercial department are estimating, costing, pricing and bid preparation (Figure 3.10).

Thus if contract negotiation is to be successfully conducted and concluded, it can be seen that organisational issues do have a bearing. To summarise, the non-specialist organisation shown in Figure 3.5 is preferred, and that in itself presupposes the existence of a commercial department whose main contract responsibilities are shown in Figure 3.10.

There is, however, one final major organisational point which is of concern, and that is the place within the organisation where procurement and purchasing take place. A distinction can be made between purchasing and what may be called major procurement or subcontracting. Purchasing can be of low monetary value or very high monetary value, but essentially the purchase orders stand independent of the contract, other than to the extent that purchased items will be supplied against the con-

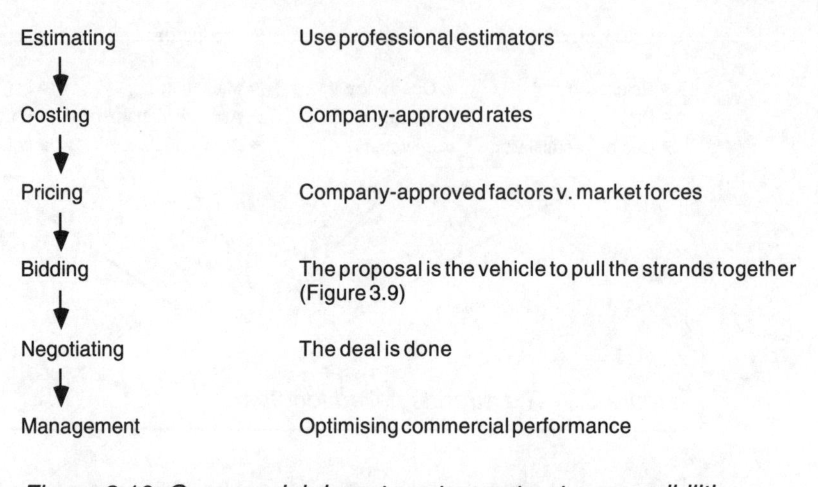

Figure 3.10: Commercial department – contract responsibilities

tract to the end customer, thus giving the company various liabilities as to the quality and fitness of those purchased items.

On the other hand, a subcontract is a purchasing instrument that needs to be a mirror image of the contract. This need can arise for a variety of reasons, of which the following are examples:

a) The customer has directed the company that certain aspects of the work must be subcontracted to a subcontractor nominated by the customer.
b) Although no nominated subcontractors are included, the contract nevertheless demands that some or all of its terms are included 'mutatis mutandis' in purchase orders of a specified type or value.
c) The work of the contract was always planned to rely upon certain major elements being undertaken outside the company.

In so far as purchasing as defined above is concerned, the activity rightly belongs in the organisation at the point which is closest to the 'consumers' of the purchased goods or services. In a factory manufacturing electronic goods, the purchasing of resistors, capacitors, and other components properly belongs to the Manufacturing Director. However, Figure 3.11 shows that the negotiation of major subcontracts under the heading of procurement is organisationally separated from the negotiation of the contracts to which the subcontracts relate.

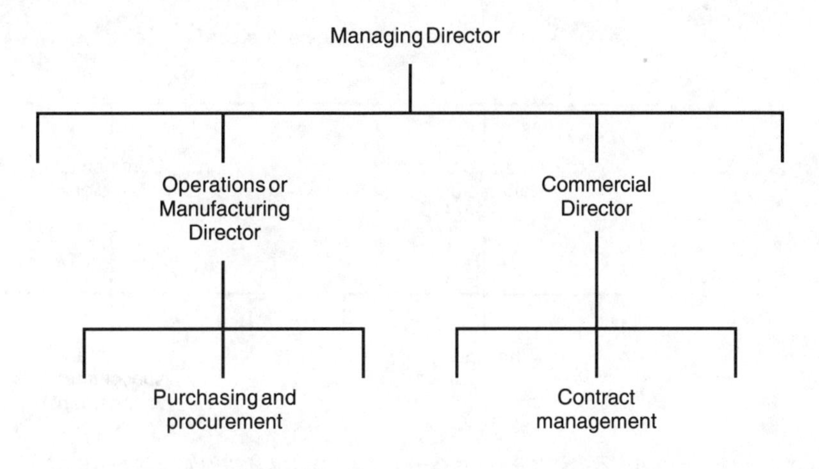

Figure 3.11: Typical placement of purchasing/procurement

This separation carries with it a significant risk to the objective of ensuring that the subcontract is back-to-back with the contract. No matter how good the internal communications, no matter the quality of the personnel involved, once these two interdependent activities are separated there is a danger that something will be missed (Figure 3.12).

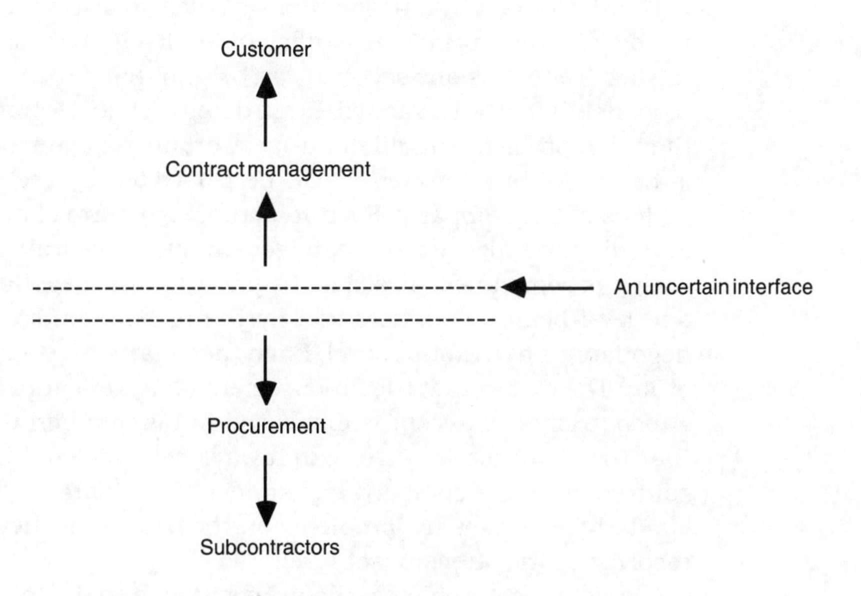

Figure 3.12: Contract management/procurement interface

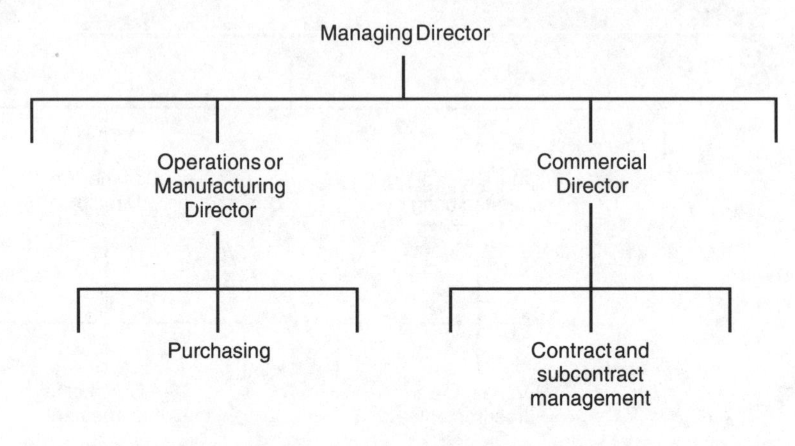

Figure 3.13: Ideal placement of purchasing/procurement

In all of these circumstances the aim of the company is to make sure that it is back-to-back with its subcontractors by 'flowing down' to them the relevant provisions of the contract. That is to say that the intent is to have the subcontract constructed in a manner that follows the contract as closely as possible.Thus it can be reasonably assumed that the subcontractor's liability to the company is highly similar, if not identical, to the company's liability to the customer.

The simple fact that negotiations at the two levels are carried on by different people is sufficient in itself to ensure that mistakes or omissions occur. It can be said that if the personnel responsible for the two activities are doing their jobs competently then this problem should not arise. Certainly a team approach is beneficial but so often it can be frustrated by the internal politics of the company. Even if factual errors are eliminated – after all, the Procurement Manager can read the draft contract – what is sometimes missed is the flavour of the negotiations at one level being misunderstood by the person conducting the negotiations at the other level. Each then starts to rely upon the other. The clause that the Procurement Manager cannot get the subcontractor to accept is dismissed in his mind on the basis that the Contract Manager can always get it deleted from the contract with the company's customer. The Contract Manager similarly dismisses his problems on the basis that they can be resolved at the subcontract level.

Against these problems, the proposition is that contract and subcontract negotiation should be integrated within a single function (Figure 3.13).

The choice of individual(s) to fulfil the role of contract/ subcontract management can depend upon the nature of the enterprise. On one hand, the choice may be of someone who is expert in dealing with the customer. Alternatively there is no reason not to select someone of a 'purchasing' background. The end objective is the same – to have a single responsibility for looking in both directions to customers and subcontractors.

3 Writing a negotiation plan

Having the company's authority and approval to negotiate is clearly an important part of the internal processes that must be completed before the contract negotiator can step outside the door. These two aspects will be covered in sections 4 and 5 of this chapter. However, experience shows that it is extremely useful to write a negotiation plan for consideration within the company. The importance of planning is a topic that will be addressed in Chapter 4. But for now the aim is to expose the advantages of writing a plan for internal agreement and to explain how to write such a plan.

Although the need to develop and maintain a sound, positive relationship with the customer is essential, the analogy of military planning is a useful one. Although the customer must not be seen as 'the enemy', nevertheless a battle plan is a good concept to have in mind when writing the negotiation plan. The battle plan might comprise the elements in Figure 3.14.

Figure 3.14: 'Battle' planning

The advantages of doing this should be clear. As a matter of self-discipline it forces the negotiator to plan the whole exercise (ie not just the prospective negotiation meeting) and to think about individual aspects. It must be the negotiator who prepares the plan as it is he who will carry it out. A far from ideal situation is one in which the negotiation plan has been prepared by others and foisted upon him. In these circumstances he may not feel committed to the plan, particularly if he considers it to be weak or less than ideal. Of course as a good company employee he will execute such a plan if so directed, but in the area of negotiation there is nothing quite like having the personal commitment of the negotiator. He must be hungry for a successful campaign and this is best achieved through his total commitment, which is easier to secure if the plan is one of his own making. Naturally the process of seeking internal approval may cause the proposed plan to be modified but this should not detract from the level of commitment brought about through personal involvement and responsibility.

Some may say that having a plan is to place restrictions upon the ingenuity and inventiveness of the negotiator. This would be entirely wrong. The plan is a means to an end and not an end in itself. The plan is a tool, a device to be used by and to aid the negotiator. Ultimately the plan can be dumped if a quicker or better means to achieve the overall aim emerges, but essentially the plan will subsist as a powerful tool against which progress can be measured and the next step formulated.

This section is entitled '*Writing* a negotiation plan'. Should such a plan be in writing, or can a plan discussed orally and carried in the head suffice? On the latter point, *all* negotiation plans must be carried in the head, at least in so far as the negotiation meeting is concerned. It would be hopeless for the negotiator at the negotiation meeting to have to refer continually to a written plan alongside him on the table or in his briefcase. For minor negotiations it is perfectly acceptable for the plan not to be committed to writing. For more complex negotiations a written plan is essential. A written plan provides a record of all the considerations; copies can be circulated to other players; other players will see what their role is and when it is to be performed. It provides a basis for internal review as the campaign proceeds. In any 'post mortem' it provides a record of why things were decided and done. It provides a basis, once the negotiation is concluded, for lessons to be learned for the future.

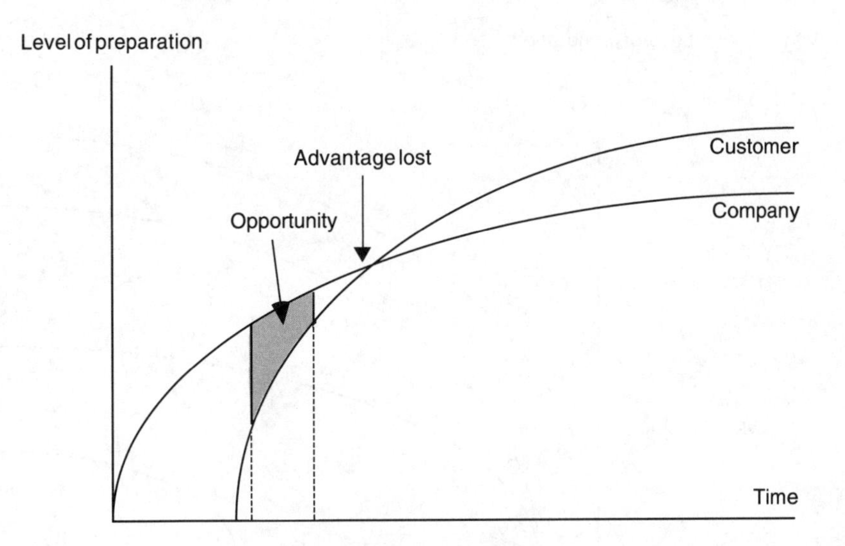

Figure 3.15: Company and customer preparation – example 1

The plan forces consideration of questions such as when to open the negotiations. This simple question allows the company to think through and to attempt to establish the point at which the gap between the company's readiness and the customer's readiness is at a maximum (Figure 3.15).

The purpose of Figure 3.15 is to show the period of time during which there is an opportunity for the company to take advantage of having prepared earlier or to a greater extent than the customer. Clearly the customer must have done some preparation or he will not be willing to negotiate at all. Where the curves on the graph cross, the company has lost that advantage and thereafter will always be at a disadvantage. This is only an example. It appears to show that the customer's preparation starts later, accelerates more quickly, overtakes the company's and eventually is more thorough. This is only one scenario. Others are illustrated in Figures 3.16 and 3.17.

In Figure 3.16 the customer's preparation is shown as A or B or C. On curve A the customer makes adequate preparation fairly quickly but never quite catches the company in thoroughness. Here the advantage lies throughout with the company. On curve B the customer starts early enough but never does enough preparation. On curve C the customer starts late and never finishes. On both B and C the danger is that inadequate preparation means that in some cases the customer is never

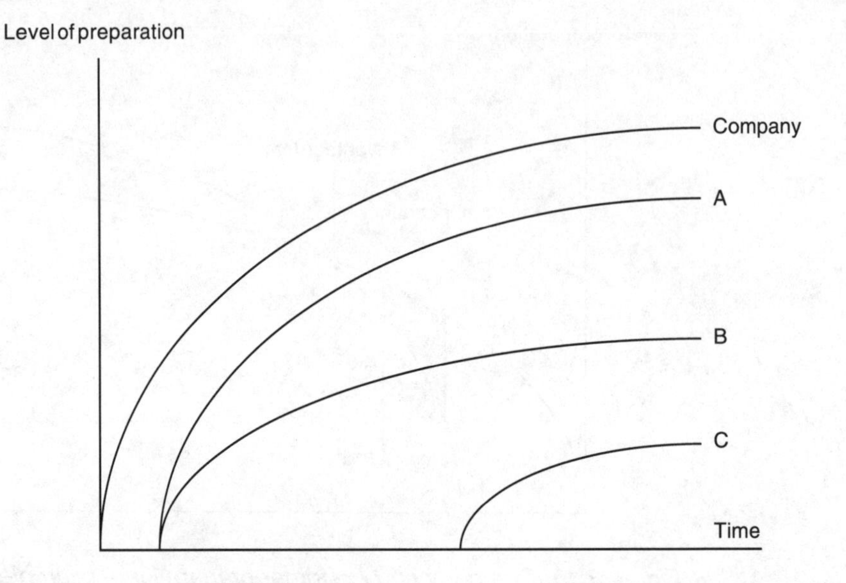

Figure 3.16: Company and customer preparation – example 2

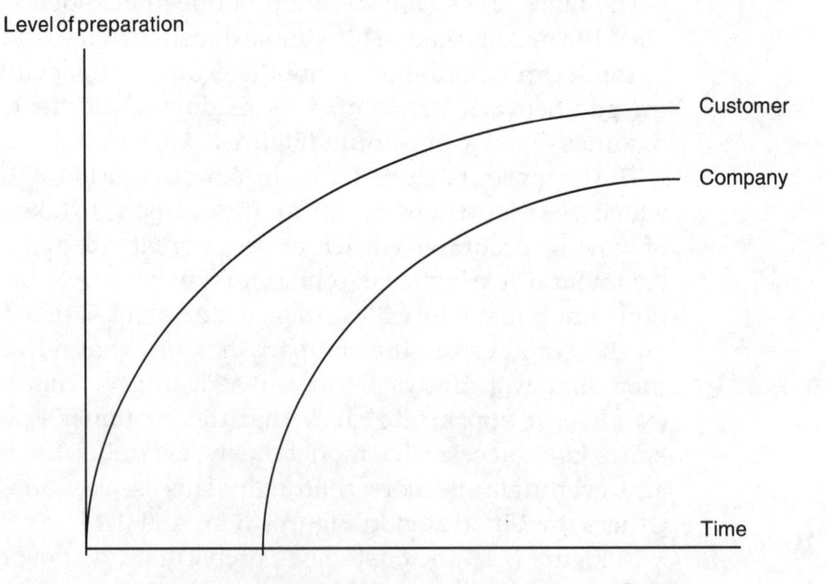

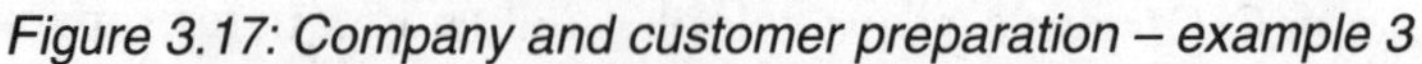
Figure 3.17: Company and customer preparation – example 3

ready or willing to negotiate – thus the company loses its opportunity and experiences a fair degree of frustration!

As far as Figure 3.17 is concerned, there is only one message to the company and its contract negotiator, which is: never let it happen!

These simple examples show the merit of using the requirement for a negotiation plan to be written as a reason to think really carefully about how and when the negotiation should be started. The discipline of doing the plan forces careful thought on all of the aspects (Figure 3.14).

What might a negotiation plan look like? Let us suppose that the negotiation is to resolve with the customer a contract price adjustment resulting from variations in subcontract work. To complicate matters, the company has the major subcontractor making similar claims against the company. Let us suppose that the contract and the subcontract are not back-to-back, and that all three parties are alleging and denying liability for the work variations.

The company's negotiation plan might include the following features:

Objective	To secure a price adjustment at least as big as any settlement needed with the subcontractor.
Problems	The contract and subcontract are not back-to-back. The position is not clear where liability lies.
Strategy	To resist making a settlement with the subcontractor unless a deal can be done in parallel with the customer.
Tactics	To insist continually that customer and subcontractor meet to resolve the dispute and costs (in such a way that the company emerges unscathed). To swamp the customer with voluminous detail to impress him with the substance of the claims. To swamp him to the extent that he cannot cope (since the detail exposes the liability problems). To find a method of putting the customer under pressure to negotiate quickly.
When to start	Immediately.
Fall-back part	If an agreement cannot be reached by 31 December then the advantage of an early negotiation and conclusion is lost and it would then be best to sit it out and wait for the customer to make a direct agreement with the subcontractor.

In this example the questions of who will open the negotiation and how or when to use reinforcements have been omitted as these points will be covered further on in this chapter.

The advantages of having this plan are clear. The objective has been carefully considered and defined in such a way that achievement can be measured. The plan is honest in so far as it identifies the real problems which, although they are there to be overcome, may be insurmountable and so at least the risks have been identified to those within the company who will authorise the plan.

4 Authority to negotiate

Before any negotiation can take place the negotiator must have both the authority and the approval of the company. The distinction being drawn here is that authority is something which should be delegated to the negotiator on an ongoing basis so that all his negotiations must be conducted within the framework of that authority. Approval is necessary only in specific cases either where the negotiator wishes to operate outside his normal level of delegated authority or where the significance or novelty of the negotiation sensibly needs to be drawn to the attention of higher management and therefore requires their blessing.

The problem of delegated authority is that it is frequently geared to only one parameter – money (Figure 3.18).

In this, the monetary limitations are clear and perhaps in a large number of cases such a simple approach provides adequate safeguards for the company. But if safeguards are necessary, surely the question is 'safeguards against what'? The answer is easy. The company needs safeguards against the wrong deal being done. Limiting by monetary value the delegated

Position	*Authority*
Commercial Officer	£25,000
Assistant Commercial Manager	£100,000
Commercial Manager	£500,000
Commercial Director	£500,000 +

Figure 3.18: Delegated authority

authority of more junior and therefore less experienced people should limit the amount of damage that could be done through a poor deal being concluded, but this really does not go far enough. After all, it is almost as easy to lose £50,000 on a £100,000 contract as it is to lose £50,000 on a £500,000 contract. If £50,000 has to be lost then is it better to lose it as 50 per cent or 10 per cent of the contract?

The point is that in any contract negotiation there are four key negotiation parameters:

1. Profitability.
2. Cash flow.
3. Risk.
4. Protection of intellectual property.

Notice that the ostensible value of the contract does not feature in this list. If these parameters become the basis of delegated authority then logically this would allow the commercial officer to negotiate a £100m contract. This would be absurd. Monetary value must appear in the rules for delegated authority but this should not be the only consideration.

Taking first the question of profitability, this relates to the required level of profit that the company aims to earn on each contract. For these purposes the word 'profit' will be used, although different companies express the need for a minimum benefit from the contract in a variety of ways. Some refer to contribution, some to margin, some to return. The definitions of these expressions also vary but the point remains the same. The company needs to have a method of defining the monetary gain which it seeks as a norm to secure from any contract.

As far as cash flow is concerned, again the company must set some formal standards for its terms of business. Are credit terms available? If so, to whom and over what period? Is a down payment required? Is neutral cash flow the minimum requirement?

In any contract for future performance there is risk. Indeed there is a variety of risks. The principal one is whether the work can be completed within the cost allowed. This risk is tied to a number of factors, one of which is the intrinsic technical level of certainty within the job. Manufacturing a thousand picnic tables to an existing design is somewhat less risky than developing safety-critical software for the control mechanisms of a nuclear power station. Thus means can be found to identify the risk in the work. For example, it is possible to define such risk by the monetary value of any design or development work required to be done within an agreed firm price. It could be defined in terms of the percentage level of risk contingency included in the price.

Not all contracts involve intellectual property, but in those that do it is essential that the company's intellectual assets are protected and that the risk of infringing someone else's rights is minimised. These are complex matters which demand a significant degree of experience and understanding. They should not be glossed over or forgotten in any contract negotiation.

With these four business parameters in mind, it is then possible to evolve a more meaningful system of delegated authority (Figure 3.19).

Although this continues to be expressed in simple monetary terms, the system now allows routine work to be handled at a lower level, requiring the involvement of more senior people only on much higher-value work or where a decision is needed to override a business requirement. So in this example (Figure 3.19), the commercial manager is free to negotiate a £2m contract provided that: the 10 per cent profit can be made; neutral cash flow can be met; no more than £250,000 is development work; and no intellectual property licences are required. The particular figures, percentages or principles can be set according to the company's individual needs but, once set, the framework provides a sound basis for delegating authority. Such parameters can include other features such as contract duration or contract terms, but the aim should be to avoid overcomplicating the system.

	All business parameters met	One or more parameters not met
Commercial Officer	£100,000	£25,000
Assistant Commercial Manager	£500,000	£100,000
Commercial Manager	£2,000,000	£500,000
Commercial Director	£2,000,000 +	£500,000 +

Figure 3.19: Meaningful delegated authority

5 Approval for negotiations

Specific approval is needed where the negotiator wishes to operate outside his normal delegated authority or where the novelty or other peculiar features require the attention of senior management.

There is one other aspect of approval which requires mention and that is the approval of other functions within the company. This is closely related to the topic of delegated authority since those other functions whose approval may be needed for quotation purposes or negotiation purposes will also be governed by a system of delegated authority. However, the purpose of mentioning such approval here is to say that whatever procedures are put in place should be designed so as to minimise sensibly the number of signatures required before the quotation or tender can be sent or before negotiations can begin. Ideally the number of functions should be no more than four:

1. Contract negotiator.
2. Finance.
3. Estimating.
4. Implementation.

In this, the word 'implementation' is intended to mean whoever will be responsible for doing the work. This might be a project manager, a manufacturing manager or a chief designer. Clearly estimating and implementation functions must work closely together and in some companies they can be one and the same person, although this is far from ideal. The implementers must be willing to sign that they will do the work at or below the estimated cost but the process of arriving at that estimated cost should be carried out by professionally qualified and experienced estimators.

There may be more functional departments involved in approving a quotation than shown in the list above. Marketing or sales departments, for example, may also be involved. However, if the approval system is to be run efficiently (and at lowest effective cost) the number of people required to sign should be kept to a sensible minimum. One short cut that should be avoided is omitting people in the hierarchy of delegated authority (Figure 3.19). It is tempting for the Commercial Officer to take his quotation for £105,000 straight to the Commercial Director for approval in the absence of the two intermediary officers. The temptation is then for the Commercial Director to quickly

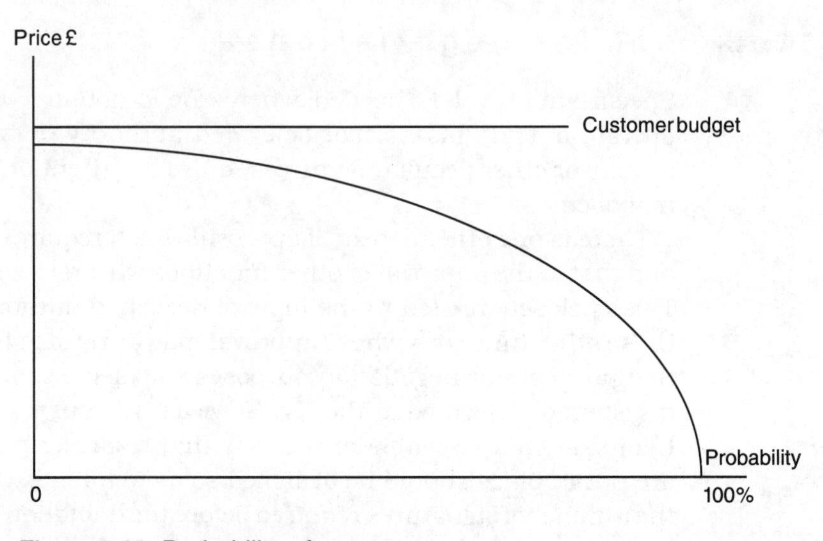

Figure 3.20: Probability of success

approve this 'trivial' quotation. Experience shows that there is a risk in ignoring in this way the detailed knowledge held by the intermediate positions and it is usually better, other than in extreme urgency, to await the return of at least one of those people.

In essence the 'core' approval shown in the above list involves the estimator signing for the responsibility that the cost estimate is accurate; the implementer signs to say he can do the job within the estimate; the finance person signs to say that the appropriate costing and pricing rates and factors have been used so that the price should generate the required profit; and the negotiator signs to say that the deal is capable of being done. In practice these responsibilities overlap and establishing the right price to quote is usually best done as a team effort.

One of the questions that is often asked of the contract negotiator during the process of approval is the probability of success. There is an expectation that the securing of the deal can be reduced to simple mathematical techniques (Figure 3.20).

Whilst it must be true that, if the quotation is for zero pounds, the probability of success will be 100 per cent, and if the quotation is above the customer's budget the chance of success must be zero, the shape of the graph in between the two extremes is indeterminable as the negotiation can depend on a large number of variables, particularly if price is not the dominant feature (Figure 3.21).

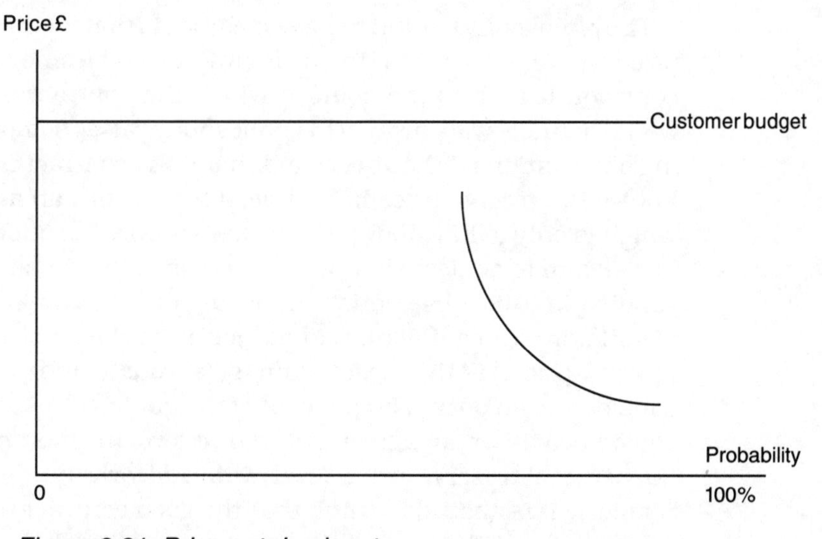

Figure 3.21: Price not dominant

Other factors to be taken into account are time frame and the personality – corporate or individual – of the other side of the negotiation.

All things considered, offering any probabilistic prognosis of success is fraught with danger.

6 Reserve position

In the previous section the percentage range of probable success was considered, but only in the context of the relationship of the price to the customer's budget.

Equally important is consideration of the degree of negotiability of the price from the point of view of the company. Mention has already been made of the need to ensure that the price secures the opportunity to make the required level of profit. Here the word 'price' means the eventually agreed price rather than the quoted price. In some environments the two will always be the same. Those trading on the basis of list prices or catalogues or those in a monopolistic position may not be prepared to consider negotiating prices, but in many contract negotiations the price, by itself or among other things, will definitely feature.

The contract negotiator must therefore know in advance not only the quoted price but also the 'walk-away' price which is sometimes referred to as the 'reserve price'.

The philosophy behind the reserve price is that it is literally the price where, for £1 less, the company really does not want the contract. It is thus the point at which the contract negotiator would actually walk away. This philosophy raises some interesting observations. It has been said that if the contract negotiator knows the reserve price he will be satisfied with an agreement which is only a little above it. If he knows only the quoted price, he will aim to achieve that price. There is only a small degree of validity in this observation. It is absurd to think that the negotiator can confidently do his job if he does not know the reserve price. If the negotiation gets rough and, all things considered, an offer of 50 per cent of the quoted price seems like a good deal, then an agreement at that level in ignorance of the 80 per cent reserve price level would clearly be disastrous. Similarly it is absurd to think that the good contract negotiator will not aim at the level of the quoted price simply because he knows that agreement at some lesser figure is acceptable.

It is also pointless for the negotiator to be told that he must aim for 85 – 95 per cent when the reserve price is only 60 per cent. This is meaningless. In this example the range is 60 – 100 per cent.

In setting the reserve price the company must take into account the opinion of the negotiator. It can be all too easy for the company to convince itself that a price of £5,000,000 would be nice and to tell the negotiator not to come back with anything less than £4,990,000. If the negotiator knows that the maximum attainable is, say, £4,750,000, then it is meaningless to set a reserve price above that value.

How then is a reserve price calculated? First it is necessary to consider that, in essence, there are only three reasons or methods by which the price can be negotiated:

1. The price is negotiated as money-related parameters are varied (eg a discount for prompt payment).
2. The price is negotiated because some amount has been added to 'give away' in negotiation (ie a simple negotiating margin).
3. The price is negotiated under pressure from the customer (eg insufficient budget).

In these instances the price negotiation is one direction only – downwards. As far as the principle of reserve prices is concerned, instance 1 does not really count. The underlying 'price for the job' remains the same. Variable factors which, because of their

	Quoted price		Reserve price	
	£		£	
Labour	500,000		400,000	
Materials	200,000		180,000	
Inflation over contract period	70,000	(10%)	46,400	(8%)
Works cost	770,000		626,400	
Contribution to overheads	154,000	(20%)	112,752	(18%)
Subtotal	924,000		739,152	
Financing cost*	92,400	(10%)	59,132	(8%)
Warranty allowance*	23,100	(2.5%)	7,391	(1%)
Liquidated damages allowance*	46,200	(5%)	–	(nil)
Subtotal	1,085,700		805,675	
Profit	162,855	(15%)	40,283	(5%)
Total	1,248,555		845,958	

* Applied to the subtotal – there are different ways of doing this calculation.

Figure 3.22: Quote and reserve prices

monetary linkage, cause the price to vary should be distinguished from the basic need to get the right price for the job. Instances 2 and 3 are similar in nature. Both represent a reduction in price not resulting from a variation in a money-related parameter. The difference between 2 and 3 is the level of intelligence which is applied. In 2 the quoted price and reserve price are conceptually the same. The 'give-away' has been added literally to be thrown away because the culture of the customer demands it. In 3 real thought is given to how the reserve price should be calculated (Figure 3.22).

In Figure 3.22 the reserve price assumes that factory efficiency will improve and reduce the labour cost. It is assumed that material prices will fall as technology moves ahead. A more optimistic view of inflation is taken. The overhead contribution is reduced from the standard 20 per cent to 18 per cent, recognising that this order will reduce the overhead load on other contracts. A more optimistic view is taken of financing costs. The warranty allowance and liquidated damages allowance are reduced to reflect confidence in the product quality and certainty of timely performance. Finally the standard profit rate is reduced, reflecting the fact that, if this contract is placed, it will bring follow-on benefits which will make it worthwhile to have taken this contract below standard profit.

It is accepted that these matters will have been taken into account in arriving at a proposed quote price. However, the purpose is to take this process through to a full conclusion to establish the point at which it would make no commercial sense to take the order.

Another way of looking at this is to say that the process arrives at the most optimistic cost estimate (ie lowest cost which gives the reserve price) and the most pessimistic cost estimate (ie highest cost which gives the quoted price), the aim being simply to secure a price which falls within that range.

7 Fall-back plans

So far in this chapter the aim has been to address the organisational aspects that affect the negotiation and the internal deliberations which should precede the negotiation. One of the difficulties to which the contract negotiator is exposed is that, once approval has been given to the negotiation plan, he is expected to go away, execute the plan and bring home the result. However, one of the recurring themes of negotiation is that things crop up which prevent such a neat and tidy conclusion. Thus it is essential that the plan identifies fall-back positions so that those granting approval are not surprised if instant success is not achieved.

In the fictional example on p. 33, a fall-back plan was identified. This is an essential part of the negotiation plan. Not to have a fall-back plan is like setting out to sea with no life raft, radio or flares. Negotiation is a bold adventure with much to win or lose. Setting out without an escape route or life preserver is utter folly.

The aim should be to set out clearly the best and the worst that could possibly happen. From this the objective should be set as closely as realistically possible to the best outcome. The fall-back plan or plans should be set at a safe distance from the worst outcome. In the example, the best outcome would be one where the customer met all the company's claims in full and the

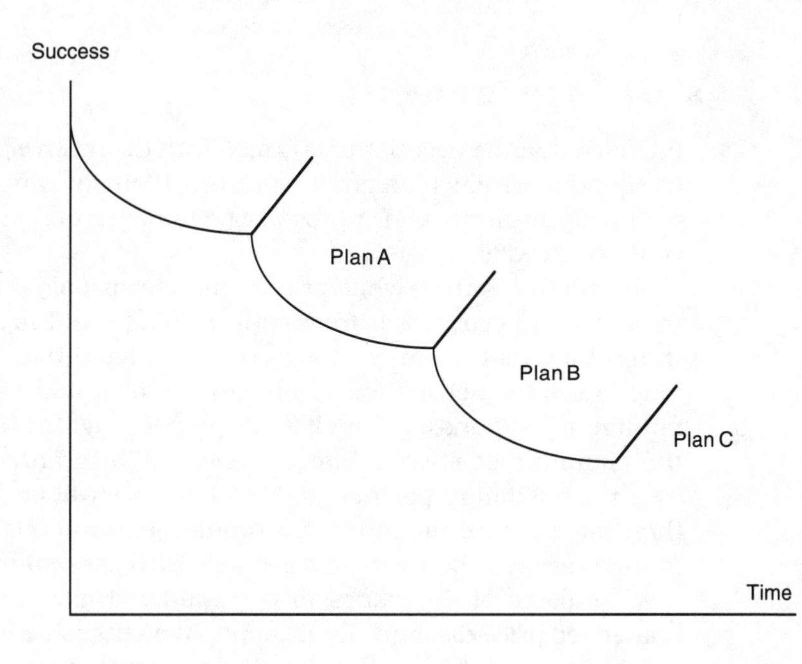

Figure 3.23: Fall-back plans

subcontractors' claims were withdrawn. This would not be realistic and so the objective was couched in terms of the relationship between the two sets of claims. The worst outcome would be the inverse: the subcontractors' claims proved in full and the customer not required to pay anything. The fall-back plan was to preclude this ever happening by forcing a direct negotiation between customer and subcontractor in such a way that the customer was responsible and liable to the company for the outcome.

If necessary there can be more than one fall-back plan to be deployed at pre-set times (Figure 3.23) or at predetermined events.

The sort of conceptualised process illustrated in Figure 3.23 is something the negotiator should keep in mind, and will be covered further in Chapter 6. For now the purpose is only to emphasise the need for fall-back plans and the need to have those identified to and approved by the company prior to the commencement of negotiations.

8 Terms of reference

Provided that the negotiatior is armed with the reserve price and the quoted price, which gives him the settlement range that is within his authority and approval, what other terms of reference could he need?

The answer is that, while price dominates people's thinking, the contract negotiator is frequently arguing about many more things than just the price. It is easy to see that if there are just four topics for negotiation, each with its own maximum and minimum positions (eg if intellectual property rights is an issue, the minimum position is that a licence will be granted royalty free, the maximum position is that no licence will be granted), then there are 16 minimum/maximum permutations with an infinite variety in between (eg a licence with 5 per cent royalties).

While some of the issues to be negotiated may be directly related (eg price discount for prompt payment) some may have external or spurious influences bearing upon them. For example, if the negotiation is for a new contract, the urgency with which the contract is wanted may have a distinct bearing on the degree to which points will be yielded or on the willingness to compromise.

With so many variables and influences dancing around, how then is the negotiator to be given some sensible terms of reference and flexibility to negotiate without the constant need to refer back for decisions or further approval?

The only good answer is that if the choice of the negotiator is well made, then he must be relied upon to exercise his judgement and make decisions on a relatively independent basis. Clearly the price range can be established. Other factors may be the subject of general or contract/customer-specific company policy. So with a sensibly limited set of constraints, the contract negotiator should be sent on his way to get the job done.

9 Managing the involvement of superiors

This might seem an odd topic but the point is this: it is frequently the case that the contract negotiator is not the Managing Director or Chief Executive. Hence the people above him in the organisation, not surprisingly, expect to have more involvement than simply authorising the quotation or approving the negotiation plan. And yet the involvement of such senior people at the wrong time or in the wrong manner can be disastrous.

The solution is to ensure that all players, whether senior managers or colleagues, have their role and the time of the entrance planned in advance as part of the negotiation plan. This means that there will be more to the negotiation than one face-to-face meeting with the other side. There may be several meetings, there will be telephone calls, there will be discussions by various people at various times. As far as possible this must be managed.

The task of these other players is to acknowledge and accept that the negotiation is being managed by the contract negotiator and that involvement must be either according to the plan or otherwise co-ordinated through him. The task of the contract negotiator is to recognise that the other players are a valuable resource which needs to be deployed usefully.

On this latter point the contract negotiator can become very protective of his baby and resent the intrusion of superiors, even when he himself has reached an impasse with the other side. Such protectiveness is misguided. An impasse can be resolved by the involvement of superiors on both sides without either negotiator losing face. If the impasse has resulted from mutually exclusive company policies from the two sides, it is right that any compromise is decided upon by the senior level of management.

Apart from that example of resolving an impasse, the most important task is for the negotiator to brief other players properly on their role. In the earlier example (p. 33) it would be likely that the subcontractor would attempt to bypass the company negotiator and appeal to a company director for early resolution. The briefing to the director must therefore be to resist the temptation to resolve one half (ie the subcontractor claims) of the problem because the agreed plan is to resolve both halves together in parallel.

If the negotiation plan is thus the focus around which the whole process is to revolve, it is sound methodology to review the plan and progress against the plan from time to time. This provides an ideal opportunity to remind the other players, and particularly superiors, of their roles and responsibilities.

One final point is to make sure that, where superiors on both sides do become involved in the process of the negotiation without the presence of the respective negotiators, they arrive at a mutual understanding of the agreement and in sufficient detail so that the negotiators can pick up the agreement and finalise or incorporate it accordingly.

10 Reporting back

One responsibility which the contract negotiator has is to report back to his management from time to time on the progress of the negotiation. This makes it sound as though every negotiation must be a tortuous and protracted affair. This is not the case. Reporting back falls into three categories:

1. Reporting the outcome.
2. Reporting progress over time.
3. Reporting during the meeting.

In point 1 it is obviously the case that, if the negotiation has reached a final conclusion, then it is necessary to advise the company of the success or failure against the objective. To digress momentarily, one of the greatest challenges facing the negotiator as he journeys back from the customer's premises is to find the most imaginative description of the result to show the brilliance of his skill, no matter how bad the outcome really was!

In point 2, if the negotiation is taking place over a period of time and across several meetings it is important to provide feedback on progress. The negotiation plan provides the basis for this so that everyone can see what was expected and how things are developing. Most importantly this process provides the opportunity to modify or adapt the plan in the light of the progress made or in the light of new information which may have emerged.

Sometimes it is necessary to report back during the actual negotiation. This may arise where the negotiation is making good progress but has changed direction significantly from that predicted in the plan. For example, as a means of reaching a compromise on one contract, the other side unexpectedly introduces the idea of doing a package deal embracing six other contracts. Although this may be well outside the plan or outside the approved terms of reference, if the negotiator can see merit in the approach he does not want to lose the opportunity through not having sufficient authority.

The balance to be achieved in these circumstances is between the need to refer back for a decision or approval and not being seen as having insufficient authority to negotiate. Referring back during the meeting can be done either in the presence or in the absence of the other side. If the point to be referred back is sensitive or if it would have ramifications which must be kept confidential, then clearly any telephone call back to base must be in private. On the other hand, it can be an impressive demonstration to allow the other side to sit while the contract negotiator calls up his Managing Director. Of course if the other side is still in the room, the Managing Director must be told that the conversation will not be in private. Occasionally one can have a little fun by calling the speaking clock and leading the 'conversation' – 'so you're saying there's no way we can accept this proposal' – again to impress the other side.

The danger in calling back to the office is that the necessary people may not be there or they may not be able or willing to make a decision on the basis of a single telephone call. So the referral back to the office has its advantages but before suggesting that a call is necessary, the negotiator must weigh up whether it is really necessary and whether the result is likely to facilitate or to stall progress being made.

11 Selecting the negotiator

Whatever the organisation may be, it will be necessary at some stage to select an individual for the particular negotiation. The three key skills to be considered in making the selection are knowledge of the job in question, a good relationship with the customer and good negotiating ability (Figure 3.24).

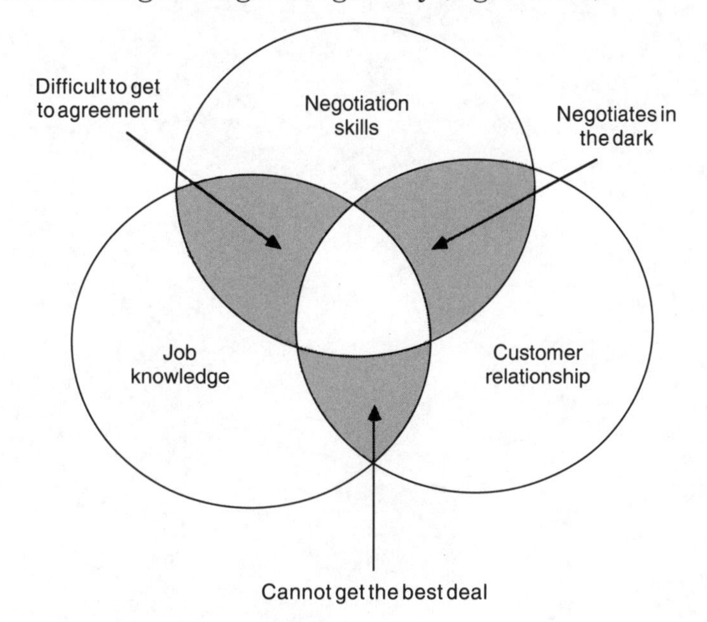

Figure 3.24: Choice of negotiator

Figure 3.24 shows that there is more to negotiation than just good negotiation skills. Someone who has only one of the three skills will be nowhere. Someone who knows the job and the customer but cannot negotiate will not secure a good deal. The ace negotiator who knows the customer but not the job is operating in the dark. The job expert who can negotiate but has no relationship with the customer will find it difficult to get to an agreement.

CHAPTER 4

Negotiation principles

1 Introduction

The aim in this chapter is to underline some of the principles that govern negotiation. Inevitably there are some topics which could be categorised either as general principles or as specific rules that apply to the negotiation itself. The actual negotiation is covered in Chapter 7. In some ways the contents of this chapter might best be described as covering the preparatory phase. This is in terms of deciding the size of the negotiating team, selecting its members, rules for the participants to absorb beforehand, planning the meeting and analysing objectives.

2 The single negotiator

If a game of chess is imagined whereby a single player is to play a team of people and where the team has a very limited ability to discuss its moves, then if all the participants are of more or less equal calibre, it is the single player who is far more likely to win than the team.

On the face of it, the team ought to win on the basis that the whole is greater than the sum of the parts. But this synergy can only be achieved if there is effective communication between the components of the team. In a negotiation such communication is naturally limited, and in any event the other side will use techniques to disrupt any intercommunication within its opposition. Furthermore, a successful team negotiation would really rely upon each member thinking the same things and going down the same track at the same time. Until the human race develops telepathic powers, team negotiations are always likely to be lost to the single negotiator.

So on balance, in most situations of contract negotiation the selection of a single negotiator is preferable to a team. Some people find comfort in the idea of safety in numbers and, while there is some merit in this (and will be covered a little further on), the experienced negotiator will not be nervous of handling things by himself. Indeed the single negotiator who will be meeting a team should rub his hands with glee at the prospect of overcoming ostensibly greater odds.

The greatest difficulty for the single negotiator meeting a team is in knowing enough about all the aspects to be negotiated. If the negotiation is about the single topic of price, the single negotiator should be able to overcome the team of six ranged against him. If the topics are price, production techniques, technical performance, engineering design, product reliability and design enhanceability, then the single negotiator meeting six experts in their respective fields is going to have a tougher time. Being properly briefed on all the topics is most important. At some stage there will be a cross-over between leaving a singleton to it and deciding to adopt a team approach.

In some circumstances it can actually be beneficial for the other side to be more expert, as it allows the contract negotiator to find a reason not to be able to make an agreement if that is what suits him. This needs to be handled very carefully as the other side are right to feel aggrieved if they think their time is being wasted by an opposition who has arrived inadequately briefed or without the proper range or level of representation.

A great advantage which the single negotiator has is in being able to exploit differences in opinion which appear as the opposition's participants each have their say. Rather as the cheetah hunts among a herd of gazelle, the single negotiator can look for the weak among the opposition and pick them off one by one.

Consider the following negotiation:

John	The single negotiator	Our side
Bill	Tough negotiator	The opposition
Ted	A soft touch	
Derek	Unsure of himself	
Peter	Sympathetic	

The first point is that, as part of the preparation, John will have discovered the characteristics of each of the opposition team. Ideally he will already know them. If he neither knows them nor is able to find out anything about them, then John will use the first part of the negotiation to learn the personalities of the others and to deal with them accordingly.

To deal with Bill, John will try to ignore him altogether. Questions asked by Bill will be ignored. John will keep his gaze fixed on the others and avoid eye contact with Bill. Body language can be used to exclude Bill from the proceedings. If Bill persists, John will diffuse his questions by bouncing them back to the others. 'Come on Peter, you know I cannot accept Bill's point.'

To exploit Ted, John will concentrate on him when it is time to make an agreement on a particular point. 'So Ted, there it is, you know I've gone further than I should, you can see it is very reasonable, now let's agree and put it to bed.'

Derek is easy prey. 'Look Ted, we've heard from Derek several times. It's obvious you're not clear on what you want so I think we must just ignore it altogether.'

Peter will fall for the logical argument. 'You see Peter, the logic of what I've said is obvious. Unless you are really trying to harm me I really don't see why you can't agree.' Poor Peter, who has never harmed anything in his life, is on hook, line and sinker.

In this example the advantages that John has are obvious. He can pick and choose when, where and how to attack, knowing that by himself he is not exposed to similar danger from the other side.

3 Negotiating in pairs

Although there are many occasions when the single negotiator has an advantage, there are other occasions when it is as, or more, beneficial for the negotiator to have a partner. As far as the simple presence of a second person is concerned, there are a number of advantages:

1. Witness.
2. Moral support.
3. Long stop.
4. Feedback.
5. Recess.

Many negotiations conclude with a set or a partial set of agreements, or perhaps an arrangement to reconvene at a later date. An agreement can only really be final when it is in writing and the written record is acknowledged by both sides as accurately representing the agreement. Prior to that point, agreements made but not reduced to writing, negotiations half completed and the like simply represent a basis or an opportunity for one side or the other to reopen closed discussions at the next meeting or to disagree with what the other side alleges to have been the agreement. After all, a negotiation is in this respect no different from any other meeting. Unless a verbatim transcript is produced immediately, people naturally forget part of what has been said. The difference with negotiation meetings is that there can be a greater incentive than is usual for people to forget on purpose. Here then is the first good reason for having a partner. He takes notes as the meeting progresses, his is a second memory as to what happened and he is thus a witness who can be used to try to stop the other side from reopening or varying agreements already made. A single negotiator attempting to insist upon his version of events is disadvantaged compared with the other side having six identical recollections.

Sometimes the contract negotiator must go into a negotiation like the fabled Light Brigade. The odds are enormous, the dangers immense and the chance of winning desperately close to zero. In such circumstances a partner to provide moral support, to soak up some of the flak, to help launch counter-attacks and diversions and to help in damage limitation can prove invaluable.

The third advantage is that, no matter how good the negotiator, there will be occasions when he cannot think of everything or occasions where he has set off on a particular path having missed some pitfall or danger that may lie ahead. In these situations a second pair of eyes provides a useful long stop to prevent the negotiator getting into difficulty.

Fourth, there is the question of feedback. Once the negotiation is over, particularly where the deal is to be concluded at a further session, it is of great benefit to be able to say to someone else, 'How did we do?', 'How should we play the next meeting?', 'What do you think they were trying to say?' and so on. This sort of hands-on feedback is invaluable.

Finally there is the recess. It is often convenient to have a break from the negotiation for each side to contemplate its position. This is a topic to be covered in Chapter 7 but suffice it here to say that a recess is much more useful if the negotiator has somebody with whom to chew over the position.

Having examined the advantages of negotiating in pairs, it is necessary to consider how the negotiation should be conducted.

First, it must be said that the two negotiators ideally must know each other well and must have a natural empathy. There should be a silent but effective understanding between them so that at the meeting neither will tread on the other's toes, they will not compete to speak and they will instinctively know when the other is in trouble and wade in to help. Even the best negotiator sometimes talks himself into a corner or up a blind alley and, while he should know how to extricate himself, it can be greatly effective for a partner to leap to the rescue. 'I think what John is trying to say is that ...' takes the discussion onto a different track (because this clarifying statement is only used to change the subject!) and the heat off the negotiator.

A primary use of the negotiation pair is to act out the hard-man/soft-man game. In this, one person takes a hard, aggressive and uncompromising approach which is designed to soften up the opposition. When the 'soft man' then appears to take the opposition's side and press the 'hard man' for a particular compromise (which is all the negotiators wanted in the first place), the softened-up opposition is only too glad to grab at the suggestion and so the deal is done.

The problem with the hard-man/soft-man game is that years of watching TV policemen act it out means that it is easy for the opposition to spot unless it is conducted in a very subtle manner. All negotiation techniques, including this one, become diluted in their effectiveness once the opposition has realised what is going on and has deployed suitable countermeasures.

A more interesting device that the negotiation pair can use is the 'side-show'. This appears in two forms with the same effect intended in each case. The pair negotiate a particular point between themselves rather than with the opposition in the hope that the other side will slip into just sitting and listening and being content with the outcome. The two variations are, first, for the pair to discuss and agree a point that they have put forward, and second, to discuss and agree a point put forward by the other side. So the dialogue is not as one would expect (Figure 4.1) but is as shown in Figure 4.2.

So in this example the opposition may have put forward a suggestion that, as part of the deal, they should be granted a licence to modify the other side's designs. Rather than argue with Bill and Peter, John and Jack argue it out between themselves:

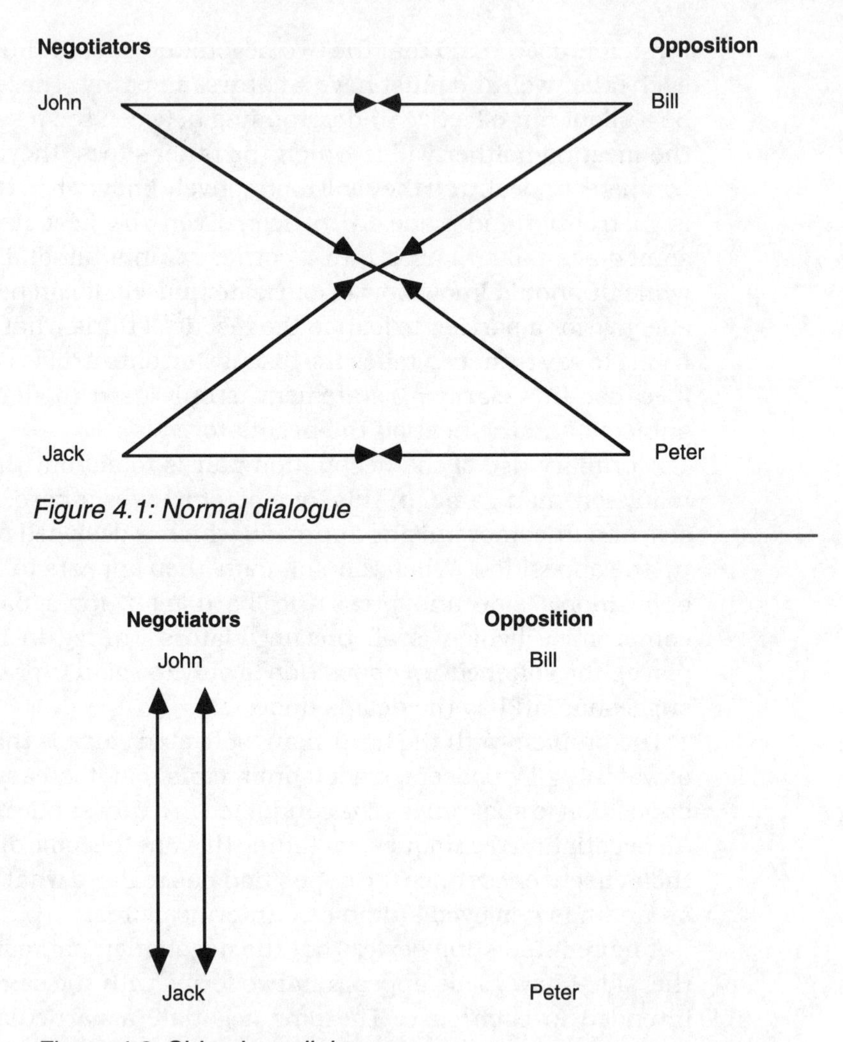

Figure 4.1: Normal dialogue

Figure 4.2: Side-show dialogue

John: It seems to me that Bill has put forward a reasonable request.
Jack: Let me see if I understand the point. Bill wants a royalty-free licence to modify our design.
John: Yes, that's it.
Jack: Of course, they haven't contributed to the cost of our background know-how.
John: Yes, I see what you mean. It wouldn't be fair, would it?
Jack: Well, I suppose if there was a 25 per cent royalty that might be OK.
John: That seems fair to me.

To illustrate the point, this example is somewhat obvious and blunt. However, it shows the aim which is apparently to debate the other side's point all the way to an apparently fair conclusion without ever actually putting forward with any strength the other side's arguments or justifications.

4 Team negotiations

As has been said, there are times when the only sensible approach is to construct a team. This may simply be because the other side will field a team and, all things considered, a single negotiator or pair of negotiators would be overmatched. It may be because the range of topics to be covered is such as to require experts in the particular fields.

It must be a truism that the rate of progress at a negotiation is inversely proportional to the number of people taking part. It must also be true that, the greater the number of people in the team, the greater the chance of somebody saying or doing the wrong thing.

So in all instances the decision to field a team which is greater in number than two or three must be carefully considered. Certainly in any major negotiation for a new contract many people may see themselves as necessarily being involved. At least the Managing Director, a brace of directors, the Bid Manager, the Project Manager, the Proposal Manager, etc, may all see themselves as having a part to play. This should be avoided. It is the task of the contract negotiator to negotiate the contract. The involvement of others in the whole process must be carefully planned and handled (see Chapter 3).

If the negotiation is to be conducted as a team effort it must be absolutely clear who the leader is going to be. Rules for the leader and for the supporters are given later on in this chapter. The need for a clear leader is twofold. First, the negotiation must be carefully managed; people must not speak out of turn or across each other. If agreements are to be reached, then decisions have to be made. Only one person can make the decisions. For these reasons a single person must be the focus of the team's efforts. Second, in most team negotiations the actual process of negotiation only happens between two people – one on each side (Figure 4.3).

Despite the multitude of discussions that might be taking place, the real negotiation happens only between our man C and their man B.

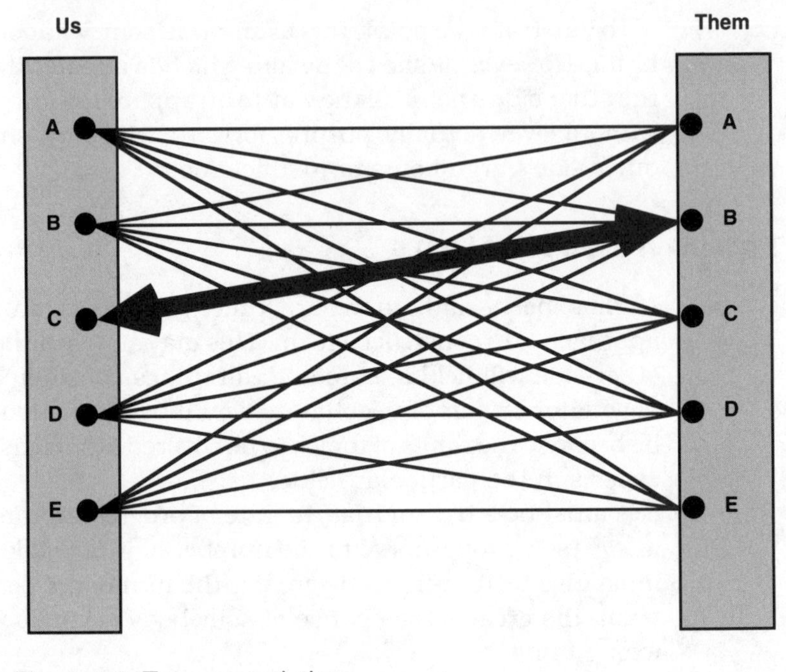

Figure 4.3: Team negotiations

5 Selecting the team

Once a team approach has been decided upon, the selection of the team members is most important. Having nominated the contract negotiator to lead the negotiation and having selected him in line with the guidance in Chapter 3, it is necessary to examine the criteria against which to select the other team members (Figure 4.4).

The three criteria are very important. The person without the technical skills in the particular field of expertise has no place on the team. Just having the skills is not, however, sufficient. At the end of the day, negotiations with customers are best conducted by people who are acceptable to the customer. This is not to say that the customer should have a right to veto those whom the company sends to the meeting, but rather that the company should always be careful not to field people who by their very nature – rightly or wrongly – would put the customer's back up. The third criteria is one of having adequate negotiation skills. This does not mean that the team member is supposed to be a fully fledged negotiator but only that he can follow the rules (set

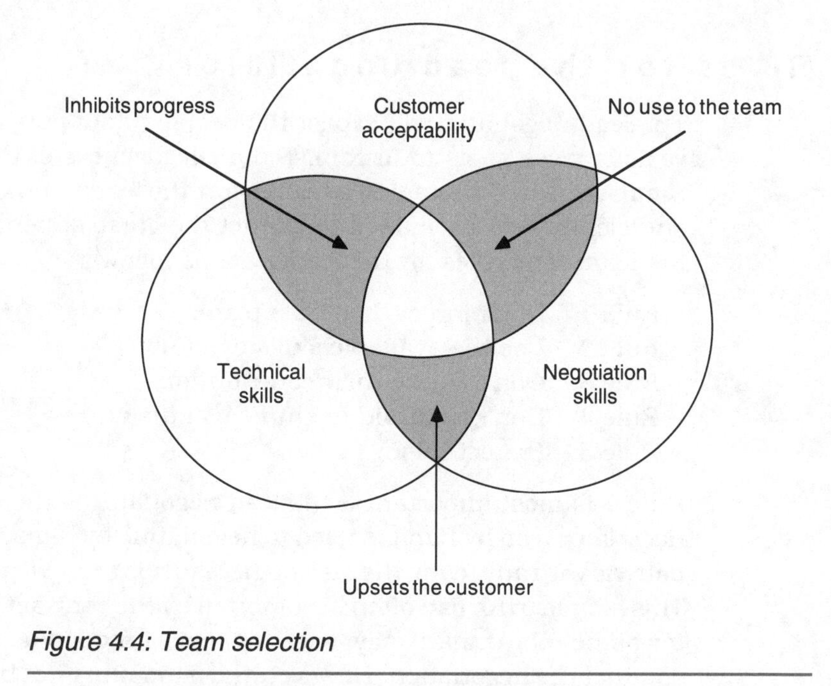

Figure 4.4: Team selection

out in section 7 of this chapter) and that he has the intrinsic characteristic of a quick brain coupled to a slow mouth!

The three skills illustrated in Figure 4.4 must be fairly evenly balanced. In selecting an engineer to join the team to argue some highly technical points it is preferable to have someone of medium technical ability who is able to impress the customer rather than a scientific genius who has not been forgiven by the customer for what he said to them last time.

Once the team is selected, the planning and preparation stage (covered later in this chapter) is very critical. However, some basic points ought to be remembered before the meeting ever gets under way. First, the team must be organised to arrive together, and if people are travelling separately then it is essential to muster near to the venue so that the team can arrive in unison. In no circumstances should one or two people allow themselves to be drawn into discussion with the other side until the full team is in place.

The final point is that, once the negotiation has been planned and the team selected, no member should be allowed to contact his 'opposite number' on the other side 'just to let them know where we're coming from'. Any such prior release of real (or spoof) information must only be part of the agreed negotiation plan.

6 Rules for the lead negotiator

The lead negotiator will expect the people in support to follow various rules so as to maximise the effectiveness of the team. Similarly, when managing a team effort the leader must also be sufficiently self-disciplined to extract the greatest benefit from his team. The rules for the leader are as follows:

Rule 1 Don't forget that it's a team.
Rule 2 Use the available skills carefully.
Rule 3 Don't ignore their contribution.
Rule 4 Don't be afraid to shut them up.
Rule 5 Protect them.

Rule 1 is most important if the lead negotiator is the contract negotiator who by habit is used to negotiating by himself or in a pair. As with any team, the task of the leader is to give leadership. This simple truth can often be forgotten by the contract negotiator as he, not unnaturally, sees his main function as being to conduct the negotiation. However, the team must not be forgotten. It requires direction and management from the leader, otherwise the team members will be either sitting quietly, wondering why their time is being wasted, or making unwanted and unwelcome intrusions into the dialogue. Also from the customer's perspective it is necessary for the team to come across as an integrated body of people.

Rule 2 says that the leader should use the available skills carefully. This captures two ideas. First, the leader must use the skills positively, and second, he must use them carefully. The former point is an extension of Rule 1, that if the skills are available at the meeting then the leader must take advantage of them. The latter point is that the leader must remember not only that the team has been selected on the basis of the individuals having the balanced skills (Figure 4.4) mentioned earlier, but also that the range of technical skills will have been chosen so as to provide a small army of experts. Thus the temptation to allow this group of intelligent experts to join freely in the whole debate should be resisted, as a free debate is unmanageable and therefore dangerous.

Imagine a negotiation team having a range of technical skills:

John Contract Negotiator (the leader)
Alec Project Manager

Tom	Engineering Manager
Alan	Programme Manager

The other side asks the question, 'Can you do the Mk II widget in six months?' All three of the supporters will undoubtedly have a view but John must prevent all three attempting to answer together, because three different answers or three conflicting answers will emerge. So John must choose his questions carefully and direct them at particular individuals:

John: Tom, what is the status of the Mk II?
Tom: Assembly is finished and we are about to start final testing.
John: Alan, how does that look from a programme point of view?
Alan: Provided there are no hiccups, four to six months is OK.
John: Alec, do you have any comments?
Alec: There may be a problem with the connecting cables because of supplier lead times.

This is much better than all three trying to answer the same question, and it leaves the leader still in control.

The third rule is not to ignore the contribution of each team member. In the heat of the moment it is easy to ignore something said which appears to be trivial or has not been said with sufficient force. In the above example, the point made by Alec about the connecting cables could be crucial. Typically a negotiation, like any conversation, will revolve around the main issue – here the delivery time of Mk II widgets. If it is known that the order would probably include the connecting cables and that these are problematic, then it would be foolish to overlook them at the negotiation stage, as the order, when offered, either would be unacceptable or could not be performed, with serious commercial consequences.

The fourth rule is that the leader should not be afraid to get his side to shut up. Any person saying the wrong thing, drifting off the negotiation plan or unnecessarily aggravating the other side needs to be stopped. There are a number of non-verbal communications which can suffice. A kick under the table, a raised hand, a hand on the arm/shoulder or sometimes a glare will suffice. Sometimes, all the non-verbal communications in the world will not stop he of the loose mouth, once in full, damaging flow, from doing his worst.

In these circumstances something needs to be said, and the leader must choose from the blunt 'shut up' on the one hand, to the less spectacular 'that's an interesting point but of course it won't really happen like that in practice' on the other. Occasionally the best method is quietly to pass the offender a written note so that the message can be conveyed in the bluntest terms!

The final rule is that the leader must protect his team from the tactics, tricks and ploys of the other side. Once they have spotted the weak or vulnerable people they will attack and try to divide and conquer. The leader can again use non-verbal communication by leaning forward in front of his people, by opening his arms as though to catch the question and by interrupting any eye contact between the other side and his people. Verbal techniques include fielding the question, answering for the other person and changing the subject.

7 Rules for the support negotiator

There are more rules for the support negotiator than for the leader. This can be rationalised on the basis that the leader, as a contract negotiator, knows what he is doing and the supporters do not, hence the guidance they need is greater:

Rule 1 Follow the leader.
Rule 2 Listen well.
Rule 3 Stick to the plan.
Rule 4 Recognise deviations.
Rule 5 Don't throw in new information.
Rule 6 Don't drop the team in it.
Rule 7 Avoid answering awkward questions.
Rule 8 Don't stray into other areas.
Rule 9 Be economical in answering questions.
Rule 10 Don't volunteer information.
Rule 11 Don't lose sight of the objective.
Rule 12 Don't forget it's tough.
Rule 13 Have fun.
Rule 14 Don't argue the other side's case.

Experience shows that, in the vast majority of negotiations, the actual process of negotiation occurs between just two people – one on each side – regardless of the respective team sizes. This is hardly surprising if the chess analogy is recalled. It would be ludicrous to think of a chess game being played equally well by a team as by a single person. The single person controls the tactics within an overall strategy, sacrifices pieces or positions and captures pieces or territory as part of an overall game plan. The golden rule must be that the negotiation is the responsibility of the leader and all other participants are there to support him.

To support the leader effectively, the supporter must develop listening skills so that he is sensitive to the line being pursued by the leader and its probable purpose, and so that he is alert and prepared to lend supporting argument if invited to do so by the leader.

One of the worst things that can happen to the leader is for one of his team accidentally – or even worse intentionally – in the heat of the moment to usurp the leader's role. If *that* problem is bad, then the seriousness is increased tenfold if the usurper deviates from the agreed negotiation plan. At best this will cause confusion and at worst is a recipe for disaster.

Diversions from the plan must be orchestrated by the leader and the team, if they have been listening well and have been sensitive to the general trend in the negotiation, will see how and to what extent the plan is being abandoned. The leader will be conscious of the need to let the team know his thinking and will find a way of bringing everyone up to speed, even if it means calling for a recess.

A further action to be avoided at the meeting is the open tabling of 'new' information. It is not unnatural as the discussion proceeds for someone to recall additional data or to see a new slant on certain things. Whatever the reason, the worst thing he can do is to table it, leaving the leader with the awful prospect of trying to recover from a self-inflicted shotgun wound to the foot. If there is new information to consider, it should be communicated to the leader. Again, it is preferable to have a recess rather than potentially destroy the painstakingly achieved progress through ill-timed presentation of extra information.

Regardless of the leader/supporter functionality, the team is nevertheless there as a team representing the company. It should be seen by the opposition as being united and of a common view. It destroys the credibility of the entire enterprise if the team appears to be divided or unequally briefed, or, in the very worst extreme, antagonistic to one another. For example, if the supporter should say to the leader, 'Actually, I disagree with you there', then the negotiation will almost certainly plummet. It is an unforgivable mistake which the opposition should ruthlessly exploit. There may very well be disagreement but it should not be made public and if the supporter believes the leader has got it seriously wrong, he must find a discreet (but rapid) means of letting the leader know.

In many cases the commercial negotiator shows a certain reluctance to take others along in support of the negotiation. This reluctance flows from a great fear that the non-expert will hinder rather than help through his not unnatural wish to answer questions. If there are technical issues to resolve then the presence of the supporter may be unavoidable. From the point of view of the lead negotiator there is a great danger that the supporter will then rush off in his eagerness to display his deep understanding and knowledge of the subject to answer all the wrong questions from the other side. Everyone has the basic intellectual desire to demonstrate that the question can be answered. In a negotiation the other side will be seeking to put questions on areas in which they perceive the company position to be weak. To answer such questions fully and frankly is to pull the proverbial rug from beneath one's feet. Far better, within reason, to feign ignorance, promise to check later or find some other way to avoid giving a direct answer.

Even worse than answering awkward questions is answering questions in areas where the person has no expert knowledge. The leader has enough problems with which to deal without having to keep his own side under control and without having to interrupt his own people to prevent them going off into the wrong subject.

Another facet of the answering of questions – where of course it is in the company's interest so to do – is to be economical with the truth. From a legal viewpoint there are significant risks in lying, as the individual and the company may be guilty of fraud, attempted fraud or misrepresentation. Economy with the truth is not free of these risks but the general objective must be to answer questions with the minimum of information.

There is good information and bad information when it comes to the actual negotiation. Beforehand all information is good, even if in itself it is bad news, but once at the meeting one of the worst statements the supporter can make begins with the words 'I don't know if this helps or not', for if he does not know, the chances are that whatever he is going to say will help the other side. In any event, he is giving his own side no more time than the opposition to consider the information and its implications.

One of the golden rules in any negotiation is not to lose sight of the objectives. It can be all too easy to get carried away and perhaps submerged in vast volumes of information, intellectual debates, slanging matches or whatever but sight should not be lost of the objective of having the meeting in the first place and it should be pursued relentlessly.

A feature of the negotiation that often comes as something of a surprise is the apparent attitude of the opposition and the atmosphere in which it is conducted. Whatever the subject of the negotiation, it is likely to have cropped up as an issue following a period of friendly relations. For example, where a contract has been running smoothly for some time, the interface between the two parties will have been amicable. Routine progress meetings and reviews will have passed off with the two sides congratulating themselves on their close co-operation and friendly manner in which the business is conducted. Suddenly there is an issue to resolve which normal activities and correspondence have failed to settle. A negotiation is necessary and the other side appears in a far more aggressive, difficult and formal manner than previously. This of course is not really surprising and indeed one's own side will be in a similar mode. It should therefore be seen as a normal part of negotiation and, while excessive aggression or rigidness is rarely a recipe for success, it should not be found off-putting.

Even though the negotiation should be expected to be tough, it is a very stimulating and potentially rewarding activity. By and large the best negotiators are those who not only have the technical and personal skills to carry it off successfully but also enjoy it for its own sake. Similarly, the supporter should see his participation in the same light and expect not only to make his contribution but also to take some degree of personal satisfaction from it.

Finally it should not be forgotten that the other side will have good points and, at one extreme, the opposition may actually be in the right and the company in the wrong. This is no reason, however, to start agreeing with him. Similarly, the supporter must resist the temptation to support the opposition's case which, at worst, can have the supporter actually appearing to change sides.

8 Planning

Montgomery said that planning is everything, but nothing ever goes according to plan. This encapsulates wonderfully the value of negotiation planning. A plan tells you where you are or where you should have been. It tells you where to go next. It helps to get you back to where you wanted to be.

In Chapter 3 the merits of a negotiation plan were discussed. In that chapter the idea of a negotiation plan was to cover the execution of tactics over a period of time in order to achieve the objective. Many of the advantages of such a plan are to do with communicating strategy within the company, seeking approval and managing the involvement of superiors. It might best be described as the internal negotiation plan. There is also the need to plan for the actual negotiation meeting with the other side. Such a plan might be described as the external negotiation plan.

The external negotiation plan needs only to be discussed with those who are going to participate in the meeting. If the contract negotiator is to be by himself, he nevertheless ought to sketch out in his mind what the plan for the meeting is to be. The plan must consider a number of aspects:

1. Venue, timing and duration.
2. Order of play.
3. Strategy.
4. Tactics.
5. Objectives analysis.

Strategy, tactics and objectives analysis will be dealt with later in this chapter. It is important to make sure that the venue and timing are planned, and this will be covered in Chapter 7. As far as duration is concerned, the contract negotiator must decide whether the meeting is to be long or short, whether the other side will cause it to be long or short and therefore to allocate sufficient time plus a contingency for the meeting. It is an unwise negotiator who promises to be home by a certain time on the day of a negotiation!

The order of play is most important. What is meant here is that, in a negotiation where several aspects are to be discussed and agreed, there are essentially only two choices. First, all of the issues can be tabled at the start of the meeting, or second, the issues can be thrown in as the meeting progresses.

The advantages of putting all the issues forward together is that at least the other side knows what is coming. Indeed if there is any doubt that the people on the other side may not have authority to deal with or settle all of the things that are to come up, then it is as well that a formal agenda is sent in advance of the meeting with a polite message to ensure that the other side has suitable authority. The disadvantage is that the breadth and depth of the topics may be such as to scare the other side off.

The advantage of feeding the issues into the meeting piecemeal is that the order of raising things or whether to raise them at all can be decided as the meeting progresses. If the first hour goes well, then that is the time to introduce the more difficult points. If it has not gone well, the difficult things can be left until later or perhaps left out altogether and held back for a further meeting. One of the judgements to be made as any negotiation proceeds is how much can be squeezed out of it without spoiling the whole thing.

9 Preparation

Preparation and planning are closely related topics. In the previous section, planning was said to cover venue/timing/duration, order of play, strategy, tactics and objectives analysis. The last three items are dealt with later in this chapter as they require both planning and preparation. Additionally there is preparatory work to be done:

1. Data gathering.
2. Preparatory meeting.
3. Rehearsal.
4. Opposition analysis.
5. Mental preparation.

Data gathering is a most important part of preparing to negotiate. Information, data, facts, records, opinions are all ammunition for the contract negotiator. If the other side is better prepared by having more data then the negotiator will be outgunned, so data gathering must be very thorough. Facts or purported facts need to be checked. Recollections must be verified as memory is notoriously unreliable. Files should be read. Letters, telexes, faxes and minutes must be reviewed. It is as though the negotiator is taking on the mantle of a barrister who must defend his accused client in one of the most adversarial environments – a court of law. If one was accused of a crime one would expect the barrister not to leave any stone unturned in the defence of one's interest – similarly with the company's contract negotiator. The company expects that he will leave no stone unturned in the defence of its interests.

The key requirement of data gathering to which all contributors must adhere is to find all the information related to the negotiation. A distinction is being drawn here between related and relevant information. If the search is for relevant information, then people will make assumptions or judgements about what is and what is not relevant. One of the difficulties is that, until the negotiation has started, it is not always possible to determine the relevance of a piece of information. Far better in the preparatory phase to gather all related information. In this way there should be no surprises at the negotiation. The contract negotiator, if he has collected all the related information, has the ability to dismiss irrelevancies raised by the other side because he is already aware of the matter and has thought through the arguments for so dismissing it. He also has the ability to dip into this pool of related but irrelevant information to find a red herring or two (of which more later in Chapter 7).

Before any negotiation, it is necessary to have a preparatory meeting. It is vital that all the players understand this need and give their full commitment. The meeting should follow a number of rules:

Rule 1 Allow sufficient time.
Rule 2 All players to attend.
Rule 3 Review the internal negotiation plan.
Rule 4 Review the external negotiation plan.
Rule 5 Review the gathered data.
Rule 6 Analyse the opposition players.
Rule 7 Review the objectives analysis.
Rule 8 Arrange a rehearsal.

All of this is really to say, 'Where do we want to get to and how are we going to get there?' In this list, Rules 3 to 8 are covered elsewhere in this chapter. Rule 1 makes the point that the preparatory meeting is wasted if insufficient time is allowed. This is not only in the context of allowing enough time for the meeting but also, and more importantly, in the context of allowing a sensible time interval between the preparatory meeting and the negotiation. If the interval is too great, the contract negotiator will not have the latest information to hand, decisions may have been overtaken by events and the players may have forgotten what was agreed. On the other hand, if the interval is too brief then the negotiator may be inadequately prepared. Sure enough, if the preparatory meeting is scheduled for the afternoon before the day of the negotiation the meeting will identify the need for more information, more checking or more decisions for which there will then be no time.

If the negotiation is to be handled by more than one person, it is vital for all the participants to be involved in the preparatory meeting. It is worse than useless to have somebody turn up for the negotiation if he comes to it cold without the benefit of involvement in the planning and preparatory stages.

One of the tasks of preparation is to rehearse the negotiation. This has the advantage of preparing the negotiator for whatever arguments the other side may come up with, but also the process in itself will convince the company that 100 per cent success is not a foregone conclusion. The internal negotiation plan (to which the company gives its formal approval) will have highlighted potential weaknesses, but the process of thorough preparation together with the existence of an external negotiation plan (which is the negotiator's crib sheet for a specific meeting) can sometimes cause the company to convince itself that it has an overwhelming case. It is a healthy reminder for the company not to bank the results of a deal which has not yet been done.

If it is to be done properly, the rehearsal must be a serious attempt to emulate the prospective negotiation. The contract negotiator and his team must head up against a small group of individuals who are prepared to role-play the other side's personnel. Experience shows that if the rehearsal is conducted in this way and the substitutes for the other side really attempt to tear down the company's case, not only can the case be strengthened but also it frequently turns out that the actual negotiation is less tough than the rehearsal!

If the company is going to appoint its best negotiator or assemble its most able team, that will necessarily take into account the experience, skills and personalities of the particular people. By corollary it would be a major omission for the preparation not to take account of the experience, skills and personalities who are likely to appear for the other side. Thus it is useful to find out in advance who is going to be on the other side. This allows the usual protocol of fielding players of more or less equivalent status to be observed. It also allows analysis to be done of the strengths and weaknesses of the other side and thereby to select specific tactics for the negotiation.

The final point to be made on preparation is that the negotiator must be mentally prepared for the negotiation. This is not the book to recommend or prescribe yoga, kung fu or maternity breathing exercises as techniques for getting into the right frame of mind. The point is simply that the negotiator is 99 per cent living off his wits. All the plans and planning in the world cannot help if most of it is not committed to memory. Mental preparation is paramount.

The topics of strategy, tactics and objectives analysis form part of the planning and preparation processes but, rather than split them between these two processes, they are dealt with in their own right in the succeeding sections of this chapter.

10 Strategy

The internal negotiation plan should embrace overall strategy covering a period of time in which several negotiation meetings may take place, and it might also address the impact on the company of the success or failure of that strategy. The external negotiation plan should cover the strategy for the particular negotiation. It is a little difficult to see how one meeting needs a strategy. Strategy is defined as 'the overall plan of a campaign' and tactics are defined as 'the art of manoeuvring one's forces', and so tactics support strategy. Surely, then, the conduct of one of a series of meetings is simply a matter of tactics. While tactics for the meeting are important, there should also be a strategy and it can best be seen as a set of optional plans (Figure 4.5), each having its own set of tactics.

So the strategy might be to have three or four different plans for one meeting:

Plan A	Don't agree to anything. Just test their resolve.
Plan B	Force them to break off negotiations.
Plan C	Use the hard-man/soft-man approach.
Plan D	Play it amicably. Compromise to get agreements.

The point is that the plan to be executed can be finally decided once the negotiation is under way and the temperature of the water has been tested. Furthermore it is possible to switch from one plan to another as matters progress.

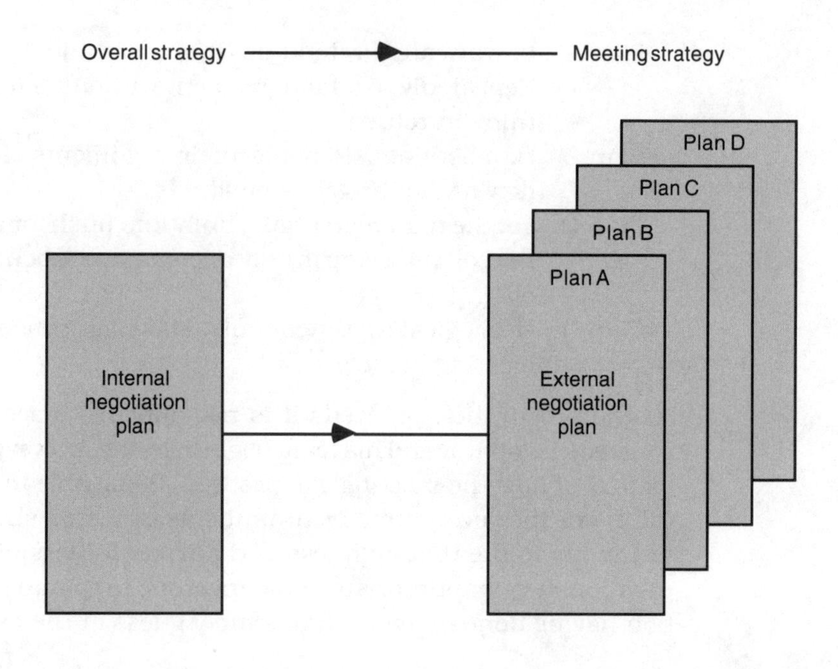

Figure 4.5: Meeting strategy

11 Tactics

In this chapter the matters to be considered before the negotiation meeting are addressed. The negotiator should have an armoury of tactics from which to choose as each negotiation progresses, but these in principle are independent of the particular negotiation. They are simply always carried and used as and when the need arises. Such tactics are described in Chapter 7. The fighting soldier always carries a semi-automatic rifle and two grenades regardless of the battle he is about to join. If he knows in advance that he will need a mortar, he makes his plans and preparations accordingly. Similarly with negotiation tactics, some can be selected in advance. Tactics selected in this way will be linked to the various plans (Figure 4.5) that make up the strategy for the particular meeting. Therefore if the example above is used, the preselection of tactics may be seen as follows:

Plan A Prevaricate. Pretend not to understand. Repeatedly ask for agreement without offering anything in return.

Plan B Be obstinate. Ridicule their arguments. Introduce new and outrageous demands.

Plan C Let the hard man argue, bully and push for more and the soft man step in only once they are about to break off.

Plan D Use logical argument only. Make agreements as the meeting proceeds.

As the preparation proceeds it is not difficult to see that the contract negotiator and his team begin to build up a very detailed picture of how the meeting will proceed. Being able to say after the event that everything went much as expected should be a testimony to the thoroughness and purposefulness of the preparation. It is inappropriate and dangerous to go into a negotiation having done no more than simply guess at the outcome.

12 Objectives analysis

The final leg of the planning and preparation stage is to analyse the objectives that each side has for the particular meeting. Again, the internal negotiation plan will give the overall objective but perhaps only in limited detail. The objectives for the meeting need to be considered in detail.

The first thing to say is that the contract negotiator should not concentrate on his side's objectives to the exclusion of the other side's possible wishes. It is sometimes assumed that the list of things which the two sides want to resolve will automatically be common. This is frequently not the case. Indeed there will be occasions when it is hoped that some of the other side's points can be deliberately kept off the list. So it is important to keep both sides' aims in mind. Perhaps all the contract negotiator wants is for the other side to restart accepting deliveries and to release frozen payments. To go into the negotiation without considering that the other side wants additional testing done and a longer period for warranty is to guarantee an unsuccessful outcome.

The objectives of each side can be analysed (Figure 4.6) in an objective way.

This provides a very detailed view of how each point for the negotiation is likely to turn out. If the company objectives are considered first, this technique forces the negotiator to sort his

Company objectives

		Opposition position		
		Impossible	Difficult	Easy
NEEDS	Must			
	Nice			
	Bonus			

Opposition objectives

		Our position		
		Impossible	Difficult	Easy
NEEDS	Must			
	Nice			
	Bonus			

Figure 4.6: Objectives analysis

objectives into must-haves, nice-to-haves and bonuses. This begins to introduce a sense of realism. With a little thought, previous experience, knowledge of the other side and some research it is not difficult to then sort the objectives by the opposition's likely position on each one. This gives more realism. Similarly, if the opposition's likely objectives are also analysed it forces the contract negotiator to think out in advance which points may have to be conceded, and as well as the level of preparedness this provides, it also tells him which potential concessions he would need to seek company approval for prior to the negotiation.

If all the points are sprinkled across the two charts then the negotiation is likely to have a successful outcome. In this sense successful outcome means that there are sufficient number of points and sufficient flexibility on both sides for an agreement to be reached. It is usually true that, the more matters there are to be negotiated, the greater the chance of there being an agreement.

If, however, all the points are in the must-have/impossible-to-yield boxes then there will be no chance of agreement. In this situation the contract negotiator has three options. First, he can abandon or postpone the negotiation and wait for the situation to change. Second, he can force a reconsideration on his side as to whether all the points are really must-haves. Third, he can proceed with the negotiation not in expectation of an agreement but merely as a data-gathering exercise to see if the assumptions made about the opposition's position were correct and also to test the opposition's resolve on the various points.

Of these three options the third is the best. Abandoning the negotiation before it starts has little appeal to the good contract negotiator and should only be followed as a last resort. Deciding upon concessions or weakening the position before even testing the temperature of the water also has little appeal, although in some cases it is obviously the right thing to do. Going forward with a proposal for new work at £2m is foolish if the customer's budget is only £1m. On balance, the third option is preferred. Going into an ostensible negotiation where the hope of agreement is futile should do little or no harm and should provide a wealth of new information with which to modify the internal negotiation plan.

CHAPTER 5

The whole process

1 Introduction

Negotiation is a process in which mutually conflicting aims are discussed with a view to finding sufficient common ground that an accommodation can be reached whereby each side goes away relatively content with its part of the agreement.

People therefore see the negotiation as a process with a start and a finish. The start is the point at which the two sides set out their wishes with supporting arguments. The end is reached after discussion when the two sides are ready to shake hands on the deal. Therefore the negotiation meeting can be seen as the start of a process the end of which will be the reconciliation of opposing views.

This view is entirely wrong in any other than the simplest of situations. In a long-term relationship such as many companies have with their customers, the negotiation or series of negotiations is just a small part in the overall scheme of things. In the case of a negotiation for the award of a contract after competitive tendering, the whole process can be seen as in Figure 5.1.

In this example it is perfectly obvious that the contract negotiations must be based upon the events that went before. The two sides could not come together in ignorance of the prior events and negotiate successfully. The negotiations are purposeful only if the aim is to reconcile opposing views that have developed over a period of time.

It is less obvious but equally important to recognise that the negotiation of a contract dispute will have considerable regard to what happened before the problem arose (Figure 5.2).

Again it would be foolish to think that the negotiators could come together cold without taking cognisance of prior events. In this example (Figure 5.2), before the negotiations have started

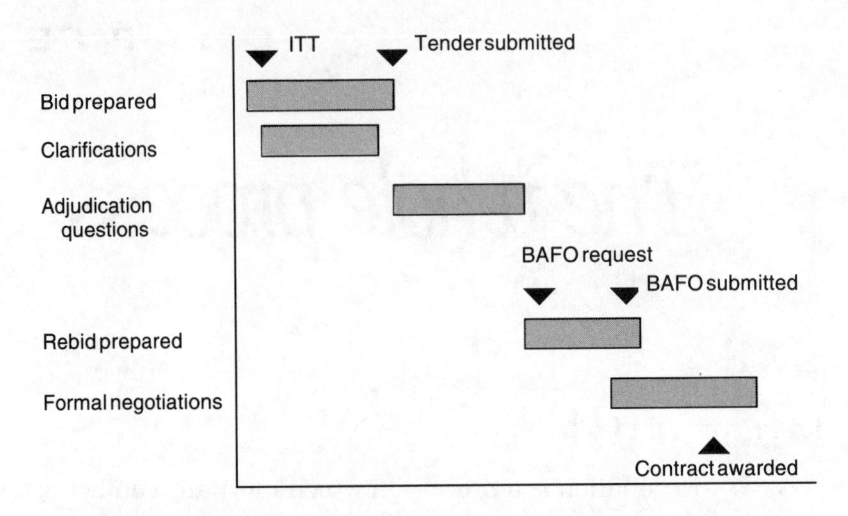

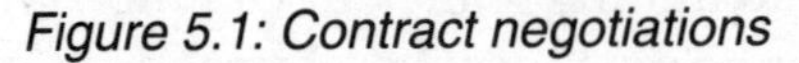

Figure 5.1: Contract negotiations

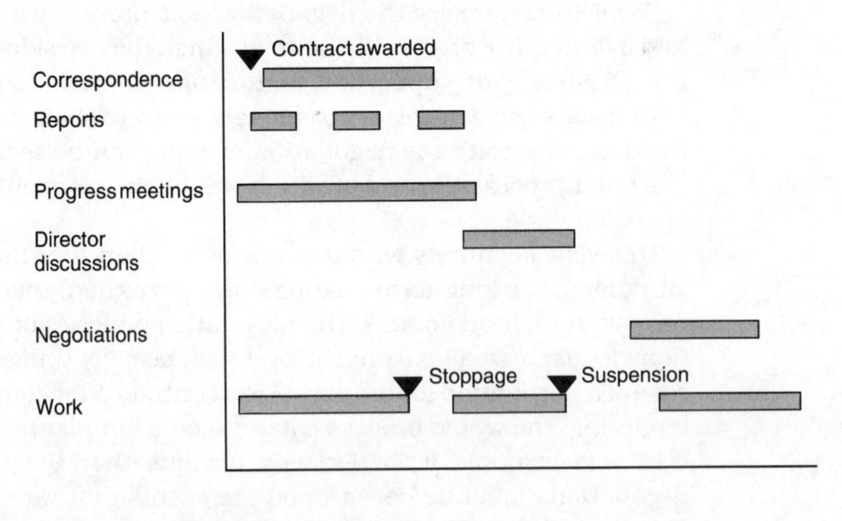

Figure 5.2: Dispute negotiations

the work has ground to a halt once and been suspended once. The parties have exchanged correspondence, meetings have taken place, reports have been sent and the respective directors have had discussions. All this must necessarily be taken into account.

The lesson to be learned here is that negotiation is not the start of a process but it is the end of a process. And yet in both examples experience shows that people conceive negotiation to be the reverse of this. It is sometimes expected that in contract negotiation, the negotiation can ignore the Invitation to Tender (ITT) or the clarification questions or the response made in the Best and Final Offer (BAFO), and simply start from the position that the company wishes at that point in time as though nothing had gone before. It is sometimes expected that in dispute negotiation the contract negotiatior can magically effect a miraculous escape for his company, no matter how deep the hole that the company has already dug itself. Both such expectations are misplaced. History cannot easily be ignored.

This point is worth repeating. Negotiation must be seen as being at the end or very close to the end of a process. It is not the start of a process. This is what is meant by the 'whole process'. It is the consideration of a whole series of events of which negotiation meetings are but a part.

2 Managing the relationship

In many businesses success or failure depends upon the quality of the relationships that the company has with the outside world. It needs a good relationship with its bank and with other financial institutions. It needs a good relationship with governmental regulatory authorities. It needs a good relationship with its suppliers. The use of partnership sourcing in place of old-fashioned buying is certainly an example of relationship-based transactions. It is vital that the company has a good relationship with its customers.

Good customer relations derive from a number of things. Attractive prices, quality goods and timely delivery are the main drivers. Advertising and public relations are also factors. The customer must feel that the company cares about him. He expects friendly and efficient salesmen. The company should aim to take care of the customer. Invitations to trade shows, entertainment and the humble Christmas card and diary or calendar all count towards a successful relationship. A good customer is a happy customer and vice versa. A happy customer comes back for more, pays his bills on time and spreads the good word that enhances the company's reputation.

All this is good motherhood material, but what about the activity of negotiation within this relationship? In the book so far, much mention has been made of the 'other side' or the 'opposition' in the negotiation. Much use has been made of military expressions such as battle planning, strategy, tactics, campaign, etc. This is quite deliberate and quite appropriate.

In any contract negotiation it is virtually impossible not to see the customer as the other side. There could hardly be a negotiation if there were not two sides with conflicting aims to resolve. In the negotiation each side naturally adopts an opposing position and hence the other side must be the opposition simply as a result of the English language. Both sides may see the negotiation as a competition. Indeed if the negotiator has no competitive drive or instinct, he will not be successful. There must be a wish to triumph intellectually over the other side. The customer holds a prize – perhaps a new order, a price to be agreed or a payment to be released – and the contract negotiator must ache to win that prize.

Similarly with the analogy to military endeavour. Every war has a number of battles. Each battle may start with initial skirmishing. Each armed encounter has a start and a finish with either an outright winner or loser, or both sides retiring to lick their wounds, regroup, replan and re-attack. The victor will usually have enjoyed the superior forces, the better equipment and the better planning. Preparation and training are essential to ensure victory and to minimise losses or casualties. The choice of strategy and tactics will depend upon the size, strength and disposition of the enemy. Sometimes a frontal attack is called for, sometimes sustained guerilla warfare; sometimes a lone sniper at a distance is needed to keep the enemy pinned down.

These images are blunt and vivid and although the author has no military experience whatsoever, negotiation experience shows that the analogy holds good as a descriptive method for this book, as a matter of what happens in practice and also as a mental directory of conceptual approaches and devices from which the contract negotiator can select his 'modus operandi' for each particular negotiation.

So it would be concluded that negotiation is an adversarial activity. The comparison between contract negotiation and the adversarial method of the English law court system is very close. In preparation for a contract negotiation, particularly where it is to be in connection with detailed contract conditions or perhaps the resolution of a dispute, the questions often asked are 'Would this stand up in court?' or 'What would be the legal position?'

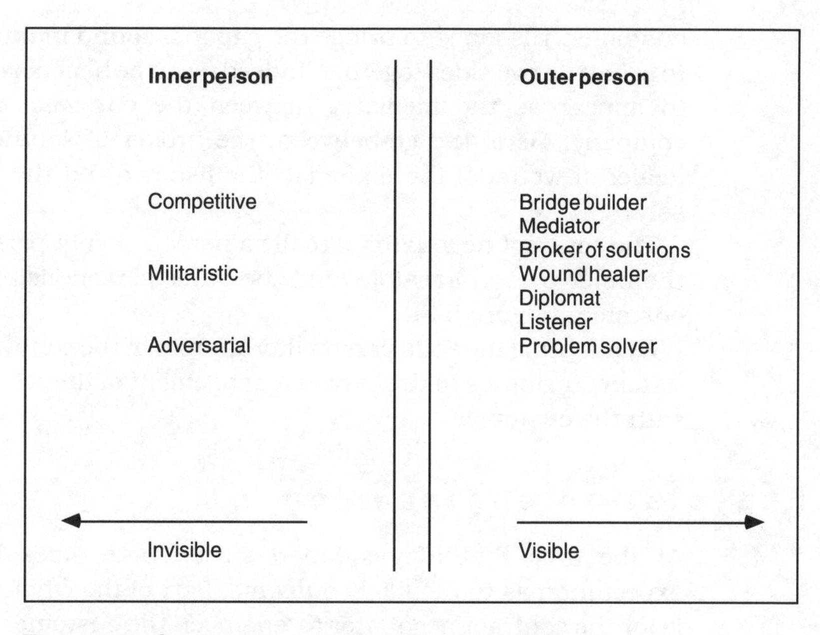

Figure 5.3: Contract negotiator split personality

Indeed, when the lawyers are asked for opinion or advice, it is clear that in their minds' eye they are imagining how the point would be argued in court. Even the terminology begins to creep in, as at the end of a discussion on a particularly difficult point the contract negotiator says, 'I rest my case'. Although commercial considerations often cause the company to set aside or ignore its legal or contractual rights, any normal contract negotiation must be conducted with regard to what the law does and does not allow.

Negotiation is therefore competitive, militaristic and adversarial. How then can this be conducive to good customer relations? The answer is in presentation. The negotiator must be competitive in order to secure a good deal. The military analogy may help in his planning. He must be ready, willing and able to debate points intelligently and articulately with his customer. But he must not appear to be charging in like a heavyweight boxer, a commando or a top criminal lawyer. He is simply there as a representative of the company whose task is to resolve any points to the mutual benefit of both sides. The customer must be pleased to see him or to hear his voice on the telephone.

The contract negotiator should see himself as a builder of bridges. Somehow there is a gap between the company and the customer. His job is to bridge the gap in a sound manner so as to bring the two sides together. Indeed it can be beneficial for him to appear as the mediator between the customer and the company. He is the go-between, the broker of solutions, the healer of wounds, the diplomat, the listener and the problem solver.

The contract negotiator is really a person of split personality: the inner person invisible, and the outer person visible to the customer (Figure 5.3).

By adopting the split-personality approach, the contract negotiator contributes to the overall management of the relationship with the customer.

3 Expectation engineering

At the time that a negotiation starts, both sides have an expectation as to the likely outcome. Part of the whole process is for the contract negotiator to 'engineer' the customer's expectation towards an outcome which is most beneficial to the company.

This expectation engineering can start at the earliest possible time and should be a continuous activity throughout the whole process (Figure 5.4).

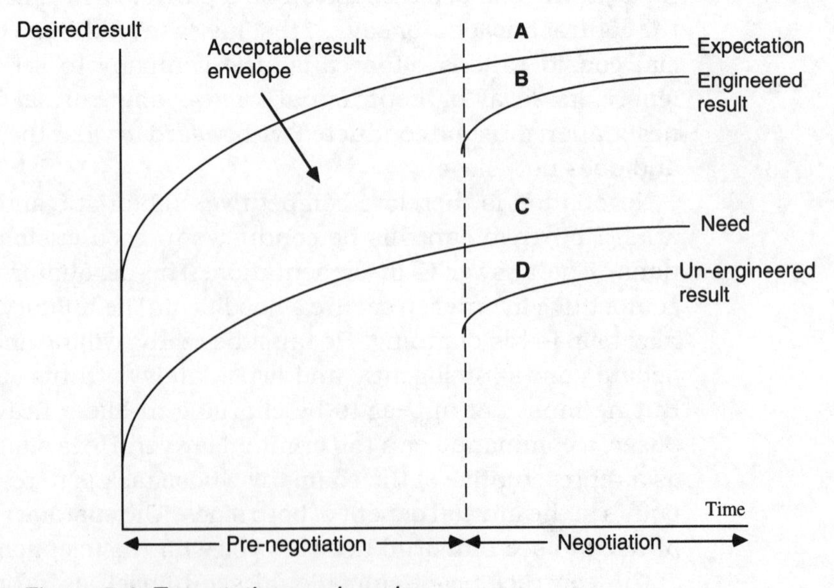

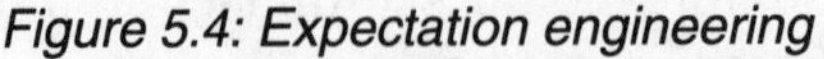

Figure 5.4: Expectation engineering

In Figure 5.4 curve C shows the level of results (whether of price, payment terms, claim settlement, etc) which the company needs. The need tends to grow over time. For example, at the outset, the company thought that agreeing a price of £100,000 would be acceptable. As time went by, it became clear that £120,000 was needed. The contract negotiator must attempt to condition the customer's thinking to expect to agree a much higher price so that the 'creeping need' is always below the envelope (the area between curves A and C) within which the price is likely to be agreed. The process of expectation engineering (curve A) ensures that the envelope is deep enough so that the customer starts with a high offer and finishes with a higher one. Without expectation engineering there is a danger that an acceptable result may never be achieved (curve D).

The rule in any negotiation must be to aim high. The customer never offers more than the company asks. The company's offer can only go down, never up.* So the purpose of expectation engineering is both to influence the customer's expectation and to facilitate the aim-high rule.

The classic mistake is made when offering a so-called budgetary estimate or quotation. It is often thought that, because such things are offered without commitment and on the understanding that any apparent offer is not capable of acceptance in the legal sense, it is safe not to bother too much in formulating the quotation or estimate and to quote low because the number can always be increased. In the strict legal sense this is true, but for the contract negotiator the damage has already been done.

Similarly in offering a range of figures: to say that the price will be £100,000–£150,000 is to alert the customer to budget for £150,000 but his expectation of a negotiated result will be no more than £100,000.

Using expressions such as 'Of course, it's negotiable' is to tell the customer that there is plenty of room for the company to back down. Such expressions must be used extremely carefully. Far better to say 'The price will be £150,000 but we might be able to negotiate if you were to drop your claim on contract XYZ'.

The objective is to convince the customer that he must settle at a high level and that the company has little room to manoeuvre. The process relies on the relationship. The customer must know that, whatever it is, it is negotiable otherwise

* This is of course a generalisation. Tactically the price can be put up at any time. The point here is simply to emphasise the benefit of expectation engineering.

excessive expectation engineering will simply frighten the customer away.

Expectation engineering is a matter not only of such things as making sure that price quotations are on the safe side (ie high), but also in the more subtle areas of choice of language and non-verbal communication. The plumber who takes one look at the central heating, shakes his head and whistles through his teeth is expectation engineering. Similarly the car salesman who shakes his head at the five-year-old trade-in muttering 'No demand, can't get the parts, insurance nightmare' is doing the same thing. As individuals we know these crude examples of expectation engineering are being done deliberately but we still cannot help being influenced by them. If it works for plumbers and car salesmen, it will for the contract negotiator.

In many ways negotiation is a game. Expectation engineering is a game. What cannot be afforded is for some other person in the company to give the game away. The plumber's mate who says 'It's alright guv, it only needs a new washer' can expect to have a tap wrench applied to some soft bodily tissue. In the company there is no room for a person in discussion with the customer to warn the customer 'I know we've quoted £150,000 but I'm sure our people will come down £50,000'. This example sounds so absurd that it is unbelievable, but it happens. Thus it is a responsibility of the contract negotiator to ensure that everybody knows that a game is afoot and not to give it away.

4 Prior events

In Chapter 4 the importance of preparation was emphasised and in particular the gathering of data and information surrounding the events leading up to the negotiation. All prior events are important and none should be overlooked. In the opening section of this chapter it was proposed that the negotiation should be seen as the end of a process and not the start. This whole process occurs over a period of time. If the preparation for the negotiation meeting looks back at prior events it should be possible at the start of the whole process to look forward and imagine the events which will later be looked back upon as the prior events. Put another way, if it were possible to look forward to the preparation meeting, is it possible to guess what prior events the negotiators would wish to have happened or not to have happened? This is illustrated in Figure 5.5.

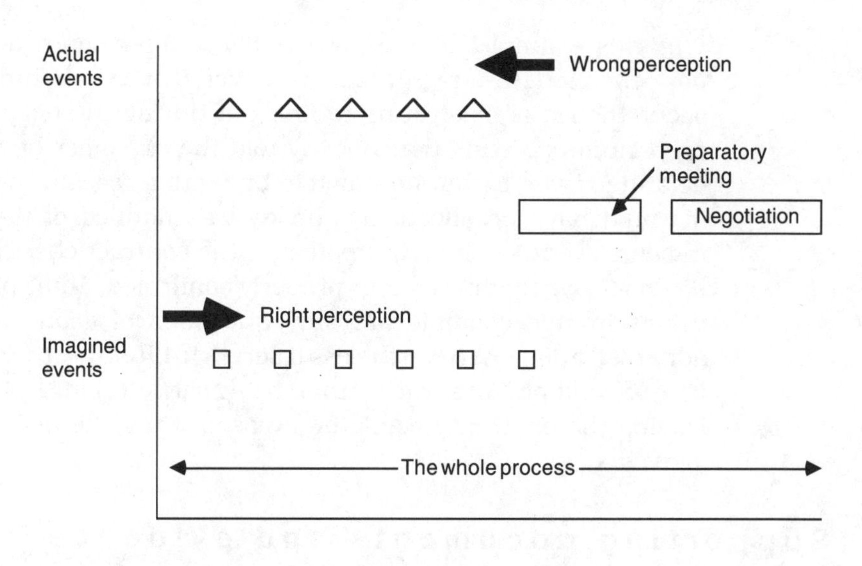

Figure 5.5: Prior-event perception

The point is that the contract negotiator must always have a weather eye to a prospective negotiation that may never happen or may not happen for some time. He thus imagines the prior events which, were they to happen, could be looked back upon as supporting his case. In this way he can plan for such events and cause them to happen.

For example, it might be foreseen that in twelve months' time there will be a negotiation with the customer to resolve a claim from the customer for liquidated damages for late delivery. The negotiator must work out what would be the likely defences of such a claim and what should have happened beforehand to substantiate those defences (Figure 5.6).

Defence	*Basis of defence*	*Ideal prior event*
A	Default of customer	A meeting to highlight the problem
B	*Force majeure*	A letter notifying the event
C	Customer altering requirement	Formal confirmation of the new requirement

Figure 5.6: Event planning

In this example, if none of the bases for defence actually happens then the strategy fails. However, if one such thing does occur then it is frustrating to find out during the negotiation preparation meeting that nobody told the customer he was in default (or worse, that he was told but with a reassurance that it would have no effect), or nobody was notified of the *force majeure* event, or the requirement of the contract changed but it is not clear that it was ever properly confirmed. Some of these things in this example are only questions of good contract administration but nevertheless it serves to illustrate the advantage of event planning rather than being carried along by events, leaving the contract negotiator exposed when the negotiation arrives.

3 Supporting documents and evidence

If event planning is a useful aid to a prospective negotiation, or in any event if any negotiation is to take account of events that have preceded it, then it is necessary to consider in a little more detail what these events might comprise (Figure 5.7).

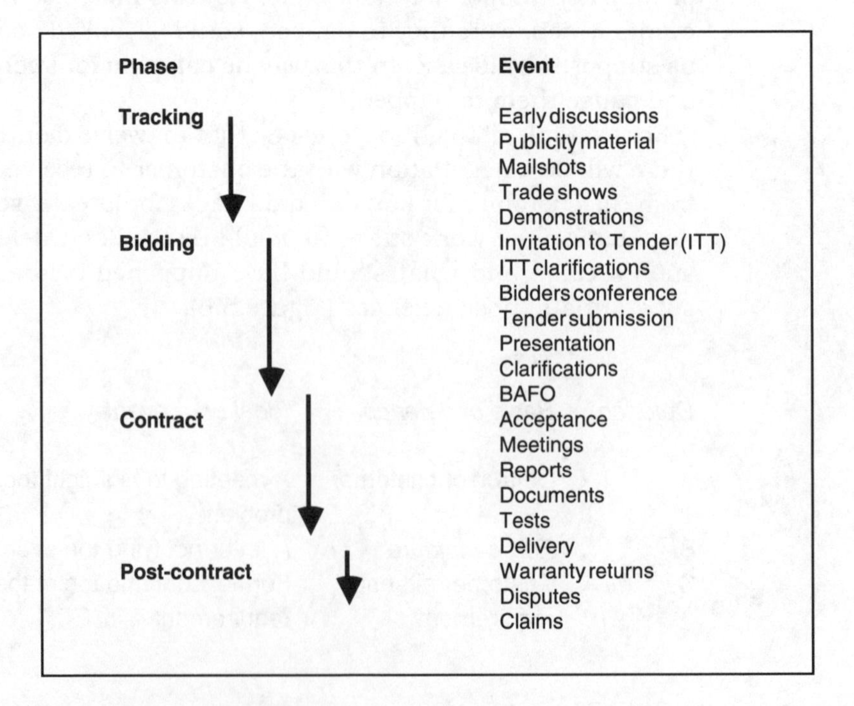

Figure 5.7: Prior events

The aim in Figure 5.7 is to illustrate some of the activities that occur during the various phases of a project. The activities shown are only those where an interaction occurs between the company and the customer. There is no real negotiation in the tracking phase. In this phase the company is aware of a potential requirement of the customer and is simply trying to position itself favourably with that customer. At the simplest level, the aim may be no more than to ensure that the customer includes the company on the tender invitation list.

At the more sophisticated level, the aim might be to influence the customer to define his requirement in such a way that the company will be the best placed among the possible tenderers in terms of submitting an attractive offer. Nevertheless, no negotiation is involved and hence the tracking phase can be largely ignored here.

In the bidding phase there is again no real negotiation. However, if the tender is successful there may be a negotiation prior to contract award. Therefore the events of the bidding phase are of much more immediacy in terms of their relevance to that negotiation. Obviously the tender itself is very important, but so too are things said or done at tender presentations, in providing clarifications and in responding to requests for Best and Final Offers (BAFOs). All of these things will condition the customer's thinking; they are media for expectation engineering. Too often, however, they are ignored on the basis that only the negotiation is important. As has already been said, there are good reasons for seeing the negotiation not as an isolated activity but as an element in an overall process.

It is fundamentally important that company and customer are absolutely clear as to whether things said or done in the bidding phase prior to contract negotiations are intended to have a binding effect or not. In Chapter 2 the difference between promissory and non-promissory representations was explained and it is important for the parties to be clear which is which. If it is left vague, the customer may find he does not get what he thought he ordered or the company may have to do or supply something it did not allow for in its price. At the one extreme, the customer would like to incorporate by reference into the contract all the things said or done in this pre-negotiation phase which are beneficial to him. At the other extreme, the company may not want to go to contract on the basis of incorporating things said or done as inducements but which were not meant as such!

For the safety and certainty of both sides, one of the functions of the negotiation is for the parties to decide exactly what each meant and then to agree that the result is what is referred to as their 'entire agreement' or 'complete agreement'. The agreement is recorded in the contract and, if described as the entire agreement, this prevents either side from seeking to rely in the future upon something said or done prior to contract which is outside the entire agreement.

Once the contract is awarded and the work is in hand, it is usual other than in the simplest of contracts for the parties to continue to interact with each other. Meetings, reports, correspondence and submission of documents all bring the two sides into contact. As time passes, deliveries and payments should be made. If all goes 100 per cent according to both sides, expectations, then such exchanges or interactions are reduced to mere formality. If, however, things do not go quite as planned, it is these exchanges and interactions which will determine the parties' positions when the time comes to solve the problem.

Ostensible completion of the contract does not mean that the relationship has ended. Responsibilities and liabilities which survive the apparent point of completion will cause the relationship to continue to be an active one. Figure 5.7 shows, among other things, claims and disputes arising in the post-contract phase. This does not mean that claims and disputes do not arise in the contract phase, because indeed they do. It is shown like this only to reflect the fact that the resolution of claims and disputes frequently drags on into the post-contract phase, even though the problem may have arisen much earlier.

Furthermore, if the final events in the contract phase list are imagined as things going wrong rather than right, then the significance of these events to a possible post-contract negotiation is clear. If delivery is seen as being troublesome – in terms of either the timeliness or quality of the delivered items – rather than straightforward, then the precise details of the problem, including how and when it came to light, are of great significance to the negotiation.

Return to the list of events in Figure 5.7, again concentrating on the bidding, contract and post-contract phases, and consider whether these diverse events have anything in common. The answer is that all these interactions between company and customer are either documented events or they are events capable of being documented. The message is therefore clear. If the negotiation must necessarily take account of prior events then the position of the contract negotiators is strengthened by the extent to which the prior events have been documented accurately and completely.

In the last sentence it was necessary to refer to the contract negotiators in the plural because the quality of the documentation may lay advantage to either side. However, in theory, if all the relevant events had been accurately and thoroughly documented then the documents would simply record the facts and the advantage would lay according to the disposition of the facts. In practice the documentation is never that good or precise, and nobody even expects it to be, so there is an advantage to be gained by the side who makes sure that documents come into existence at the times and in the manner that would best support its position in the prospective negotiation. This is definitely not to suggest that documents should be invented or that facts should be misrepresented because to do so is to step into or dangerously close to illegal activity. The point is purely to say that because no activity or series of events is ever completely documented then it is legitimate for either side to keep a canny eye open for the times when ensuring that documentation does exist would be to its advantage.

A good example to illustrate this proposition is the occurrence of routine meetings between company and customer during the course of a contract. Such meetings are frequently required by the terms of the contract and are usually to cover such mundane things as progress reporting, technical management or project management. In addition to such predetermined meetings, other *ad hoc* meetings will arise to solve problems, resolve ambiguities or simply to ensure that company and customer remain in personal contact.

There are a number of inherent risks and dangers in these meetings in so far as the recording of their results is concerned. First, as with all meetings, nobody wants to take the minutes and so no proper record exists. Where a minute-taker is appointed (in some contracts there is a contractual duty on one side or the other to provide secretarial support for formal meetings) the reluctance persists and minutes are inaccurate, incomplete and usually appear no more than one day before the next meeting, by which time everyone has forgotten or lost interest in what was actually said or agreed. Second, many such meetings are carried on between what might loosely be described as the technical (perhaps engineering or project management) staff of the two sides. Technical staff are notorious for having discussions and making agreements without considering the full commercial implications. Thus records of technical meetings are often sketchy or ambiguous or entirely absent on the basis that the two technical sides agreed that no minutes or notes were necessary because everyone understood what was agreed!

A classic instance of this problem is where the Technical Manager comes to his contract negotiator pleading for help because the customer keeps demanding more work and changing the contractual requirement, thus causing a significant overrun in contract costs and time.

The contract negotiator enquires how this has come about and the wretched Technical Manager waxes lyrical about a long series of meetings during which the sorry state of affairs has come about. The negotiator who is keen to get in to bat against the customer calls for the evidence, the minutes of meetings and the confirmatory correspondence, only to find of course that what documents do exist tell either no such story or a completely different story.

It is thus important for the contract negotiator to ensure that all company staff who will interact with the customer are briefed on the need for and in the art of keeping proper records to support the company's position. Such records are very necessary to show not only what was agreed but also things not agreed.

Many things under the contract are required to be documented. Delivery should always be documented. Indeed, in the legal sense delivery can occur on the basis of documentation only. Payment is always accompanied by documentation. Suffice it here to say that where the contract requires documentation, then the documentation, whether held electronically or on paper, must be clear, precise and in accordance with the prescribed terms of the contract. Failure in this respect has not only the obvious consequence of deliveries being rejected or payment not being made but also that of weakening a negotiation position.

As the work of the contract progresses, interactions between the company and the customer result in decisions being made or agreements being reached. Where this happens in formal meetings, the recording of accurate minutes is important. Where it happens in informal meetings (in this context, meetings not expressly required under the contract) or in discussions, especially those conducted over the telephone, it is essential that the agreement is confirmed in writing.

Confirmation in writing strengthens the negotiator's position if at some later date the customer denies the agreement, or does not act upon it, or seeks to vary the agreement. This sounds an obvious point but it is so important. If someone relies upon the word of another and as a result puts himself to some cost or detriment, or as a result the other party accrues some benefit, then the law is keen to ensure that he whose word was relied upon honours what was said. Thus, if there should be a dispute, it is essential that appropriate evidence is available. The company negotiator who waits for the customer to confirm in writing is running an enormous risk. The customer may not confirm, either intentionally or through tardiness (the problem of 'unagreements' will be covered in Chapter 8). It is so much better for the company to take the initiative. Again, this is not to say that the company should invent an agreement and write to 'confirm' it so as to impute substance to the invention. The law has never seen a reason to enforce the 'unless I hear from you to the contrary, you owe me a tenner' scam!

An important thing to realise about confirmation in writing as a negotiating device is that oral agreements are never as simple as they seem. Certainly if the only issue to resolve is the price, and the parties telephone each other to split the difference between the price offers that each made as their closing positions at the time the meeting ended, then there is no complexity to confirming that the agreed price was £100,000. Where the issue or set of issues is more complicated, then two possibilities arise. First, the negotiation concludes with progress having been made, but not all matters finally agreed. Second, the negotiation concludes with a final agreement on all matters. In both cases oral agreements, whether whole or partial, will appear at the time to be unambiguous. However, when an attempt is made to reduce the agreement to writing it is not always as clear as it seemed to be. In both cases this gives the contract negotiator an opportunity to write to confirm in such a way that improves his position. In the first case this will be with the objective of improving the opening position at the next meeting. In the latter case the objective is to improve the agreement without expanding the agreement so much that the other side is inclined to simply disagree with the written confirmation.

Platform building

A platform is a place from which to start. A railway platform is a place to wait before a train journey starts. A swimming platform is the high diving board from which the swimmer launches himself. The armed forces use the word 'platform' to describe a ship, an aeroplane or a tank, places from which weapons are launched. The importance of the railway platform is to know from where the journey starts and the destination. The swimming platform needs to be solidly built. The weapons platform needs to be stable, flexible, under control and immune from attack. These same features characterise the nature of the platform that the contract negotiator needs for his task.

The platform is developed from the internal and external negotiation plans described in Chapters 3 and 4. Chapter 3 (p. 33) outlined an internal negotiation plan for a prospective negotiation with the customer in respect of claims for price increase in connection with additional work and claims from a major subcontractor. As a platform for negotiation, a simple request for more money can be visualised in a way that shows how ineffective it would be (Figure 5.8).

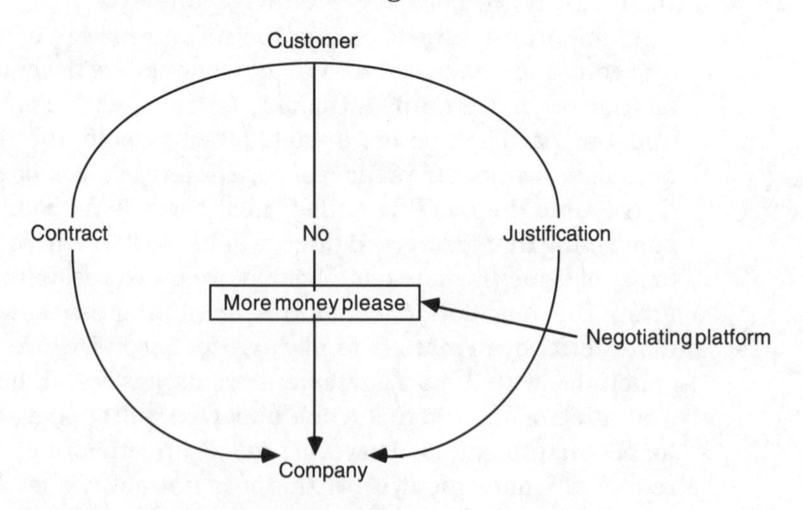

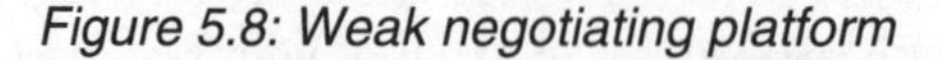
Figure 5.8: Weak negotiating platform

The company's request can be countered with a simple 'no'. The customer can attack the company for having no justification and no contractual right. A stronger platform is called for (Figure 5.9).

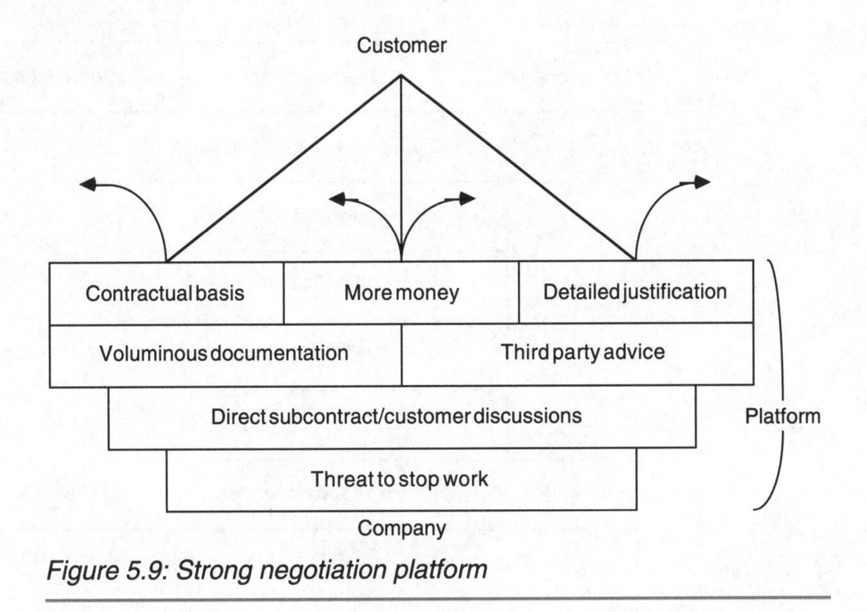

Figure 5.9: Strong negotiation platform

In Figure 5.9 the platform is broad and deep to make it resilient to attack. The claims have been made according to contractual terms and justified in detail. If this does not work, the platform is supported by a huge volume of documentation and by approaching the customer's third party adviser to persuade him to endorse the claims. If this does not work, there is the proposal that the matter should be resolved by direct discussions between subcontractor and customer. The final sanction is to threaten to stop work. Conceptualised in this way, the company has built a strong platform for the negotiation. Imagining the platform in layers allows decisions to be made as to when to deploy each device, keeping the ultimate sanction in reserve until higher layers have been breached.

A pitfall to watch out for is not to be lulled into a false sense of security. Any negotiation plan or platform is capable of being demolished and it should not be thought that the simple existence of these things is a guarantee of 100 per cent success.

As well as conceptualising the platform, it also needs to be built materially. This is done by a process of discussions, hints and rumours. For example, it is of little use to turn up at the negotiation meeting and, after thirty minutes of onslaught from the other side, to threaten to stop work. As will be seen in Chapter 7, the use of head-on threats (particularly of stopping work) is fraught with danger. It is far more effective for the

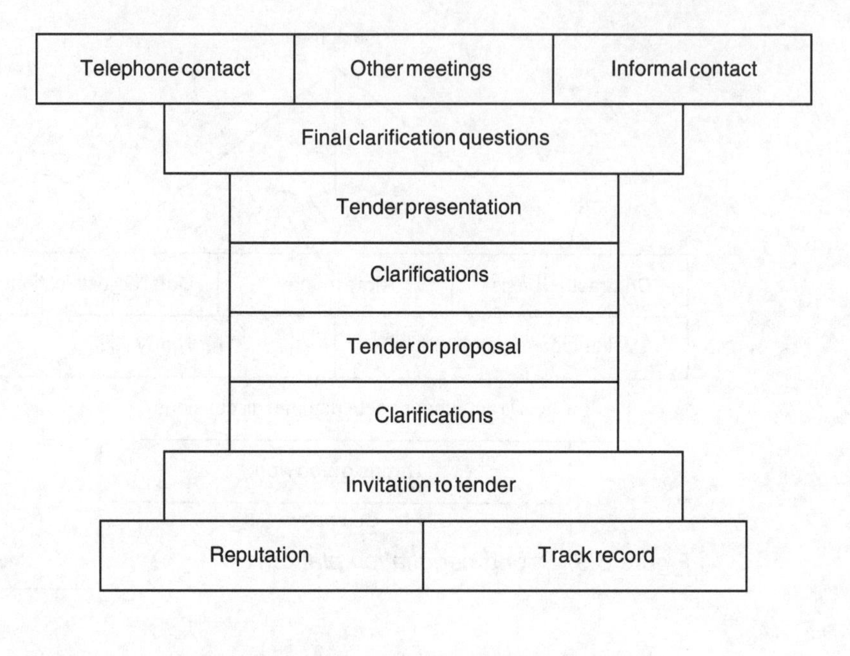

Figure 5.10: New contract platform

customer to know already that this is an option that the company is considering. This intelligence must therefore have been trickled into the customer at some earlier time and in an informal manner.

In essence the platform is constructed from everything said or done which is to the advantage of the company. The platform for a negotiation of a new contract is easy to formulate (Figure 5.10).

In this case one of the merits of the platform is its use as an *aide-mémoire* that there is more to sell than simply that put into the tender or proposal.

Both as a technique for event planning and for platform building, the well-thought-out and well-written business letter is an excellent tactical device. Consider the following exchange of correspondence (Figures 5.11 and 5.12).

In Figure 5.11 the problem has been set out clearly and concisely. The writer has been careful not to prejudice his position and to demand in precise terms the desired remedy. In response (Figure 5.12) the supplier has attempted to offer a helpful resolution which will cost him nothing, to blame somebody else and to introduce extra factors (price discount, order

Williams-Hanks Ltd
St Andrews Road
Derby
Derbyshire
D28 7JA

P J Wolfe & Sons plc
Friars Road
Wilkenthorpe Road
Basingstoke
Hampshire
BA43 2RC

FAO Mr W Williams

10 June
Your Ref: 2133/WW/BT
Our Ref: A/Wid/JW/281

Dear Sirs

WIDGETS
ORDER NO 21469/ST

Under the above order a quantity of 100 widgets was due for delivery on 3 June. In the telephone conversation (Williams/Wilfe) of 20 May you confirmed that delivery would be effected on time.

We must point out that delivery did not take place until 8 June. Further we have discovered that 25 of the units failed to operate when connected to their power supply. It would appear that this is due to a quality problem as the connectors appear to be corroded. This is only an opinion and is offered without liability or prejudice.

As regards the 75 units which appear to be satisfactory we reserve our rights as regards the lateness of delivery. You are hereby advised that the 25 failed units are rejected. Please arrange to collect them and supply replacement units in accordance with condition 15 of the order.

We must express our extreme disappointment in that the order has been delivered late – with 25 per cent rate – against the background of a confirmatory promise to deliver on time.

Yours faithfully
for P J Wolfe & Sons plc

John Wolfe
Commercial Administrator

Figure 5.11: Letter of complaint

P J Wolfe & Sons plc

William-Hanks Ltd

14 June

Your Ref: A/Wid/JW/281
Our Ref: 2133/WW/BT

Dear Sirs

WIDGETS
ORDER NO 21469/ST

Thank you for your letter reference A/Wid/JW/281 dated 10 June.

We regret that you have experienced difficulty with 25 of the units. If you wipe the connectors with the standard 4121 cleaning fluid before connection to the power supply there should be no further difficulty.

We apologise that delivery was made late, this being due to industrial action at Customs which was completely beyond our control.

Although we consider that we are not at fault we would be prepared – without prejudice – to offer you 5 per cent discount of our quoted price against your next order, provided this can be placed by 31 August.

In the meantime we enclose our invoices for the 100 units under this order and request payment within the next seven days.

Yours faithfully

William-Hanks Ltd

Figure 5.12: Platform-building reply

receipt date, outstanding payments), thus building a platform ready for negotiation if that becomes necessary.

In using correspondence as tactical devices, the importance of the precise use of language cannot be overstated. Imagine that the company must provide an urgent quotation for some work which has already been the subject of extensive technical debate. The company is concerned that the technical definition is still unstable and nowhere fully committed to writing. It can therefore quote including the caveat that 'the work is as per the definition at 30 June'.

It is much better to say that 'the work is as per the definition as understood by us at 30 June'. The difference is very obvious when written out in isolation like this but the latter statement by itself (ie not in contrast to the former statement) buried in the midst of a long letter of quotation may not be noticed for the protective measure it is. But sure enough, when the time comes for negotiation the letter can be produced to limit the extent to which the company's price is linked to the customer's understanding of the status of the technical requirement.

7 Defensive measures

A defensive measure is a step taken against a foreseeable but uncertain event. Military defences are built against an attack which may or may not happen. Coastal defences are constructed against the possibility of abnormally high tides which may never occur.

To be effective such defences must be well planned, well built and put in place well ahead in time of the possible occurrence of the event against which the defences were designed to protect. Last-minute attempts to stem the tide, last-ditch attempts to slow the enemy advance are panic measures and are unlikely to succeed. The illustrations are evocative and the parallels close in considering defensive measures in the process of negotiation.

By analogy, negotiation defensive measures are not created at the time of the negotiation meeting but well beforehand as part of event planning. This concept of pre-planned defensive measures is best illustrated by example. Imagine a contract for the supply of 10,000 widgets to be delivered over a specified period with payment being made at an agreed unit price as and when each widget is delivered. The company is to be separately paid under the same contract for the activity of managing the programme. Payment for management is to be in equal monthly instalments paid over the period of the contract from inception to the end of the agreed delivery schedule for the widgets (Figure 5.13).

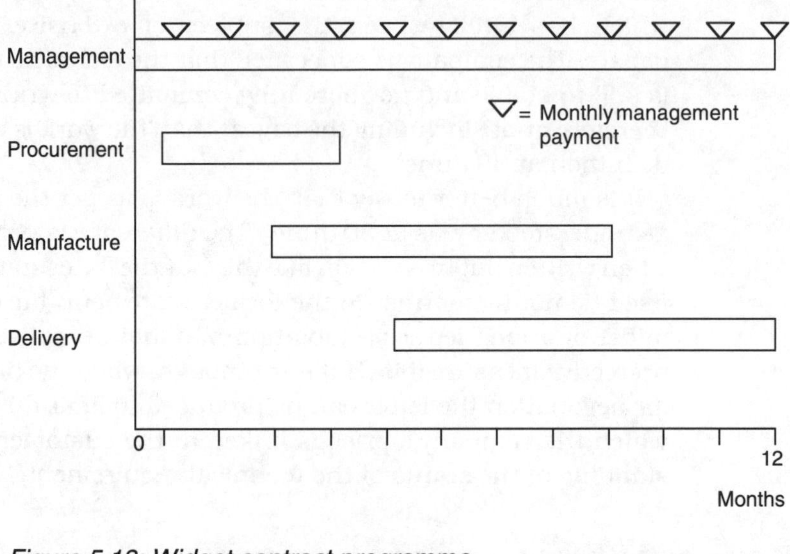

Figure 5.13: Widget contract programme

As work progresses, difficulties are encountered and the production programme slows down and thus deliveries are forecast to occur behind schedule. However, the wording of the contract regarding management allows that the management fee will be paid in twelve equal instalments commencing one month after the date of contract, and thus there is no automatic slowing-down of management payments even though delivery is slipping. This causes concern with the customer, who declares that he will unilaterally adjust the number, value and time period of management payments to reflect the different forecast of widget deliveries. Of course, the company argues that this is unfair, saying that the customer has no contractual right, that the cost of managing a programme in difficulty is higher and that, had the original delivery programme been accelerated, no doubt the customer would not have revised the management payments to reflect the shorter programme. All good arguments, but all to no avail.

Notwithstanding any legal or contractual arguments in its favour, the point which is really concerning the company is that the customer may terminate the contract for anticipatory or actual breach of the delivery condition. A defensive measure is needed to reduce the risk of such a termination being effective.

A head-on confrontation at this stage would not help. The company could offer some benefit (eg a price reduction) to the customer in return for his formal agreement to adopt contractually the revised delivery forecast. This is thought unlikely to work: the customer may wake up to the company's real concern and may take the unfortunate step of writing to formally reserve his rights to terminate for default. In any event, no one wants to offer reduced prices or other expensive palliatives.

The defensive measure put in place is to nudge gently, by low-key telephone contact, the customer into taking his action to revise the management payments by issuing a formal amendment to the contract. Now amendments need to be accepted, so the trick is to reply at great and verbose length (to ensure that it would not be read thoroughly) to the amendment and to slip in the words 'we accept the detriment to our cash flow resulting from the revised management payment terms in consideration of you having accepted the revised delivery programme'. The letter is sent by second-class post to a low-level official in the customer organisation so as to avoid any great ripples being caused. With luck the customer never responds to this and thus the defensive measure is in place.

In this example the defensive measure is not guaranteed to prevent an effective termination but it certainly helps. The customer did not reserve his right to terminate (such right can be lost if he waits too long); the customer continued to treat with the company (hence it could be argued that the customer adopted the late programme by his actions); and it can be shown that the customer acted to the detriment (by revising the management payments) of the company and the company accepted the detriment in consideration (a good legal glue) of the customer agreeing to the new programme.

This ploy could only help if it was done at the time of the customer changing the management payments. It could not help if done much later and certainly could not work if done during a negotiation following a purported attempt by the customer to terminate the contract. It also has the advantage that reference can be made (to the amendment and the nature of the acceptance) quietly in the customer's ear at some time in the future to undermine his conviction that he has got the right to terminate, if it is believed that termination has entered the customer's mind as a possible course of action.

In this example the benefit of a defensive measure is clear, although the customer may never have actually considered termination.

Time bombs

If defensive measures are put in place to deter or to repel a future attack which may or may not ever come, then the military analogy can be developed a stage further. In some situations it can be foreseen that an attack will definitely come. The timing may be a little uncertain but not greatly so. A wonderful countermeasure is the time bomb. Carefully placed and timed to go off just ahead of the attack, the time bomb can be devastating. The timer may be set for an hour, a week, a month or a year. It does not matter, the end result is the same. There it sits, undetected, undisturbed, ticking away until the crucial moment. Event planning can make much use of the time bomb in the whole process of negotiation. Again, an example will serve to illuminate the concept.

Imagine a long-term project that starts with initial study work, carries through into development and implementation and concludes with the support phase, during which enhancement and improvements will be developed (Figure 5.14).

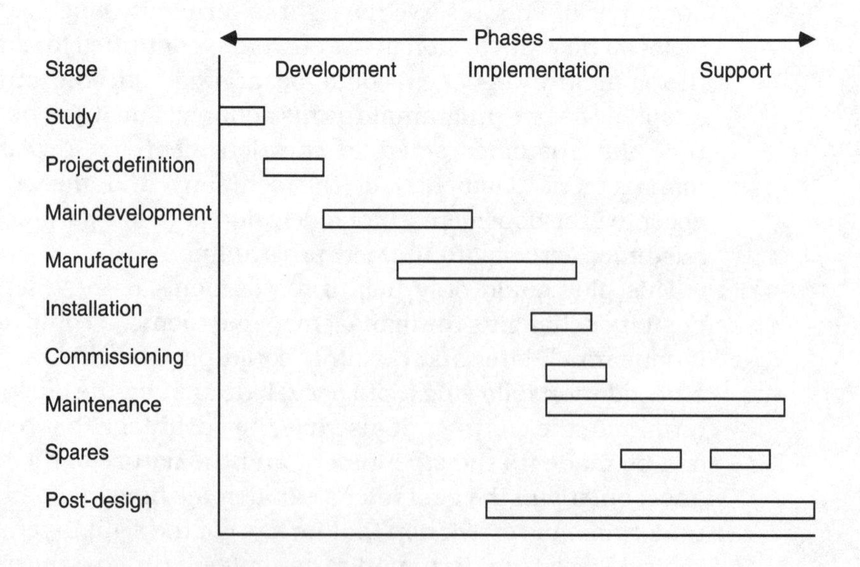

Figure 5.14: Major project phases

The customer has decided to appoint a consultant to help him oversee the work of the company. The customer also wishes to avoid being tied to the company for all stages and all phases of the project. The company naturally wishes to maximise its chances of securing as many contracts in as many stages and phases as possible. To achieve this it needs to have a long-term strategy for the project and, where possible, to build time bombs into the negotiation for individual contracts. Having successfully completed the study and project definition phases, the company knows that the customer is tied to it for development and implementation. However, at the time that contracts are negotiated for those early stages, the company must have an eye to the future in terms of securing, for example, the post-design services contracts which might be five years or more in the future.

The company should therefore consider in the early days how its position might be threatened in the future. Taking post-design services, its future position could be threatened by the customer having sufficient rights in the intellectual property generated in the early stages to invite other companies to compete for the work. It could be threatened by a consultant to the customer who will have had access to all the technical and engineering designs and data created by the company. Therefore the company should aim to limit the customer's intellectual property rights and to restrict the use to which the consultant can put any design data that it acquires during the early stages.

The intention should be to secure these limitations and restrictions in such a way that no particular attention is drawn to them during the negotiations. They should be buried in a heap of other matters to be resolved. In this way these contractually binding limitations and restrictions tick away until the evil day when the customer tries to break his ties to the company. The bombs go off and the attack on the company's position is repulsed.

9 Corporate, general and personal relationships

In the early part of this chapter, mention was made of the need to effectively and productively manage the relationship with the customer. This topic is worthy of a little more examination to round off the idea of the whole process. There is in fact a hierarchy of relationships (Figure 5.15) which provides a basis for further analysis.

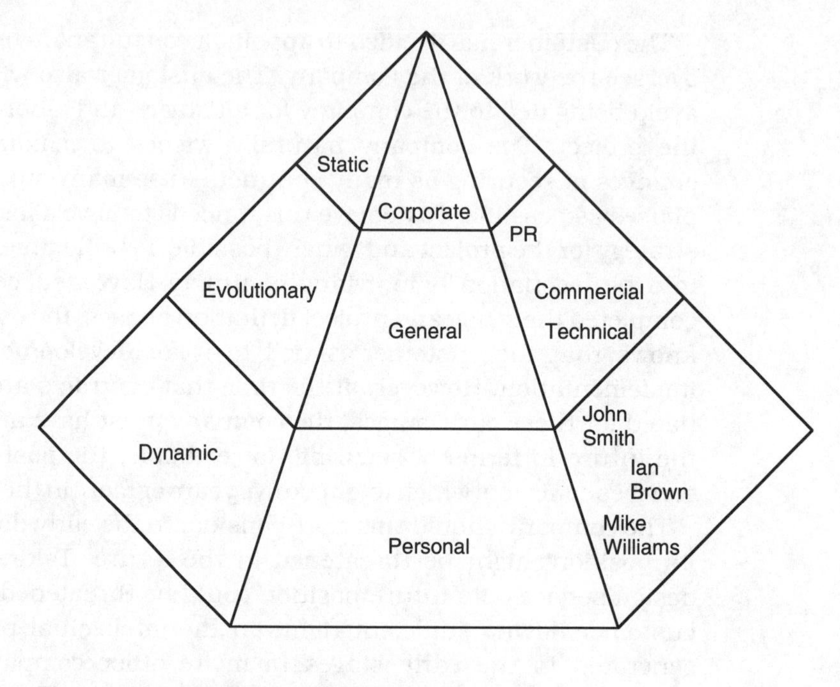

Figure 5.15: Hierarchy of relationships

The relevance of the corporate relationship from the point of view of the contract negotiator is that it is his job to reflect the desired corporate image in the eyes of the customer, to be sensitive to customer perceptions which are at variance with the desired image and to respond accordingly. The corporate relationship is largely a static one. Individual deals, specific contracts and performance do not generally alter the customer's perception of the company as a corporate entity.

On the other hand, the general relationship is an evolutionary one. At this level it can be seen that the customer will have different pictures of the company on a functional level. The company may be seen as having a glossy PR image but nevertheless is seen as commercially naive. If it is accepted that good negotiations are facilitated by sound relationships, then the general relationship needs to be evolved in all interfaces to achieve the desired image. The contract negotiator cannot negotiate in isolation from the customer's perception of the company.

At the personal level the relationship is crucially important. The contract negotiator must foster the relationship (Figure 5.16) so that his face and voice are always welcome.

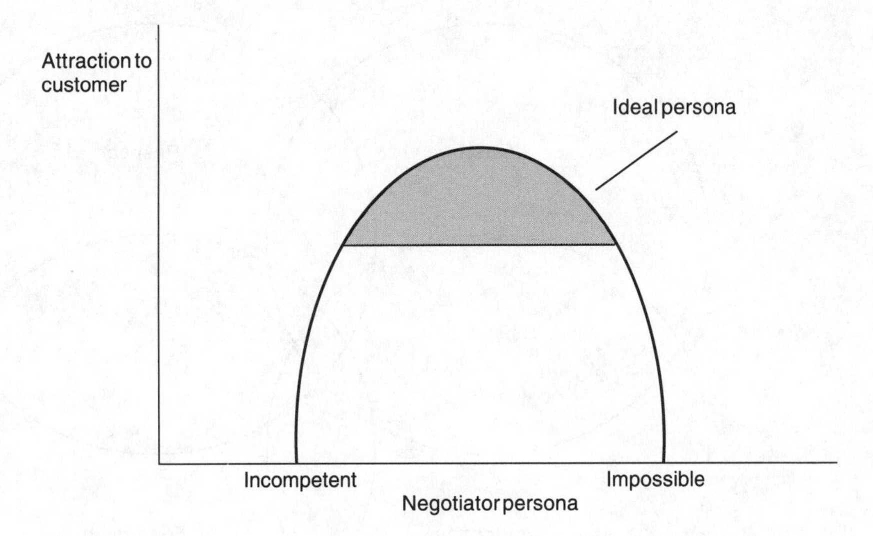

Figure 5.16: Personal relationship

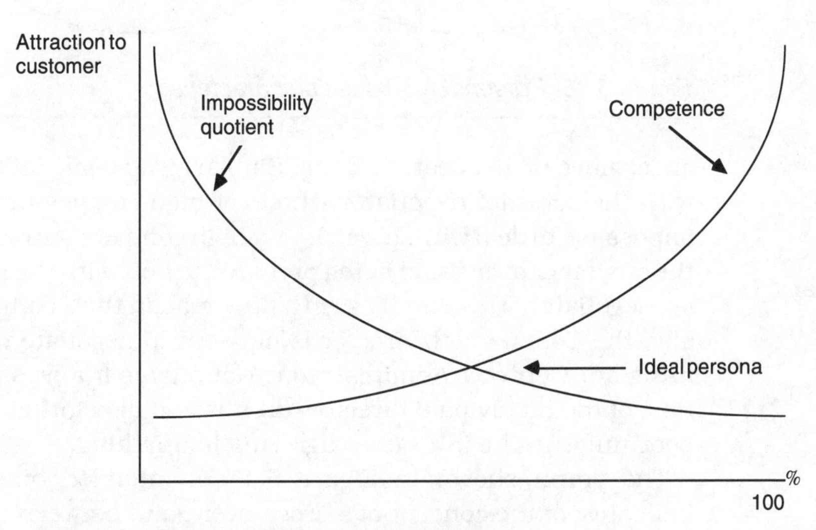

Figure 5.17: Impossibility and competence

The customer will want to deal neither with an incompetent nor with somebody who is impossible. Another way of looking at this is to consider the cross-over point (Figure 5.17) between competence and 'impossibility quotient' (a 100 per cent score indicates the person who is impossible to deal with).

Figure 5.17 shows that the customer will not wish to deal with the 'soft touch' (low impossibility quotient) who is of low compet-

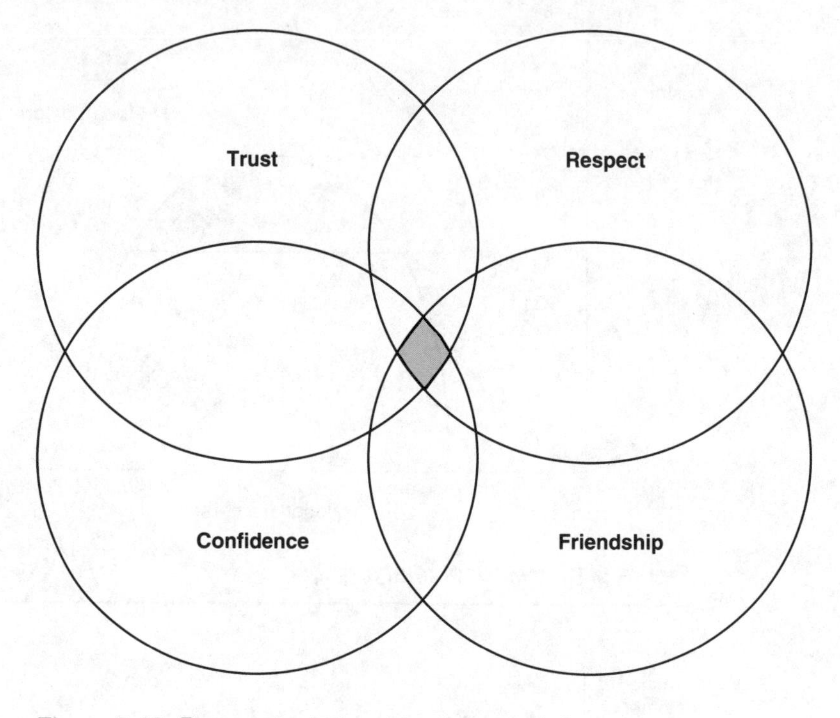

Figure 5.18: Personal relationship characteristics

ence, since no deal can be done. Similarly, no deal can be done with the contract negotiator who is of high competence but is impossible to deal with. Indeed, very high competence may scare the customer away from being prepared to deal with the particular negotiator. This can be seen as the reason that, conventionally, the Commercial Director is not sent to negotiate with the Assistant Contract Administrator. Not only is it a waste of the time of the highly paid director but it would also intimidate the poor unfortunate into never agreeing to anything.

The graph shown in Figure 5.17 is intended only to be indicative of the concept of a cross-over point between competence and impossibility quotient as seen by the customer. It is not intended to show that the ideal negotiator is someone who is only 50 per cent competent! This idea helps to condition the contract negotiator's attitude to the person on the customer side with whom he must deal. It may help him in his task to conceal or suppress his level of competence so as not to intimidate the other side. If he is proud (he should not be!) of his reputation of being difficult to deal with, it may help to tone down this appearance in order to get to a deal.

Earlier in this chapter (Figure 5.3), the idea was introduced of the contract negotiator needing to have a split personality: the inner person being competitive, militaristic and adversarial, the outer person being the bridge builder, the mediator, etc. The outer person can now be analysed further in terms of the features which should characterise his personal relationship with the customer (Figure 5.18).

These four principal characteristics must be fostered and developed by the contract negotiator. The individual on the other side must be able to trust his word. He must have respect for the position, stature and competence of the negotiator. He must have confidence that, if the negotiator agrees to do something, it will be done. Finally, if the relationship can be built around friendship, this too will facilitate successful negotiation. This latter point is a question of balance. Excessive friendliness will inhibit or prejudice a good agreement. Unfriendliness is of course wholly unproductive.

CHAPTER 6

Self-preparation

1 Introduction

The most important activity for the contract negotiator in the time leading up to the negotiation, once the planning and preparation described in Chapter 4 are out of the way, is self-preparation. The negotiator must be physically and mentally in the right condition. Negotiation can be very demanding on both body and mind. There is a lower chance of success if the negotiator is tired, suffering from a cold or is hung over from the night before. If there is a long journey to make to meet the customer, he should travel the day before and get an early night.

Similarly, he should contrive to be at his best mental pitch. It is well known that there are 'morning' people and 'afternoon' people. That is, some people are at their very best first thing in the morning. Others do not come alive until the evening. The aim should be to fix the start time of the meeting as far as possible according to the negotiator's best time of day.

Another helpful trick is to use music as an aid to self-preparation. As people drive their cars the type of music they listen to can have a profound effect on their behaviour and manner of driving. Loud, noisy rock music can produce aggressive driving. Quiet, easy-going, relaxing music can produce calm and considerate driving. If music can attune the human state of mind to its characteristic, then why not use it to help in mental preparation for a negotiation? For example, if the negotiator is travelling to the customer by car then he should listen to something with triumphant, victorious, exciting overtones.

Returning to the point about physical preparedness, there is the question of eating. Generally speaking the negotiator should eat properly beforehand – for some people an empty stomach might produce an extra-sharp edge to their negotiation skills but usually it produces an element of tetchiness, an energy loss as body sugar levels drop and an impatience to finish the meeting in order to get out and get something to eat. An impatient negotiator makes mistakes and concedes points unnecessarily in his rush to finish. Conversely, a big meal beforehand should also be avoided. The body's natural reaction to a large meal is to want to sleep. Needless to say, a sleepy negotiator will hardly be effective.

It is, however, the state of mind of the negotiator, his mental preparation and his ability to analyse the processes of negotiation that are the main themes for this chapter.

2 Mental imaging

A very powerful technique for the contract negotiator is what might be called mental imaging. The idea is to visualise the process of negotiation as an aid to self-preparation and as an aid during the negotiation meeting. Understanding how something works rather than just what it does always gives a greater insight. Insight into the processes of negotiation is a powerful tool that assists in securing a successful result.

Mental imaging is of benefit in many different spheres, particularly where personal performance is paramount. Consider the common features (Figure 6.1) of giving a presentation, of a job interview and of a negotiation.

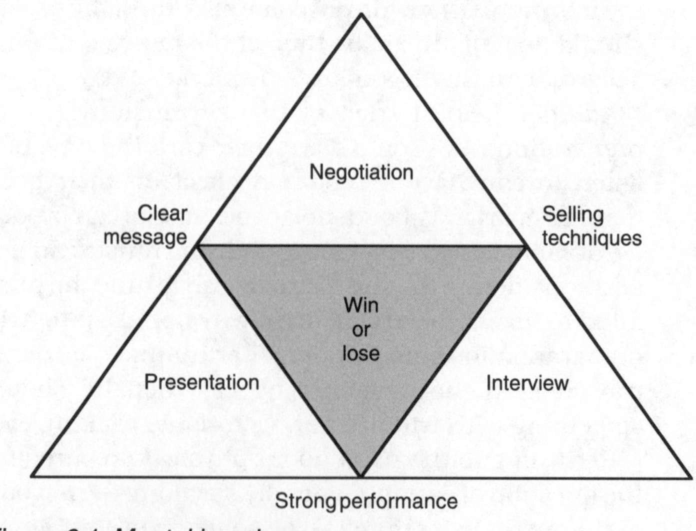

Figure 6.1: Mental imaging

The process of negotiation has a lot in common with giving a presentation or being interviewed for a job. In a presentation it is most important that the presenter has a clear idea of the message he is going to get across to the audience. A clear message by itself does not make a good presentation. The message has to be 'sold' to the audience and this is best achieved if the presenter puts it into his mind that he is giving a performance in the theatrical sense. This does not necessarily mean that drama or histrionics are called for (although these enliven a presentation if used well), but only that an ineffective presentation is given by someone whose approach and tone of voice is no more than they might use in speaking on the telephone about some innocuous topic – a presentation needs a strong personal performance. Without it the presenter will lose the support and attention of the audience.

Similarly with a job interview. The interviewee must have a clear message – 'these are my qualifications, this is my experience, this is what I bring to the job'. He must sell himself to the interviewer – 'it is me you want because I am the best, don't waste your time with the others'. Again this is best done through giving a strong performance. Interviews are not successful if the interviewee speaks as though he were chatting to his neighbour about the weather. Without a strong performance the job will be lost.

And so with negotiation. The negotiator must be clear as to his message – 'these are the points I must win, these are the facts and arguments that support my case'. His selling job is the same – 'you can see I'm right, this really is the best deal for you'. A distinction with the negotiation is that, tactically, the negotiator may not want the whole message to be immediately clear to the opposition; nevertheless it must be clear to himself. It may very well be that if the true intent is concealed throughout from the opposition and the negotiation is a success, the person on the opposition side may wake the next day thinking, 'Merciful heaven, what have I done?' So the message and selling analogies hold. So too does the idea of performance.

There are a few lucky people who are naturally talented negotiators. Others will have to step out of their usual personality to deliver a performance. Without a strong performance the negotiation will be lost. It is suggested therefore that the negotiator holds in his mind the simple checklist of 'message, sell, perform'.

3 Performance imaging

It is in the area of performance that mental imaging can really help (Figure 6.2).

The purpose here is for the contract negotiator to fill his mind with positive images before the negotiation starts. As far as his picture of the start of the meeting is concerned, he should imagine himself excited by the challenge and eager to get on with the fun. He should imagine the negotiation finishing with his boss congratulating him on the result. Negative thoughts such as 'why me? I must get this over with' spell disaster. The person who plans in his mind how he is going to apologise for the result even before the game begins is in no frame of mind to negotiate. Indeed for the negotiator who suffers this 'double negative' there is perhaps a question mark over his career prospects, certainly as far as negotiation is concerned. It could be said that to put this double-negative person into a negotiation is nothing more than a failure by the company in selecting the negotiator in the first place (see Chapter 3). However, it is not a perfect world. The company may not always have complete freedom (such as where the customer has a preference for dealing with a particular

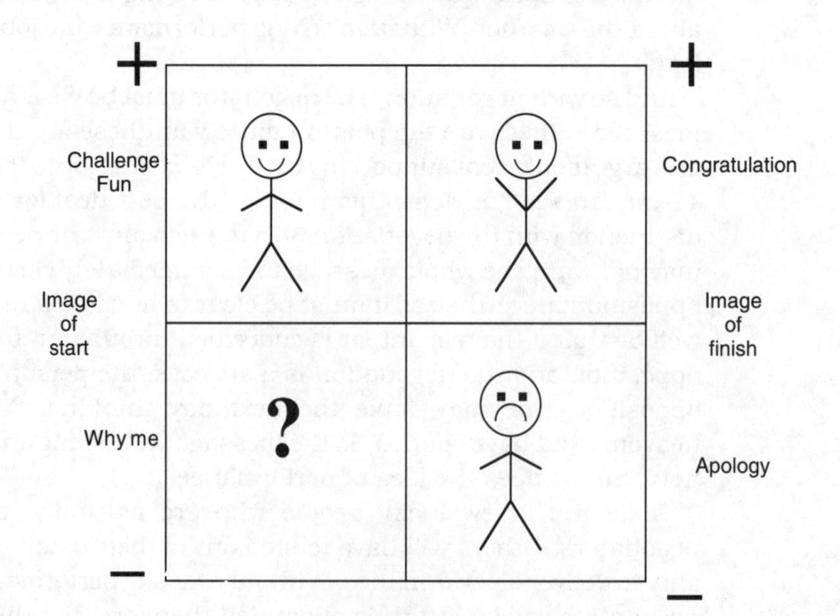

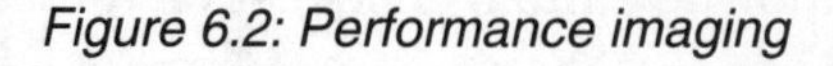
Figure 6.2: Performance imaging

person) or circumstances (eg where there is no one else available) may dictate the choice of a certain individual. From this perspective it is one aim of this book to assist the non-expert negotiator as well as those people for whom contract negotiation is a principal activity.

4 Game analogies

Another source of helpful mental images is games such as chess, poker and pool. The choice of game to imagine does not matter, provided it is a game which the contract negotiator enjoys playing and at which he is quite successful. Taking chess as a first example, what does this teach that could be helpful in negotiation? When someone first learns the rules, a game starts with both sides moving pieces virtually at random until by good fortune a piece can be captured. This process continues until both sides are left with a king and one pawn. The game feels to have been unsatisfactory and a proper result has been frustrated or denied. On the other hand, the grand master plans the whole game from the first move and executes his plan with ruthless efficiency. Moves by the other side are countered with subplans and at all times he concentrates on all the pieces, the whole game and upon refining and adjusting tactics as the game proceeds. Crucially he is thinking as many moves ahead as is humanly possible. These are the rules for the contract negotiator. Have a plan and stick to it, other than in the last resort. Think ahead. Predict what moves the other side will make and make ready to counter them. Do not lose sight of the whole game. Make sacrifices in order to make gains. Do not react impetuously. Consider each move. Take advantage of mistakes.

Playing a card game such as poker teaches a different set of ideas. In chess both sides start with the same number of pieces, the value of each piece is known and each player can at all times see the disposition and strength of the opposing forces. Only the plan of campaign is concealed. In a card game all is different. Each player's hand contains different cards of different value. The game starts with neither player being able to see the other's cards. Cards may be revealed as the game progresses and the element of bluff is very important. In contract negotiations the parallels are close. It is not always possible to know what cards the other side holds; it is not possible to assess immediately the strength of the company's cards in comparison with those of the other side. If bluff can be described as making the most of one's cards, no matter how trivial their real absolute value, then it can be seen just how important bluff is in contract negotiation.

A game such as pool provides another model of negotiation. In pool the aim is to pot balls more quickly than the other side. The first to finish by potting the 'eight ball' is the winner. There are basically two ways of playing the game. First, a simple approach of potting every available ball as soon as the opportunity arises. Second, a more sophisticated approach whereby balls are gradually positioned over the holes and then all are potted in quick succession. Both methods can be disrupted by the play of the other side but patience, thought and accuracy usually win through. In contract negotiation the message is similar. Rushing to score points does not always work. It can be better to develop things gradually before choosing precisely the right time to strike. Play by the other side will intentionally or accidentally disrupt progress but persistence will triumph.

Imagining these various game analogies before or during the negotiation can be helpful. The negotiator can ask himself these questions: 'Is the other side following a tactical plan? How can I spoil it? Is my move predictable?' This is the chess analogy. 'When shall I reveal my hand? Does he have better cards? Who holds the aces?' This is the poker analogy. 'Can I set him up? Can I spoil his play? When shall I strike?' This is the pool analogy.

Particular games such as the ones mentioned are useful aids. The overall message is that a negotiation is a game. All games should be played for fun and played to win.

5 Self-induced feedback

This rather odd section heading is intended to describe another facet of mental imaging. Just as it is helpful for the negotiator to look ahead and imagine himself being congratulated by his boss after the negotiation, it is also helpful during the negotiation to imagine himself as the proverbial fly on the wall, observing events as they unfold. This ability to stand outside one's own mind is a very useful trick. It allows the negotiator to review his performance and its effect on the opposition. As the negotiator proceeds with his careful think-before-speaking approach his mind should be racing many times faster, examining his performance and its effect (Figure 6.3).

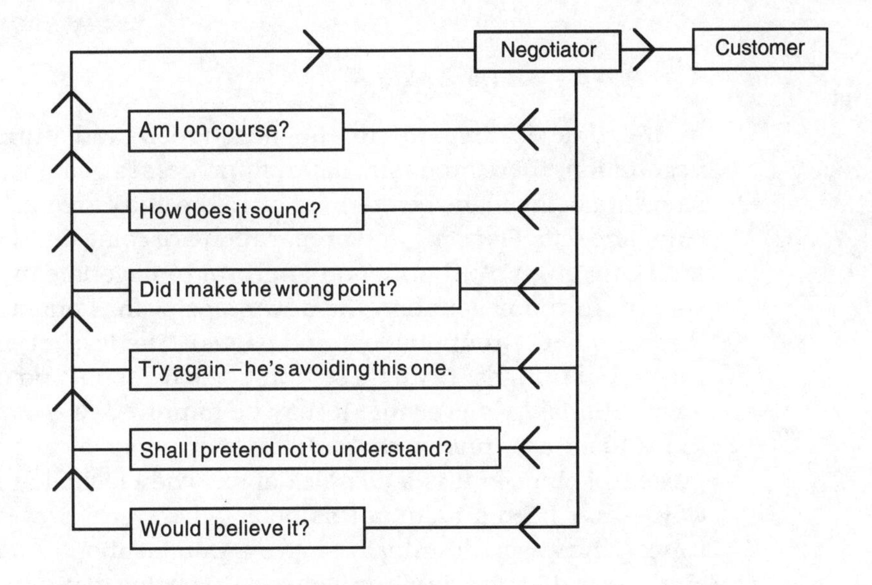

Figure 6.3: Self-induced feedback

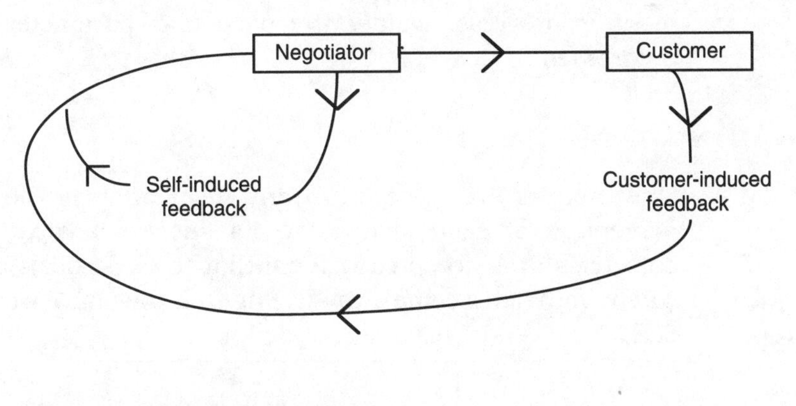

Figure 6.4: Combined feedback

The point is that this process of self-induced feedback stems indirectly from the reaction of the other side. It genuinely comes from an objective assessment by the negotiator of his words, as though he were the one listening to them.

Combined with reacting to feedback stemming directly from the other side (Figure 6.4), this provides a useful tool to allow the negotiator to optimise the course of discussion.

6 Process analysis

In the time leading up to the negotiation and during the negotiation, there are many different processes going on. Decisions are being made beforehand as to the choice of negotiator, team size, etc. Planning and preparation are going on. Briefings are being given. Authority and approval to negotiate are being sought. In the negotiation the advantage swings one way and then another. Ground is lost and gained. The level of emotion peaks and troughs. In all these things the personal and corporate relationship is evolving. It may be improved, it may suffer. Individuals are influenced by their own personal and career pressures. Indeed it is a complex affair when looked at in this way. It has been an aim of this book, wherever a process or a concept has been described, to give a visualisation as a graph, chart, flow diagram, table or picture. This helps to put the point across. However, it is also helpful to the negotiator to have these visualisations in his mind in order to help him analyse the processes that are going on during the negotiation and to monitor progress against the particular parameter as time progresses.

7 Win-win

One process that goes on in any negotiation is the evolving perception of each side as to its success against its own objectives. It is accepted wisdom that the best deals are those where both sides come away feeling that they have won (Figure 6.5).

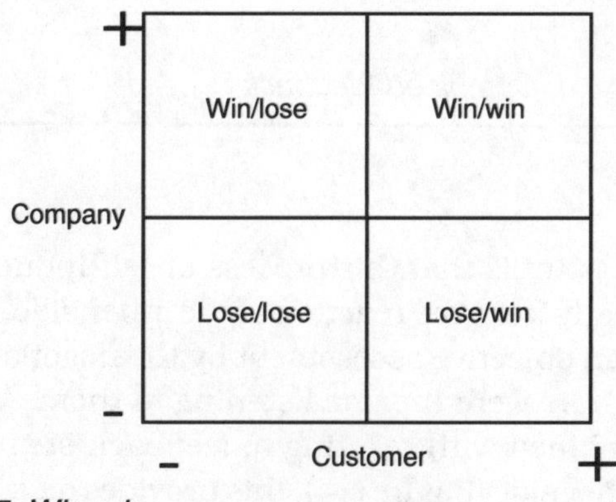

Figure 6.5: Win-win

The important factor about win-win is that the other side must *feel* that it has got itself a good deal. It may be that the negotiator has won virtually every single point and conceded almost nothing. Win-win does not mean necessarily that the other side should be given a real concession for free just to balance up the deal (although in the extreme this might become necessary if, for example, there is to be another negotiation in the near future with the same customer on another matter and it is important for him not to be in a defensive or vengeful mood). Normally the aim should be to balance the deal as perceived in the customer's eyes by overselling the advantages to him of the small concessions that he has won or by convincing him of the paucity of the deal from the company's point of view. This latter approach can be achieved by convincing him that relatively minor points which are easy to give up are actually very hard to concede (see the objectives analysis diagram at Figure 4.6 in Chapter 4). This can be done by the contract negotiator giving the impression that, in agreeing, he is exceeding his authority, or by telephoning back to the office (or to the speaking clock!) for approval or simply by arguing for an hour over the trivial point.

8 Transactional analysis

In any negotiation or indeed in any discussion between two or more people the attitude adopted by each can be analysed. This is called transactional analysis. The attitude adopted by each person falls into one of three categories (Figure 6.6). Each person's attitude can move continuously between these categories.

This shows that everybody talks in one of the three modes. Adults speak with intellect, intelligence, logic and courtesy. Children whine and whinge to get their own way and use stupid arguments to try to win their point. Parents should respond to their children with firm admonishment but sometimes, if aggravated, slip into responding in an equally childish way.

The principle behind transactional analysis is that an individual should always be in the adult mode and that he should try to drag the conversation up to the level of adult/adult interchange. For a negotiation this means that, where one side falls into a childish approach, the other should try to restore the exchange to an adult one (Figure 6.7).

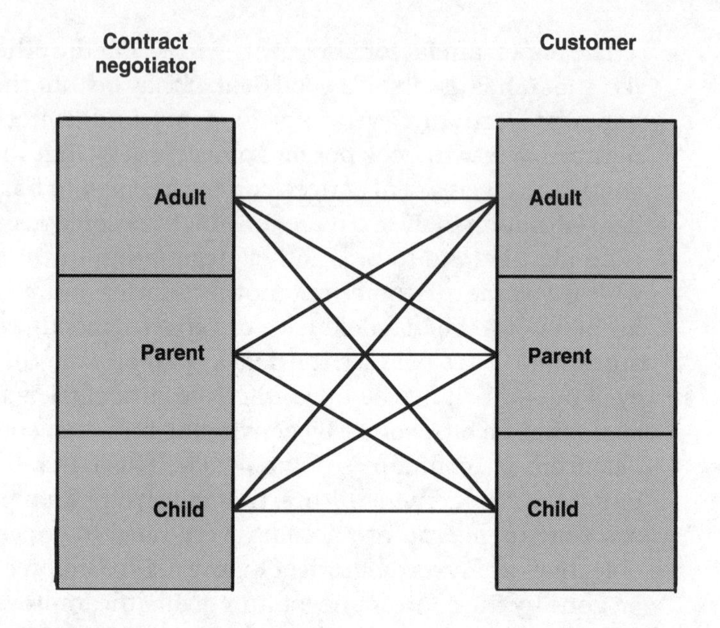

Figure 6.6: Transactional analysis

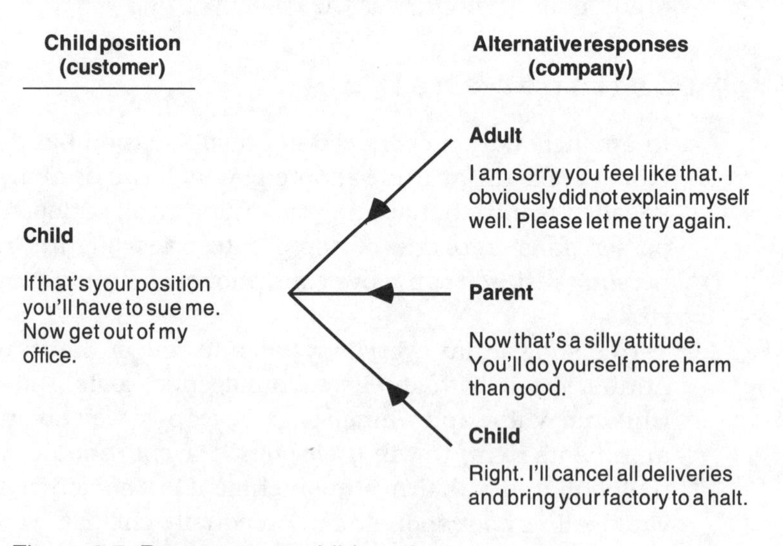

Figure 6.7: Responses to child mode

This shows very clearly that the mode of response to a childish stance can dramatically alter the direction of the negotiation. The childish response of meeting an unfortunate threat with a bigger threat (probably neither side would wish to carry their threats out) is patently stupid and will make matters worse, not better. The parental response is almost as bad as it would be received by the other side as a condescending and pompous attitude which will not heal the wound. The adult response is sensible and soothing. It includes two of the key (and much under-used) words – 'sorry', 'please' and 'thank you'. It is designed to grab the negotiation from the edge of the precipice.

When seen in black and white like this, it is obvious that remaining in the adult mode at all times is the most productive manner in which to conduct the negotiation; yet people, as emotional creatures, drop subconsciously into the parent and child modes. Occasionally it may be beneficial to drop intentionally into a different mode, just to see what happens. That is a risky experiment but it helps to explore the personality of the opposition and to test the volatility of the attitude that he has taken. However, the point is that it must be an intentional ploy.

9 Gap closing

Whenever a negotiation starts there is a gap between the two sides. Bridging the gap is one way of looking at the aim of negotiation. Therefore one of the processes that goes on is the shifting of positions as attempts are made to meet that aim. The successful negotiator is the one who can mentally stand back from the proceedings and ask himself 'What is happening here?', 'What is going on?', 'How am I doing?' As has been said before, the knack of visualising all the processes is important. The process of closing the gap can also be visualised as the negotiation starts (Figure 6.8) and as it proceeds (Figure 6.9) to a conclusion (Figure 6.10). Occasionally a negotiation meeting ends unsuccessfully with the gap wider than ever (Figure 6.11).

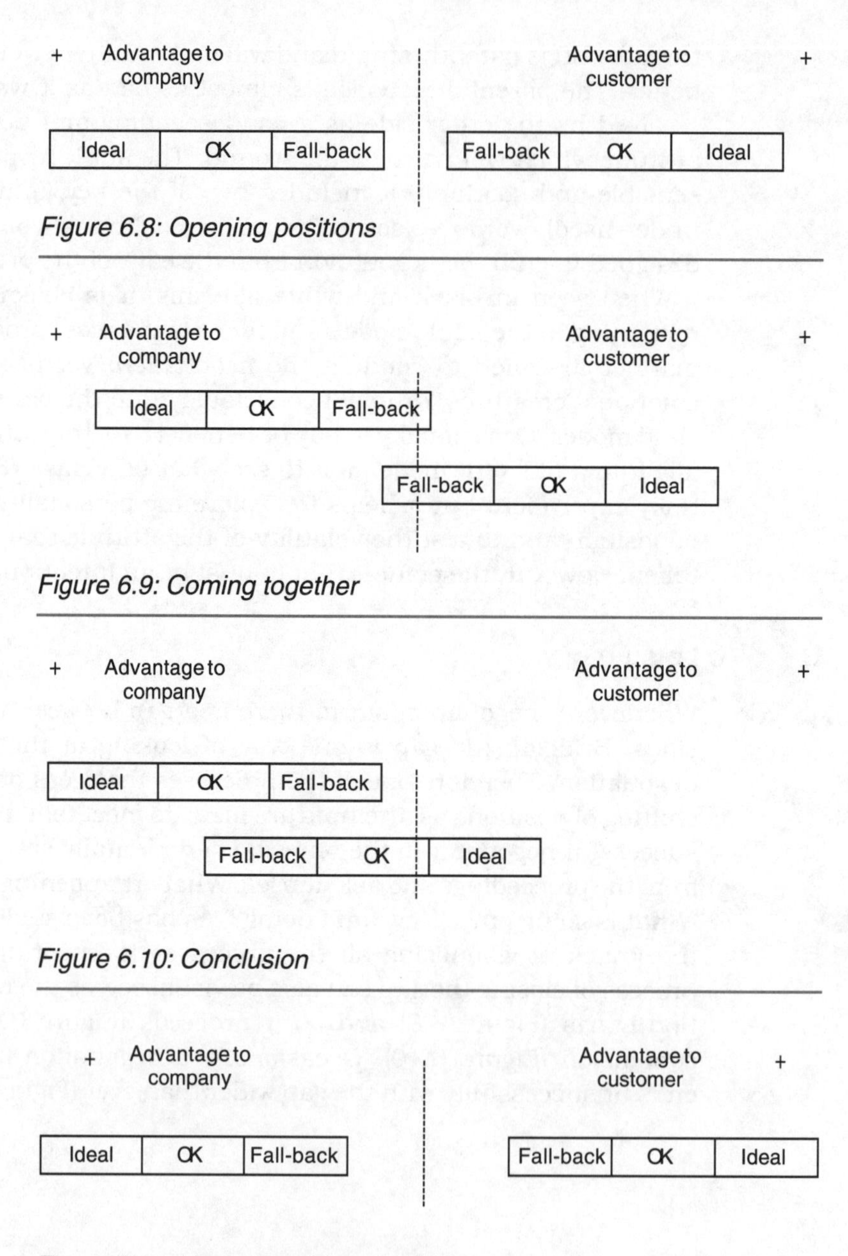

Figure 6.8: Opening positions

Figure 6.9: Coming together

Figure 6.10: Conclusion

Figure 6.11: Unsuccessful – gap wider

These pictures show how tug-of-war-like negotiation can be: pulling hard, yielding ground, win a little, lose a little, and so on until one side collapses exhausted.

CHAPTER 7

The negotiation

1 Introduction

In a book about successful contract negotiation it is perhaps surprising that the negotiation meeting itself is not addressed in detail until Chapter 7. This serves well to illustrate one of the fundamental principles, which is that there really is a much longer process in train and it is that process (Figure 7.1) which must be managed successfully and not just the actual meeting with the customer.

Having said that, all can be won or lost at the meeting and it is there that the contract negotiator must excel, his performance should be worthy of an Oscar as all the skills, preparation, planning and rehearsal are brought together at the same time. He must set himself the task of winning the 'un-winnable'.

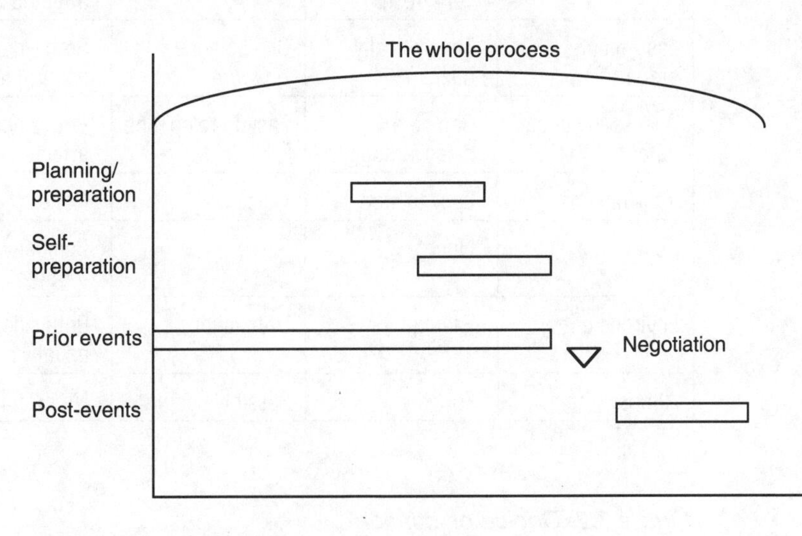

Figure 7.1: Manage the whole process

Location, timing, agenda and opening shots

The first thing to consider is the location of the meeting. There are only three choices. The customer's premises, the company's premises or neutral ground. Each choice presents advantages and disadvantages. These can be described under the headings of home, away or neutral ground (Figure 7.2).

On a simple analysis it is fairly clear that a neutral ground is preferred. Surprisingly, this is a possibility which is usually completely overlooked. Custom and practice normally evolves so that one party most often visits the other. The customer likes to feel he is in control and prefers the meetings to be on his site unless the company happens to be located somewhere where there is an ulterior attraction: London is popular at Christmas, Germany is good in September (Oktoberfest), far-away places are good for those collecting 'air miles', etc. The suggestion of a neutral ground can be made from time to time. If the proposed place benefits from one of the aforementioned attractions, the better it will appeal to the customer. Of course the real reasons

	Home	Away	Neutral
Travelling	None: negotiator very fresh	Fatigue	Both sides equally affected
Last-minute preparation	Theoretically easier	Can be done *en route*	Both sides equal opportunity
Access to people/ data	Can be a disadvantage	Easy to telephone	Both sides equally affected
Interruptions	Easy to stop	Nuisance	None
Cost	None	Some	Company pays for both!
Environment	Familiar	Unfamiliar	Both sides equally affected
Atmosphere	Friendly	Possibly hostile	Neutral

Figure 7.2: Choice of location

are to take the sting out of a potentially difficult meeting, to make the customer subconsciously feel beholden to the company and, most importantly, to isolate the customer from back-up support or data.

If a neutral ground is not appropriate or acceptable then convention demands that the meeting will be at the customer's premises. The contract negotiator should be aware of the disadvantages and work actively to counter them. For example, he should get to know the customer's location, building and office so that going there becomes a routine and familiar activity. He should be on friendly terms with as many people as possible in the customer's organisation. He should feel able to send away people who interrupt the meeting. In other words he should be in control of the situation.

The question of the start time of the meeting was mentioned in Chapter 6. The negotiator should aim to contrive things so that the start time best suits his purpose. There is also the question of the finish time or duration of the meeting. The first rule here is that, for a meeting starting at 9.00 am, he should expect to finish at midnight! Prepare for the worst and anything better is then a bonus. Pressure to agree by a certain time is an enormous burden under which to work.

Sometimes there might be a real deadline. For example, if agreement of a price for the provision of an engineer to go overseas is required before the engineer gets on the plane, then clearly if agreement is not reached by flight departure time the deal cannot go ahead. This is a real deadline and its negotiating advantage would lie either with the customer or with the company, depending upon the particular circumstances. More often than not, deadlines are not real and usually obviously so. The contract negotiator's performance has to be believable to be effective. Inventing obviously spoof deadlines will not help and the respect of the other side will be lost. Real but irrelevant deadlines are also to be avoided. Declaring an aim to finish by 4.30 pm in order to get the 5.00 pm train from Waterloo is to hand the other side a free and powerful negotiating weapon.

Careful thought needs to be given before sending to the customer a proposed agenda for the meeting as there is a balance between too much and too little notice of the items to be discussed (Figure 7.3).

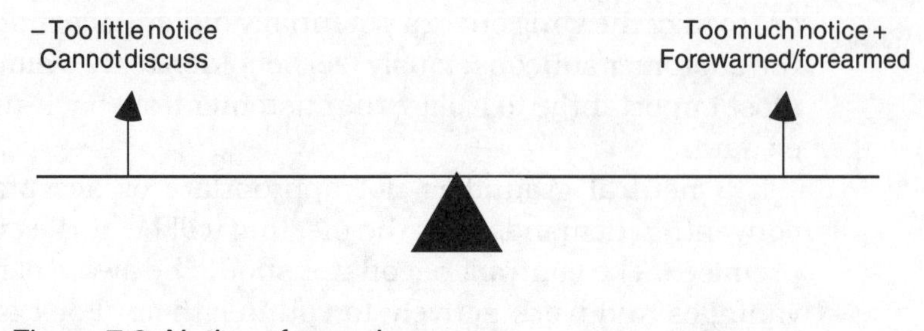

Figure 7.3: Notice of agenda

A decision should be made in each case as to how much time and how much detail to give the customer in advance of the meeting. On the one hand, no notice may mean that the customer would be unable to discuss anything. On the other hand, too much notice may give the customer sufficient time to prepare thoroughly and research his position. This decision depends upon knowing the customer well, knowing his willingness or otherwise to negotiate from cold, how well or badly he would react to a last-minute agenda and so on.

Moving on from this is the question of how much to reveal right at the start of the meeting. It may be better to list straight away all of the things requiring resolution, or it may be better to drip-feed them into the discussion, choosing the timing and method of tabling points according to the success, tone and direction of the meeting. Again this decision should be made on a case-by-case basis, taking full account of the personality and skills of the opposition negotiator.

A further decision to be made is what opening shots to use. The principal decision is whether to speak first or not. Some people always prefer to seize the initiative and speak first. This can be advantageous. However, the risk is that the wrong thing might be said which would have a spoiling rather than a beneficial effect. Alternatively, letting the customer speak first allows the negotiator to gauge the depths of the customer's preparation, the extent of his arguments as well as his mood and tone of voice. While the customer is speaking the negotiator can carefully frame his opening remarks or response to ensure maximum effect. Many a negotiation has been won or lost in the first few minutes. Even if not won or lost straight away, the gambits of the two sides will dictate the tone, direction and length of the meeting.

3 Single and series meetings

To return to the military analogy, thought needs to be given to the company's preference for a short, sharp single battle or, at the other extreme, a long-drawn-out war of attrition.

A single meeting has the advantage of a quick result, saving time, money, energy and resources on both sides. Both negotiators are freed to get on with other work and, if the result is speedily arrived at, it should be reasonably clear as to what the agreement is, and it can be committed to writing in a short period of time.

From a strategic or tactical point of view it may be that a series of meetings suits the company much better. A long campaign may be the ideal approach. This sounds odd, but only because there is an automatic supposition that it is usually the company which wants something (an order or money) from the customer and hence a quick agreement is desirable. This is not always so. The customer may have a valid claim against the company which the company does not want to meet. What, in those circumstances, could be better than a long delay? With a bit of luck the customer may lose interest, personalities might change, circumstances might change or, if enough time goes by, the claim might even be debarred under the statute of limitations.

In the normal course of events, however, it is usually in the interests of both sides to come to an agreement as quickly as is sensibly possible. Sometimes, though, where a single meeting is planned but complete agreement has not been reached by the end and a further meeting is scheduled, the parties should have it clear between them whether the whole negotiation is to continue or just that part which relates to the unresolved issues. In other words, are agreements made during the first meeting absolutely fixed or is either side entitled to reopen points at the concluding meeting?

As each meeting progresses it should not be assumed that the rate of progress is directly proportional to the rate of elapse of time or that the progress rate is fixed throughout the meeting. It is the more likely that these relationships vary as time goes by (Figure 7.4).

The shape of the progress/time graph is endlessly variable. In the example shown in Figure 7.4, period A marks the initial phase when some good progress is made. Period B shows the

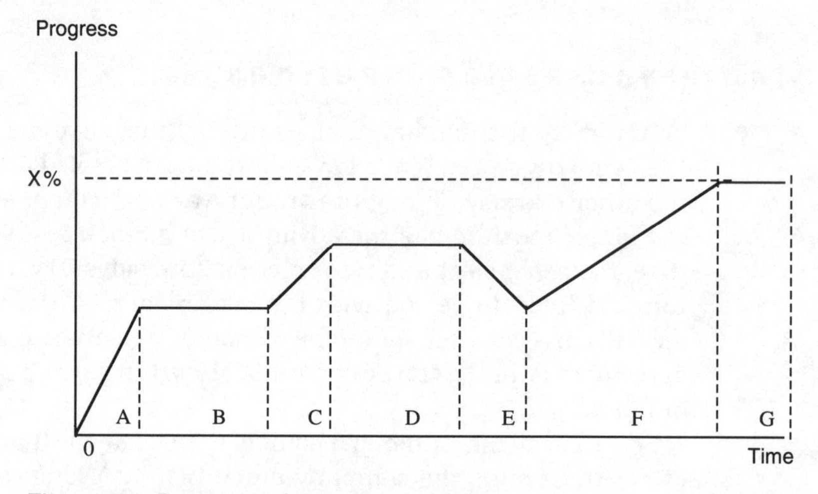

Figure 7.4: Progress of the negotiation I

negotiation stagnating until a breakthrough in C, but this is then followed by further stagnation in D and then unfortunately a backwards step in E. Period F sees a steady resolution of issues before endeavour toils off in G, right at the end of the meeting. By this time X per cent of progress has been made where X per cent could be in the range of, say, 30 –100 per cent. That is, 100 per cent might be a reasonable expectation where there are no contentious issues; 30 per cent may be a hopeless result or a very good result depending upon the number and seriousness of the problems to be solved.

There is no such thing as a typical progress/time graph. The example shown in Figure 7.4 might just as easily have looked completely different (Figure 7.5).

In some ways it is more pertinent to consider, not progress against time, which measures the rate of getting the set of issues resolved, but gain against time. Gain against time means the relationship between what the customer can be pushed to on a particular parameter such as price and the time spent pushing him there. This is definitely not a linear relationship (Figure 7.6).

The precise shape of the curve and the exact location of PNRFG can vary. Some people will go from their opening to closing positions in five minutes. Some may take five hours. But the characteristics of the curve will always be present. Some negotiators will carry on past the PNRFG and try to push the customer for a little more over lunch, or on the telephone the next day or by letter the following week. It is for individuals to decide

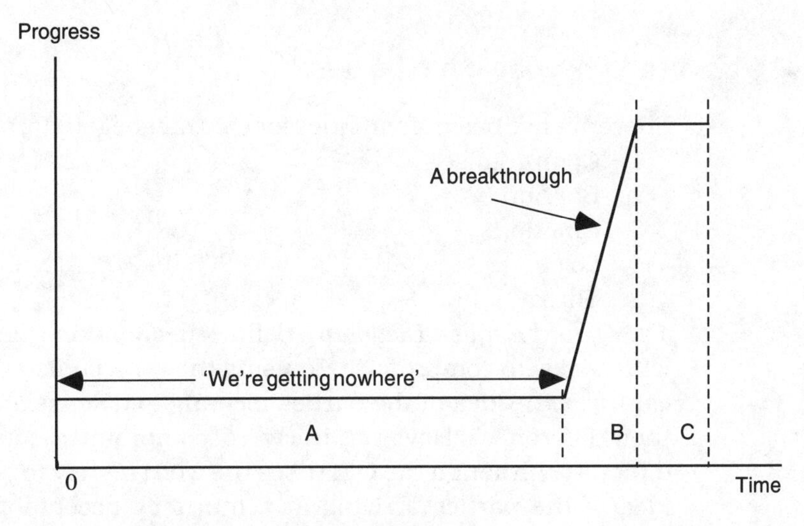

Figure 7.5: Progress of the negotiation II

where along the curve it is time to stop, but it should not be thought that twice as much time will produce twice the gain. Indeed, if the negotiator does not strike while the iron is hot and make the agreement, the delay may cause the customer to re-examine his position and thus whatever has been gained can be lost.

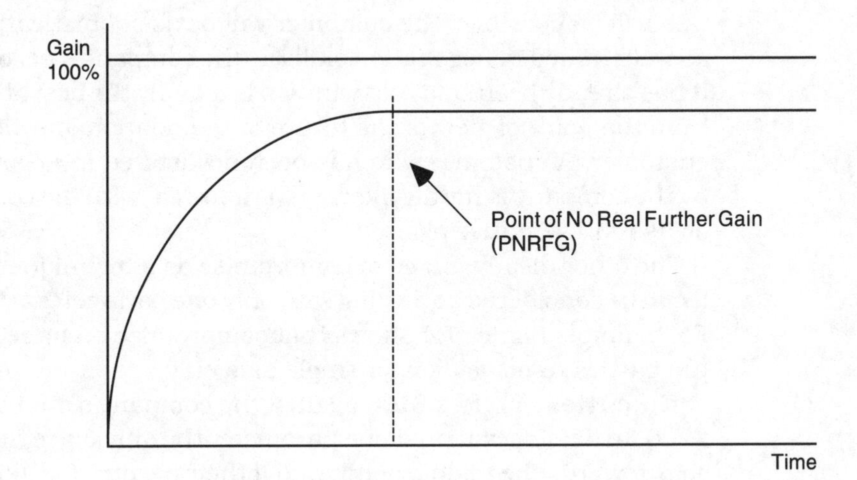

Figure 7.6: Gain against time

4 Negotiating techniques

There are five basic techniques for contract negotiators to utilise:

1. Compromise.
2. Bargain.
3. Emotion.
4. Logic.
5. Threat.

The *Oxford English Dictionary* defines negotiation as conferring with a view to compromise. In using the verb 'confer' this nicely captures the idea of the parties meeting to discuss and resolve their differences. However, the word 'compromise' causes some difficulty. Although the *OED* uses the word merely to convey the idea of the parties arriving at a mutually acceptable accommodation, compromise nevertheless smacks of what is sometimes called the English disease. That is a ready willingness to concede ground in order not to cause a fuss, a hastiness in meeting the other side half-way so that the negotiation does not take too long and that everybody can see that it is fair.

This concern over the nature of compromise is a fair one and the contract negotiator should be aware that, in this sense, a readiness to compromise should be seen as a negotiation technique to reserve for use towards the end of the meeting. His initial aim should be to win everything and concede nothing. However, in complex business matters it is rarely the case that this will be possible. The customer will be as sophisticated and as well trained in negotiation skills as the company's negotiator. It has already been said that win-win is usually the best outcome from the point of view of the future of the relationship with the customer. A customer who has been devastated in negotiation by the company is hardly likely to want to deal with the company or its representative again.

The other disadvantage of compromise as a technique is that it can be considered as dealing with only one parameter at a time. For example Figure 7.7 shows that compromise on price allows the parties to move along a single axis only.

The customer offers £100 against the company's quotation of £200. In dealing with just one parameter the only place they can go is towards the middle point, and if their negotiation skills are evenly balanced, they will end up at £150. Splitting the difference to close the gap is all right provided it is used at the finish (Figure 7.8) and not the start of the negotiation.

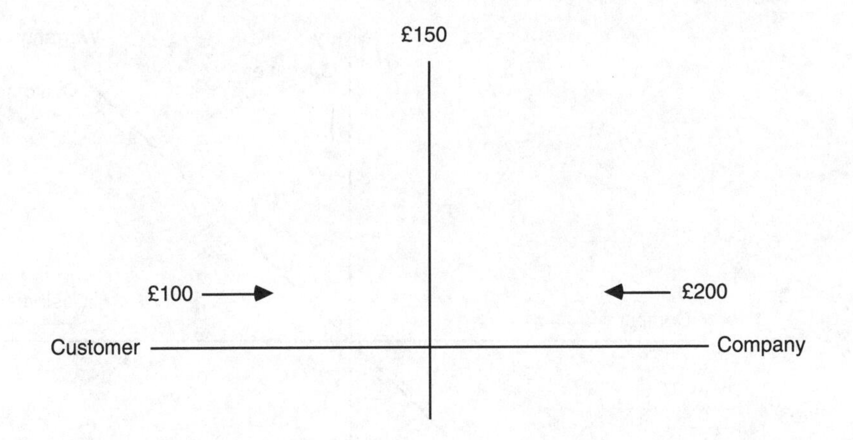

Figure 7.7: Compromising – a single axis

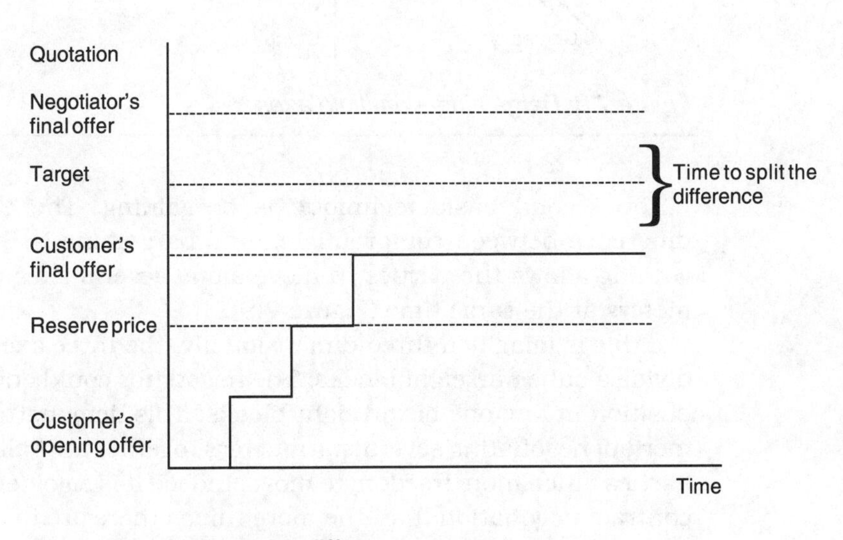

Figure 7.8: Splitting the difference

Figure 7.8 shows the company negotiator pushing the customer up and up beyond the reserve price (see Chapter 3) and towards a target which he will have set himself. If the customer sticks at an offer which is below this target then, at the appropriate moment, it is time to suggest splitting the difference. The negotiator should have sufficient powers of mental arithmetic (or a calculator) to ensure that his final offer and the customer's final offer equate on a simple average basis to the target.

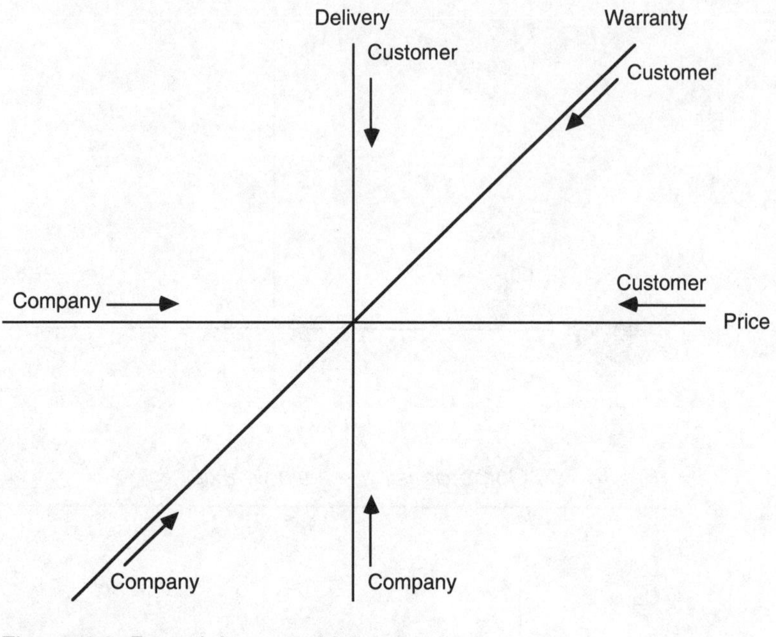

Figure 7.9: Bargaining – multiple axes

The second basic technique is bargaining. The essential difference between compromising and bargaining is that bargaining allows the parties to move along several axes of parameters at the same time (Figure 7.9).

If this is imagined three-dimensionally, the three axes would divide a cube into eight blocks. The negotiator could end in any position in any one of the eight blocks. This demonstrates the merit of negotiating several parameters together as it allows the parties much more freedom to move. Indeed it is a golden rule of contract negotiation that, the more things there are to discuss, the greater the chance of an overall agreement being reached.

The only exception to this rule is where one side's negotiator is much stronger than the other's. In this situation the stronger one should attempt to negotiate each parameter in turn so that he secures exactly what he wants on each parameter without the risk of an overall diluting effect by making a composite agreement.

Emotion is the next basic negotiating technique. It is interesting that, in countries such as the UK, it is often overlooked as the two sides aim to conduct their negotiations in a gentlemanly and seemly fashion. Somehow emotion seems out of place in a contract negotiation. However, if it is accepted that the good negotiator is actually undertaking a performance (see Chapter 6) in the theatrical sense, then it should be obvious that emotion can have a very important part to play. It must be remembered, though, that just as with a theatrical performance where the emotion must appear real, it is nevertheless only an act. Emotion in a contract negotiation must likewise be an act. It must be convincing to be effective but it is only an act. It is rarely the case that the negotiator who genuinely loses control of his feelings and responds emotionally is going to get the best deal, although it is true to say that getting the right deal must be important to the negotiator on a personal level. Just as real emotion on the one extreme can be counterproductive, then so also can too little feeling be unhelpful. Somebody just going through the motions will not succeed.

Emotion ranges through quite a wide scale of states (Figure 7.10).

The plus scale in Figure 7.10 shows an increasingly tough line being taken with the emphasis in the language changing from the negotiator to the customer. Apparent loss of temper, table thumping, jumping up, throwing things and increasing use of

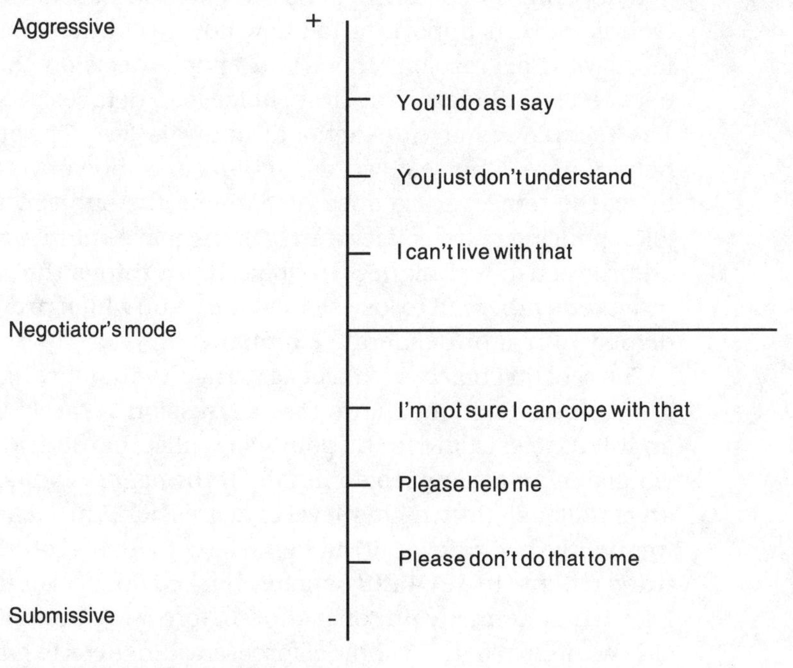

Figure 7.10: Scale of emotions

Anglo-Saxon all characterise the aggressive mode and, used sparingly, the effect can be devastating. It does no good always to appear bad-tempered and always to be swearing but, used just at the right moment, these things can be just enough to tip the discussion in the negotiator's favour. It shows how serious the point is, how important the point is to the negotiator. It convinces when other methods of persuasion have failed.

The minus scale in Figure 7.10 shows the often forgotten, other side of emotion. Because the contract negotiator in his inner self (see Chapter 5) is competitive, aggressive and militaristic, it is difficult to drop into a submissive, pathetic mode, but in such a mode it is an extremely tough person on the other side who can ignore the pleas of another human being. Again it is a technique which by its very nature can only be used infrequently.

It is sometimes said that children are the best and most natural negotiators. Certainly they use all the methods of persuasion known to humankind and emotion is no exception. Children happily and without inhibition oscillate from the aggressive mode to the submissive mode and generally do very well from it.

When on the receiving end of emotion-based negotiating techniques it is important to know how to counter them. When faced with aggression, there is a simple decision to be made between two choices. The first choice is to defuse the situation. The techniques of transactional analysis (see Chapter 6) are helpful here. Choice of words, actions and tone of voice can all bring the temperature down. Changing the subject, making a joke, pouring more coffee or suggesting a five-minute recess are all productive techniques. In doing these things the negotiator must remember not to lose sight of the issue which prompted the display of real or deliberate emotion.

The second choice is to meet aggression with more aggression. The animal kingdom shows that aggression is rarely used with an intent to escalate to the point of conflict, battle and injury. It is used in an attempt to dominate. If the aggression is met with an equal or slightly higher level of aggression, the aggressor will frequently back down. This behaviour is also seen in human transactions. In 1964 Khrushchev backed down over the 'Bay of Pigs' when Kennedy put on a show of force. Presumably neither side wanted to fight. A show of force, a willingness to gamble and a lot of nerve won the day. In contract negotiation, aggression can be used to counter aggression but it must be based upon a calculated decision that such a response will call the other side's bluff rather than make matters worse.

Dealing with submissive emotion is easier. Again there is a choice: first, to pull the emotion level back to the neutral zone by using adult/child or parent/child interplay. Otherwise, the second choice is simple. If the other side is playing wounded or is really in a weak position, then go for the kill. Show no mercy, but just be nice about it.

Logic is both a powerful and disappointing negotiating technique. As intelligent people contract negotiators should be able to muster a range of logical arguments to support their position. The arguments can be either prepared beforehand or fabricated out of thin air as the situation demands. Two reasonable people should each be able to put forward their respective arguments, to listen to the arguments of the other side and on a logical basis to decide and agree between them which set of arguments is the stronger. Logical negotiation is therefore easy and the outcome must logically be acceptable to both sides without any further debate.

However, the disappointing feature (or rewarding feature, depending upon whose argument is the stronger) of logical argument is that it is entirely vulnerable to the simple word 'no'! The intention is not to diminish the value of logical reasoning, only to say that by itself it may not prove sufficient. Indeed if the contract negotiator's position is actually the weaker, he must at best avoid logical argument or at worst resort to attacking the logic of the other side's argument rather than try to defend his own logically.

Where the negotiator knows he has the stronger set of arguments, his first task is to persuade the other side that the negotiation will be based upon logic only. If the other side agrees then the battle is won before the game commences. The phrasing of this suggestion should be handled carefully. Suppose the principal aim of the negotiation is to agree a price for a job for which the company has quoted £100,000. If the basis of agreement has not been preconditioned as described, then the customer can attack in a number of ways:

Compromise: 'I only wanted to pay £80,000. Let's compromise on £90,000.'

Bargain: 'I'll agree £100,000 if you give me three years' credit.'

Emotion: 'How dare you charge that much?'

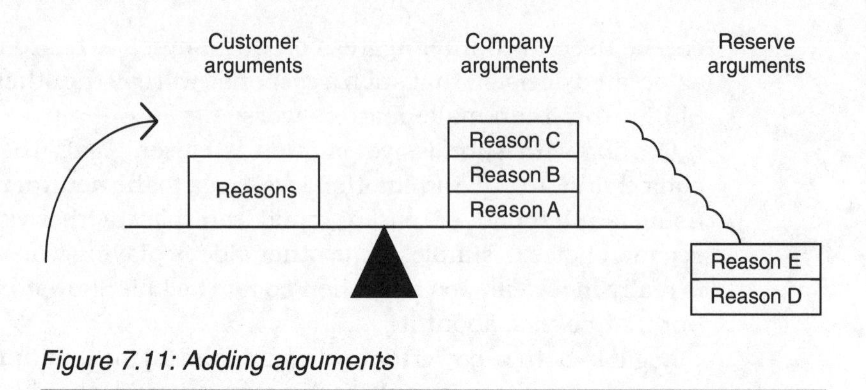

Figure 7.11: Adding arguments

Whereas if the negotiator says beforehand, 'If I can demonstrate that the job will take four people six months, will you agree that the price is £100,000?', and the customer agrees, then all techniques but logical reasoning have been excluded from the negotiation. This is a trivial example and, as with all negotiating techniques and ploys, there is no guarantee of 100 per cent success but at least it serves to show what can be done to precondition the nature of the negotiation.

The final observation about logical reasoning is that it is usually best not to volunteer all the assembled arguments in one go, but to use each one to add further weight only to the point where the customer gives in (Figure 7.11).

The reason for this is that, as in any professional game, the aim is to do just enough to win. Once the negotiation is won, unused arguments can be stored away for another day. Proffering lots of arguments can stimulate the customer into thinking of lots of defences. Indeed some arguments turn out to help the other side more than the company. Psychologically it is also reassuring to have won the battle knowing that some ammunition is left in reserve. To illustrate these principles, imagine a battery of logical reasons to dissuade the customer from going to other suppliers to compete with the company for the further development of one of the company's designs:

Reason A Takes more time.
Reason B Higher technical risk.
Reason C No technical support/assistance from designer.
Reason D Invalidates existing warranties.
Reason E Might be more expensive.
Reason F Interchangeability problems.
Reason G Insufficient intellectual property rights.

It is possible that any one of these would dissuade the customer. It might take two or three. Reason G would win the argument all by itself. However, the customer may not realise that he has insufficient intellectual property rights for his purposes. This realisation in itself may cause a lot of problems and so the decision might be made not to deploy this argument unless and until all others have failed. If the battle can be won on Reason A, why waste all the other reasons? The most powerful in particular might best be saved for another day, when perhaps the other reasons are less convincing or are inapplicable.

The final basic negotiating technique is threat. To describe threat as a technique is perhaps somewhat inaccurate. Technique seems to imply the careful use of some craft or skill. Threat is a very crude and blunt instrument but nevertheless it can be an effective device. It cannot be used frequently and, to be used at all, the negotiator must be able to ensure that the threat will be carried out. Empty threats are usually obvious and fairly pointless. The company must be in a very powerful position to be able to threaten convincingly to stop work or hold up deliveries. Customers rightly do not take such threats seriously. If a threat is called for, the negotiator must be absolutely sure that the company is willing and able to carry the threat out.

The problem with a blunt threat is that it will be met with an unfavourable response and matters will have been made much worse. If threat is to be used at all, it is much better to use it in as subtle a fashion as possible. Expressions such as 'I think we need to explore the consequences', or 'What would you do in my position?' or 'Of course if you said that to XYZ company they'd have stopped work by now' provide much better introductions to the difficult task of putting a gun to the customer's head. Indeed, threat is a technique that can be used only when its possible adverse effect (in the boomerang vein) has been analysed, thought through and appropriate countermeasures prepared.

5 Ploys

At the heart of any negotiation is the use of ploys, tricks, devices and diversions. The contract negotiator should have a mental armoury of such ploys. He should also know how to recognise them when used by the other side and how to counter them when on the receiving end. The following list describes such ploys and their counters.

1. Bacon rolls

Ploy: As part of any negotiation planning activity, the question should always be asked as to the likely mood of the customer on arrival for the start of the meeting. If it can be seen that he is likely to be in an aggressive mood, possibly upset, then a ploy is needed to diffuse the atmosphere. One such ploy for meetings that start early in the morning is to take bacon rolls, Danish pastries or whatever the customer likes into the meeting and offer them around. This usually works, as it is difficult to be angry with somebody who has just offered hospitality and fulfilled a basic animal need – food.

Counter: Although it is unlikely that the customer would use this ploy, the counter is easy: 'Thank you, I've had breakfast already so let's get on with the meeting'.

2. A favour

Ploy: Another useful way to diffuse a hostile atmosphere before the meeting starts is to have done the other side a favour. 'Good morning John, I remembered to bring with me *Fly Fishing* by J R Hartley which you asked to borrow.'

Counter: As with a lot of negotiating ploys the best counter is to expose the ploy for what it is. 'Thanks, but it's no good trying to butter me up.'

3. Good news

Ploy: Good news is always well received. The idea is to have done something unexpected to please the customer. 'Good morning John. Before we start, I thought you would like to know that we finished stage 2 acceptance ahead of schedule and that means there's a refund to you under the contract.'

Counter: Recognise but be dismissive of the news. 'Good, about time too. Now if you can just do as well on this one I can start to feel happy.'

4. Red herrings

Ploy: There is nothing quite like a good red herring to divert attention from a weak point. It is important to be absolutely serious and stick at it until the weak point has been forgotten.

Counter: Do not lose sight of the original point. If the red herring has to be discussed, make a note on a piece of paper of the original point and return to it time and again.

5. Wild goose chase

Ploy: Similar to the red herring but more developed. The aim is to take the customer along one apparently logical path and then onto another and another until the conversation is a mile away from a difficult point.

Counter: Again, make a written note and come back to the first point. 'That's all very interesting, but will you now answer this question?'

6. Apology

Ploy: Apologise for something whether or not an apology is warranted. Apologies cost nothing but can do wonders for softening the customer's attitude.

Counter: Be dismissive. 'It's no good you apologising, that doesn't help at all. Now, this is what I want you to do.'

7. Instant agreement

Ploy: To unnerve the other side, smile broadly and agree instantly with a proposition (provided it is not really important) to worry them that they have made a mistake.

Counter: Be sure of your ground and look for any unfortunate implications of the agreement. If there are any, retract the agreement immediately. If it is only a ploy, tell the other side they should agree to everything as quickly.

8. Kite flying

Ploy: Ask for something completely outrageous just to see what happens, but keep a straight face.

Counter: Say the suggestion is ludicrous and threaten to call off the meeting.

9. Sell it

Ploy: Whatever the proposition, it must be sold as attractive from the customer's point of view. One of the skills of the negotiator is to convince the other side that what is bad for him is really good for him.

Counter: Dismiss it for the twisted logic it undoubtedly is.

10. Change the argument

Ploy: If a point is being lost because the argument in its favour is being overwhelmed by the other side, dump the argument and find another one.

Counter: Drag the other side back to the original argument and force them to concede upon it.

11. Feign misunderstanding

Ploy: This is useful in avoiding defeat by a good argument. 'Well, that sounds very clever, but it's beyond me. I don't think anybody could understand it, let alone believe it.'

Counter: Challenge the feint. 'You know very well what I mean.'

12. Take an action

Ploy: Say that the point cannot be discussed and take an action to write back after the meeting, and then delay or avoid doing it.

Counter: Insist on discussing. Offer to get the other person's boss to join the meeting. At worst, write and confirm after the meeting. Do not wait for the other side.

13. Why

Ploy: A logical argument can be put in such a way that it conceals the real reason. Always challenge to find the real reason. 'Why are you saying that? What is it you are getting at?'

Counter: Repeat the logical argument in more depth and at greater length.

14. Cold shoulder

Ploy: In team negotiations, identify the weakest person on the other side and then cold-shoulder the others to exclude them psychologically and to some extent physically from the discussion.

Counter: Prevent the others in the team from speaking. Move seats to confront physically the lead negotiator on the other side.

15. Sit it out

Ploy: Make it clear that you are there for the duration. Book a hotel. Telephone your spouse during the meeting to say you will be very late. This puts the other side under pressure to make concessions in order to avoid a late night.

Counter: Apologise but say firmly that you must leave by a specified time. Call the other side's bluff by immediately suggesting that a further date is fixed to continue the discussion.

16. Comparison with others

Ploy: Make the other side feel unreasonable and uncomfortable by comparing them with others. 'I don't know why you are being so difficult over this, all our other customers are very happy with this arrangement.'

Counter: Do not be fooled by what is probably a fictional statement. Do not be dragged into even discussing it. 'What others do is of no concern to me, I'm only interested in my position.'

17. Policy

Ploy: Refuse to agree, explaining that it is not company policy. The danger here is that, if it is true, there is no way to compromise. If it is not true and a compromise is reached, it will be apparent that it was an untruth.

Counter: Challenge, based on previous knowledge or experience of the other side's policies. Suggest that a more senior person who can discuss policy is hauled into the meeting.

18. You've got to be joking

Ploy: Literally laugh at the other side's suggestion, dismiss it as a joke and move on to the next issue.

Counter: Stern face and reproachful voice. 'Unfortunately for you I'm not joking. Now let's discuss this properly.'

19. Humour

Ploy: Use humour to lighten the atmosphere or to obscure an important point.

Counter: If it is preferable to keep the atmosphere heavy, do not join in the humour. Let the other side have their laugh and then continue. If the atmosphere needs to be lightened, allow it but look for the important point which is being skipped over or obscured.

20. Persistence

Ploy: Keep coming back to the same point. Children repeat the same request over and over, knowing that on a percentage basis they have a high chance of succeeding. Do not be put off by having apparently exhausted all the arguments. Negotiation is not like an exam. More than one chance is allowed to win a particular point.

Counter: Meet fire with fire. If the arguments are successful, keep repeating them. Tell the other side they are wasting time going over the same ground.

21. Patience

Ploy: Just keep at it. Patience is an important characteristic of the contract negotiator.

Counter: Find ways to niggle and irritate the other side until their patience cracks.

22. Shelve the issue

Ploy: If it appears that no real progress is to be made on a particular issue, drop it and come back to it later. This can be done either covertly by wandering on to a different topic or overtly by suggesting that the issue is parked for now. This allows time for the other side's mood to change and time to think of a more persuasive argument.

Counter: If on the point of winning an argument, do not allow it to be shelved. Insist that it is concluded straight away.

23. Stone wall

Ploy: Just keep arguing. Keep going. Do not yield anything. Wait to see what happens. The other side may volunteer concessions just to achieve some progress.

Counter: Trying to break through a stone wall is exhausting, futile and pointlessly 'uses up' good arguments. Find the weakest point and attack that or wait for the other side to get fed up with repeating themselves.

24. Divide and conquer

Ploy: In a team negotiation, get the other side to argue among themselves. Pick up inconsistencies between their statements and provoke disagreement.

Counter: Seize control. Get the others in the team to shut up. Restate or summarise the inconsistent arguments in such a way that they appear consistent after all.

25. Challenge their competence

Ploy: Interrogate the other side's propositions. 'Where did

you get that from?', 'What research have you done?', 'You obviously did not read our letter of two years ago', 'Can you explain that from first principles?'

Counter: Refuse to be drawn. Throw the ball back. 'You know perfectly well what I mean.'

26. Ghost agreements

Ploy: Refer to an agreement (real or imagined) made orally or by custom and practice with a predecessor of one of the other side's team.

Counter: Do not be drawn into finding out whether the alleged agreement is real or not. Simply say that this is now and the past is immaterial.

27. Mountains and molehills

Ploy: Make a minor point seem very important so that when it is given away, the other side think that they have won a major concession.

Counter: Always retain a sense of perspective. It should be obvious which are major and minor points.

28. Silence

Ploy: Sit in total silence and wait for the other side to crack.

Counter: Silence is an old chestnut and is an obvious ploy. It is best met with silence. After five minutes, suggest that both sides stop playing games and invite the other side to move on.

29. Old chestnuts

Ploy: Old chestnuts, such as sitting the opposition with their backs to a radiator and staring into the sun, putting place names on the table so as to separate physically the other side's players and not providing thirsty visitors with a drink are all tired, old ploys which can still sometimes work.

Counter: Do the obvious. Sit where you like. Get a drink beforehand or bring a flask of coffee (and only one cup) to the meeting.

30. Recess

Ploy: Taking a break for both sides to reconsider can provide a real opportunity for a breakthrough or, if things are going badly, to allow breathing space.

Counter: If the other side look weak and on the point of collapse, do not allow a recess. Press for an agreement.

31. Speak their lines

Ploy: To take the sting out of a difficult meeting, open by voicing the concerns of the other side but in such a way that it diminishes the venom.

Counter: Emphasise the level of concern. 'I'm glad you understand the concern but you seem to have seriously underestimated just how bad things are.'

32. Dummy summary

Ploy: Summarise the agreements so far, omitting some things, including others not actually agreed and twisting things to improve the position.

Counter: As the meeting progresses, make written notes of the agreements and check these off as the other side offers its summary.

33. Back scratching

Ploy: Link unrelated matters. It is easy to negotiate related matters such as price and payment terms. It is more difficult where there is no actual linkage, such as between two separate contracts. Nevertheless, suggesting a compromise on one to get a deal on the other can be useful.

Counter: Avoid broad deals unless it is certain that there is an overall advantage.

34. Facts reversal

Ploy: Take the opposite situation as an analogous basis to defeat the proposition: 'If I had delivered a week early, you would not have paid a bonus, so why should I reduce the price because I delivered a week late?'

Counter: Stick to the real facts and the relevant principle. 'Early delivery is not allowed under the contract. Late delivery is breach of contract which I'm not bound to accept. A price reduction would help make up my mind.'

35. Let's be reasonable

Ploy: State or imply that the other side is being unfair or unreasonable. Appeal to their ethical and moral values. Ask why they have a vendetta.

Counter: Ignore the insult and explain the extreme reasonableness of the position.

36. Let's go to lunch

Ploy: A good opportunity to break a deadlock is the business lunch/dinner. Attitudes relax in a less formal environment. Up to a point, food and drink stimulate the imaginative processes and new solutions can be found.

Counter: If a meal break is inconvenient, do not suggest one (it is usually at the company's initiative) or suggest that a break is taken once a particular point has been agreed. Alternatively, have sandwiches and soft drinks brought in so that the meeting can continue without interruption.

37. One more thing

Ploy: Just as the deal is being closed, ask for one more concession. Asking never hurts. If you do not ask, you do not get, so always slip in that final, last-second request.

Counter: Refuse. The deal is the deal. Any further concessions must be matched by the other side. Alternatively, threaten to reopen the whole negotiation.

38. Look at the options

Ploy: When the other side will not agree a particular point, paint a series of options all of which are much less beneficial to the other side.

Counter: Do not be diverted. Stick to the position and only concede in return for something else.

39. Attack

Ploy: Attack is the best means of defence. Defend a weak argument by counterattacking on another point.

Counter: Never be diverted once a weak point has been exposed on the other side. Promise (but forget) to deal with the counterattacked points later, once this main point is resolved.

6 Human interaction

Any interaction between people occurs simultaneously through all six senses (Figure 7.12).

Taking the six senses in turn, it is probably the case that taste is not actually used in many contract negotiations! All other

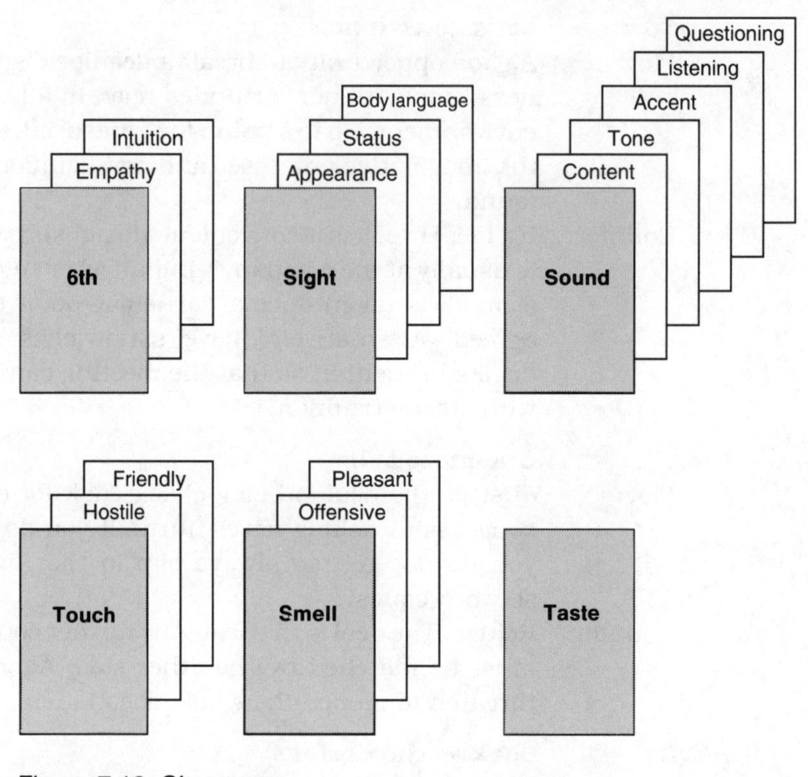

Figure 7.12: Six senses

senses are, however, in play. The good negotiator must use his sixth sense to develop empathy with the customer and he must similarly exercise intuitive skills to 'know' how the customer is feeling and what he is thinking. Smell might at first appear not to be a factor. However, there is nothing like bad breath to guarantee the other side being turned off from a positive co-operative negotiation. Not a lot of touching goes on in most negotiations, but what there is carries important signals. Just consider the opening ceremony of a handshake (Figure 7.13).

So a deliberate choice can be made to provide a sensory signal to the other side as to what to expect. Generally a warm, firm handshake is the best preconditioner. This may mean holding a cup of hot coffee beforehand or wiping the palm dry of perspiration in order to conceal a real sense of fear or apprehension, but the right signal will influence the result. During the negotiation a very occasional touch to the other person's arm may prevent something unfortunate being said; it may remove a barrier; it enhances intimacy. It all helps to build a relationship.

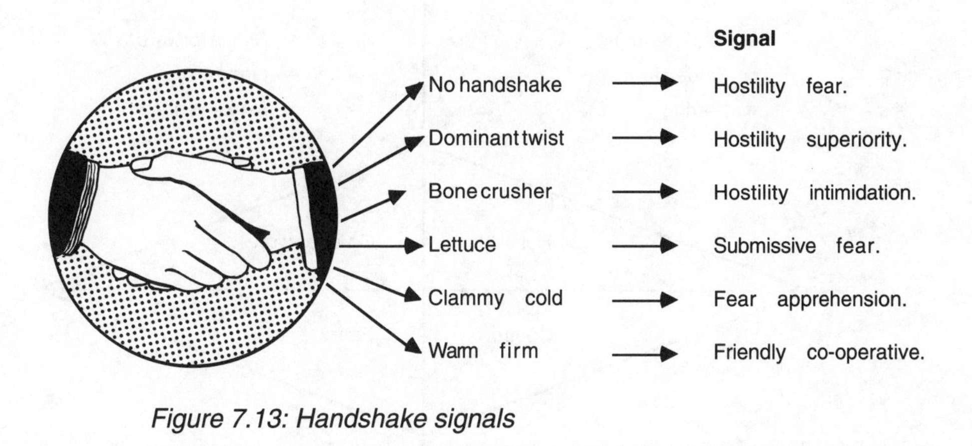

Figure 7.13: Handshake signals

Sight and sound are both crucial. The choice of appearance can influence the other person. Expensive suit, power hair style and smart car all impress and establish a status and position in the other person's mind. When overdone, it can intimidate. The level of formality of the meeting can dictate or be dictated by the choice of dress. Body language is a key, visual negotiating technique which will be covered in detail further in this chapter. The receptive sense of listening is combined with the projective power of speech to produce the most important negotiating feature of all: sound. Negotiation can be conducted by sound alone (on the telephone) and it is thus unique. All other senses are therefore supportive. It is sound which is the principal device.

Listening and questioning skills are very important, and are dealt with later in this chapter. Clearly what is said is important but equally the choice of words, method of expression and tone of voice can have similar influence. Accent can raise or lower barriers between people. The flexible negotiator should, within reason and if necessary, be able to fall into the mode of speech and perhaps accent of the customer to facilitate the discussion.

7 Body language

Body language is a great source of influence. The subconscious adoption of different postures or mannerisms transmits strong signals about mood and intent. Body language should be used as a positive technique. The negotiator should be aware of his

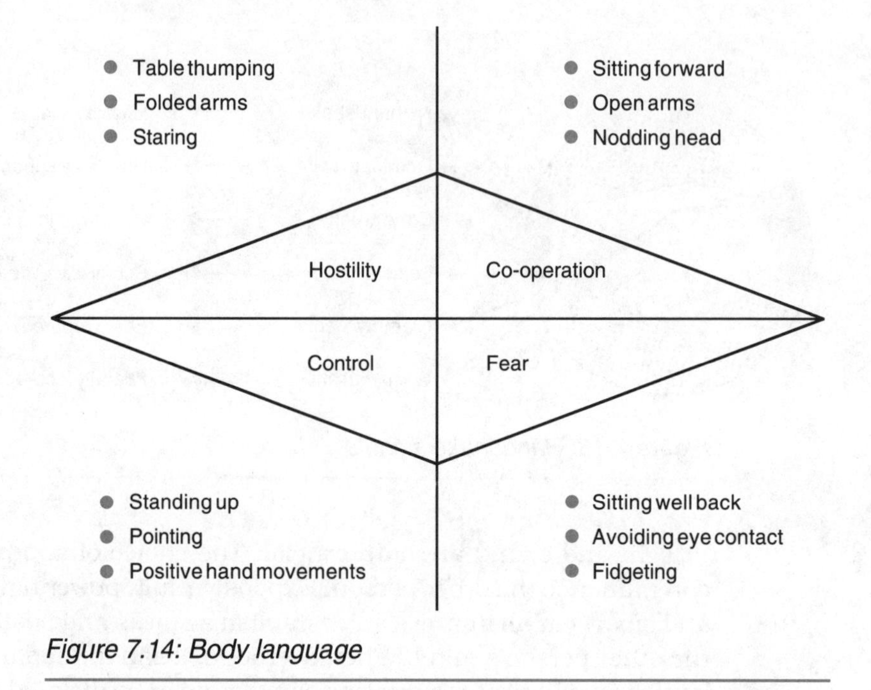

Figure 7.14: Body language

own feelings and adopt postures to conceal the wrong feelings. It can be used to transmit positive and negative feelings as the situation and tactics demand. It can be used to read the feelings of the customer.

Body language can be divided into four categories (Figure 7.14) of hostility, co-operation, control and fear.

When used effectively, body language can produce some interesting results. It is also a source of fun for the negotiator. To move from co-operative body language to hostile body language half-way through the other person's point can cause him to dry up and give up.

8 Listening skills

One of the difficulties that any negotiator faces is that of forcing himself to listen properly to the other side. It is easy to fall into a transmit-only mode and this can be disastrous. Skilled listening occurs on four levels (Figure 7.15).

It is easy to listen to level 1. Level 1 is the words themselves. At level 1, the words could just as well be written as spoken. The words have a literal meaning but this is only part of the overall

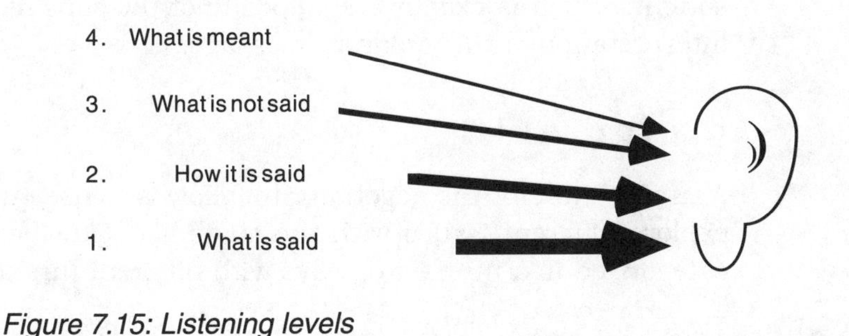

Figure 7.15: Listening levels

message. It is important for the negotiator to be attuned to level 2, to listen for the style and tone of expression and to analyse why this style and tone have been used. As important as the words actually spoken are the words not spoken, the things not said. In Britain there is a wonderful practice of people not saying what they mean or saying the opposite of what is meant, or speaking in cryptic fashion. Listening for the missing bits is just as important as listening to what is said. This is level 3. Each of the levels is progressively more difficult to hear. Level 4 is the hardest to hear. Level 4 carries the real message and it is this that the negotiator must listen for most of all. Sometimes this hidden message is actually present in the speaker's words because he intended it to be there. At other times the hidden message can be found only by interpretation or inference. Either way, to ignore the hidden message is a perilous course of action.

The simple question 'Will you license us your IPR?' invites either a yes/no/maybe answer or a search for more information about the reasons behind the request. Nevertheless, the question is at level 1 and could have been asked in writing rather than orally. However, the same question put differently implies some ulterior thought: 'We assume you would not license your IPR but we have to ask'. The range of answers could be the same but the style of question perhaps accompanied by a searching look begins to indicate that there is more to this than meets the eye (or ear!). This level 2 message prompts the negotiator to ask himself, 'What didn't they say that they would have said if they were serious?' They did not say that agreement to a licence was a prerequisite to the placing of the new contract. If this level 3 inference is correct, perhaps what they really mean is that they hope the answer is 'no'. So the level 4 message, if it has been correctly interpreted, means that a negative answer is being sought, which is exactly the opposite of the sensible, obvious interpretation of the apparent message.

9 Questioning skills

A useful habit for the negotiator to follow is to use questions to explore different issues with the customer. Questions can be categorised in a number of ways with different functions:

Type	*Example*	*Function*
Open	Why, how, when, etc	Information gathering
Closed	Can you provide transport?	To establish fact
Leading	Would you agree that this is reasonable?	Conditioning
Pressure	Will you confirm within 48 hours?	Tying things down
Defensive	How would you feel?	To gain sympathy
Exploratory	Would you consider …?	Searching for common ground

As a technique this is no more than one of any array of devices which the negotiator should hold in his mind and use as the need arises. As the conservation flows he should alternate seamlessly between these different methods of asking questions.

Four phases

All negotiations go through four phases and it is usually as well to let these take their natural course:

Phase 1	Opening.
Phase 2	Testing.
Phase 3	Moving.
Phase 4	Agreeing.

In the opening phase it is important to set the scene and to strive to create the warmest and most productive atmosphere. The testing phase is used to test the strength of the other side's position, the strength of their arguments and the depth of their feelings. It is also the time to try out the strength of the company's arguments, to see how much resistance they will meet and to discover how much analysis and preparation has been done by the other side. Once this phase is complete, one or both sides will have to move their position in order to reach agreement. The negotiator should aim to get the other side to move first. One technique to use or avoid, as necessary, is the 'I've moved, now it's your turn' philosophy. This is a trap into which the unwitting may fall. Therefore it should be used against the customer's negotiator but should be resisted if the company negotiator is on the receiving end. A substantial move from the other side can be met with a little movement, but a minor movement from the other side should be dismissed as trivia. The final agreeing phase is one in which the negotiator should aim to have the initiative, summarising the discussion to his advantage, adding extra concessions from the other side and omitting things which are of value to the other side.

When the negotiators on the two sides know each other well and have conducted many negotiations between themselves, it is possible that time can be saved by eliminating or truncating the first three phases and jumping to the agreeing phase. It can certainly be fairly pointless to repeat well-tried and well-known arguments when both negotiators are astute enough to have analysed each other's positions and are capable of going straight to the heart of the issue. However, this approach of negotiating at a 'high level' (ie skipping over the detail) is particularly advantageous where the negotiator knows his own position to be weak or his arguments flawed. Therefore it is important to look out for the situation where the other side is suggesting a high-level negotiation as this may be to conceal weakness rather than to save time.

11 The buzz

A final word on the negotiation itself: rather like the tingle produced by a favourite piece of music or by a moving theatrical performance, there is a real sensation which could be called 'the buzz' that comes when the negotiation is going well. When it has been handled well, the techniques and ploys have been utilised successfully and the other side are figuratively on the run, a sense of real excitement rushes through the veins. It is a wonderful feeling and a strong motive to do well. The negotiator should always set out with the aim of getting the buzz.

CHAPTER 8

Post-negotiation activities

1 Introduction

The negotiation itself may be over once hands are shaken to seal the deal, but there is much more to it than that. Throughout the book the theme of the whole process has been followed. It has been suggested that the negotiation is not the start of this process but an event which occurs towards the end of the whole process. It is not at the start; it is not right at the end but *towards* the end. The purpose of this chapter is to describe the activities that complete the process.

2 Summarise

The first and most important activity is to summarise the agreement. Whether before or just after hands are shaken does not really matter, provided it is done before the meeting breaks up. Assuming that customer and company hold exactly the same view of the agreement, then it is surprising how quickly memory fades. What is clear in everybody's mind as the meeting finishes at 5.00 pm can become distinctly fuzzy by 9.00 am the next day. If customer and company perceptions of the agreement do not exactly coincide, then the intended meeting of the minds is even less likely to have been achieved.

The contract negotiator should take to the negotiation meeting a written checklist of the issues to be resolved. The objectives analysis and negotiation plan must be carried in the head but a simple written list of the issues should always be taken. This ensures that nothing is forgotten in the heat of the moment. It also means that if all the issues are resolved, the agreement is complete. This saves the delay and embarrassment inherent in having to telephone the opposition the next day to raise a new issue that had been forgotten. To do this is fraught with difficulty. The opposition are unlikely to agree to an additional point without securing some concession in return. Knowing this, there can be a temptation to forget the issue altogether. This is hardly good news for the company.

The list can be used overtly or covertly. It may be convenient to have the list out on the table. Alternatively, if the aim is to trickle the issues into the negotiation and thus not reveal the overall objective, a covert means must be found. A list printed with a tiny font size is useful because it can be left on the table with the negotiator secure in the knowledge that it is too small to be read upside-down and from a distance by the opposition. A list which is concealed among a sheaf of papers is well-enough camouflaged. Otherwise, if the list is written out cryptically so as to be unintelligible to the other side, this will usually suffice.

For an element of fun the list can be used to convey disinformation to the other side. A list which is clear enough to be read upside-down from a distance can easily be written to include spoof or misleading information just to throw the other side off the real track.

As the meeting progresses, written notes should be kept recording the agreements in some detail, albeit abbreviated; this facilitates making a summary of the whole agreement at the end of the meeting.

The negotiator should seize the initiative and use his notes to summarise the meeting. This gives him the chance to flavour the summary to his own advantage, to add bits in his favour and to omit things he does not like. The onus is on the other side to confirm or deny each element of the summary. Innocent apology should be used to deflect any allegation that the negotiator's summary is not an accurate reflection of the meeting. Needless to say, if the customer is giving the summary then his words should be checked very carefully by the negotiator.

The summary is most important and should not be left to chance. Even between opposing negotiators who know each other well, the summary should be precise and specific. Phrases like 'we understand each other' or 'yes, I know what you mean' should be avoided.

If, in making the summary, the negotiator realises that he has made some awful mistake and conceded something of huge value, this is his last chance to remedy the error. He should not be afraid of reopening the discussion. It is far better to upset the other side and lose a fraction of their respect than to have to explain to the boss the next day why the company has been sold down the river. It can also be useful on the key points to summarise the positions and arguments of both sides and the process by which the differences were reconciled. When debriefing company colleagues on the progress and results of the negotiation, it is easy for armchair critics to pontificate on how bad a deal has been done. It always helps if the arguments and processes can be replayed in order to explain and justify the agreement.

3 Check the relationship

The negotiator should always take pains to check the relationship with the customer after any significant negotiation. In Chapter 5 the relationship between the two parties was described (Figure 5.15) as being on corporate, general and personal levels. At the corporate level, the aim should be that the negotiation will not have disturbed and will have enhanced the perception that the customer has of the company as a body corporate. At the general level, the evolution of the relationship should have taken a step forward. At the dynamic level of the personal relationship, the outcome could vary from the extreme of 'That was good, look forward to the next time' to 'Never darken my door again'. It is the responsibility of the negotiatior to ensure that, at all levels, the relationship has been nurtured and not diminished.

The first rule is never to show exuberance during or at the end of the meeting. No matter how well the meeting has gone, it is just stupid to reveal any feeling of triumph or victory. The moment after shaking hands can be a moment of huge anti-climax. The excitement is in working towards a conclusion. Once the conclusion has been reached there is a vacuum to fill as the overcharged atmosphere and pent-up feelings dissipate. In this period there is a tendency to relax and to exchange feelings. This should be guarded against. It is better to change the topic and give the emotions a chance to normalise. In this awkward time it is better to say nothing than risk an unfortunate slip which could upset the relationship.

So the first rule is essentially for the negotiator to guard his own feelings. The second rule is therefore to be sensitive to the feelings of the other side and to respond accordingly (Figure 8.1).

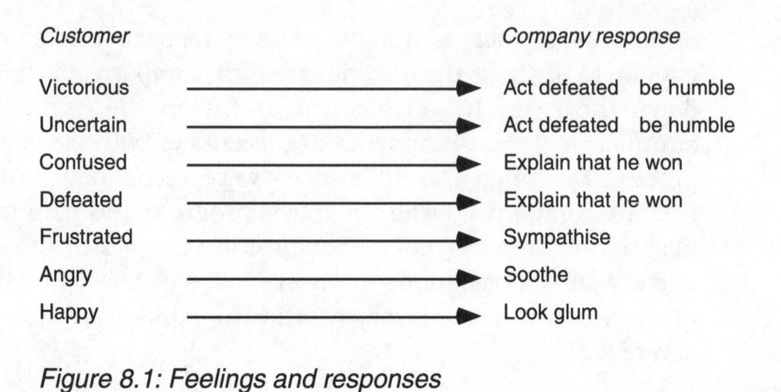

Figure 8.1: Feelings and responses

To explain this, it must first be understood that there is no such thing as the customer really achieving an overwhelming victory against the company's negotiator. If the negotiation is really proceeding that badly, he will find a way to frustrate an agreement. So when the customer feels victorious it can only be because he does not really understand what went on. Nevertheless, customers who feel victorious are happy customers and should be encouraged. Nothing should be done to disabuse them from their happy state. It does the customer good to feel he has scored a victory. If the customer is not sure whether he won, the negotiator should act defeated anyway. If the customer is confused as to how the result was arrived at, the negotiator should clarify it for him in such a way as to show that, on balance, the customer came off the better. Indeed a lot of good work can be done in helping the other side to write up the result in a way that makes their negotiator look as though he did well.

A defeated customer is an unhappy customer. The negotiator should find the silver lining in the customer's cloud for him. A defeated customer does not happily and readily return to the table for the next meeting. He becomes difficult to get hold of. He becomes unresponsive and uncommunicative. This is no way for a customer to be feeling and the negotiator should be at pains to restore the relationship. If the customer is frustrated because he could not get what he wanted, the negotiator should sympathise. 'I know how you feel. I wanted to help but my hands were tied because of that wretched subcontractor.' Solidarity with the customer over a real or invented common enemy is always useful.

The angry customer is a dangerous customer. Looking for revenge or a victim on whom to take things out, the angry customer is somebody to be avoided. It is a failure of the negotiator in the first place if he has allowed the customer to become angry, but if it happens then the customer must be cooled off before the negotiator departs. On the other hand, if the customer is happy then the negotiator should let him wallow in it. Looking glum, hurt and pained may even earn some sympathy for next time.

Lunch or a drink after the meeting provides an excellent opportunity to gauge the mood of the customer and to repair any damage that may have been caused. It is important to do this before the customer's negotiator has had any chance to convey any negative feelings back within his own organisation. Choice of restaurant, choice of food and number of drinks all reveal little bits of information about the customer's mood.

Some aspects of the negotiation may have been left to be resolved in the informal atmosphere of a restaurant or pub. If so, the timing of when to discuss them is all-important: too soon and the mood will still be that obtaining during the meeting, which prevented an agreement; too late and the enthusiasm for resolving the issues will have evaporated. Nevertheless, the hostelry provides a good forum for gathering information. 'John, how do you think Bill (John's boss) will react to the deal we've just done?' 'Who else has to endorse our agreement?'

Apart from any action immediately following the meeting, it is a good idea to make telephone contact the next day to test the temperature of the water, to say 'thank you' and to detect whether the agreement caused any negative reaction on the customer side. If the deal is one of high visibility or if there is some adverse reaction on the customer side, it is also helpful for the contract negotiator to arrange for his own boss to make contact at the appropriate level with the customer to further this aim of maintaining a sound relationship.

4 Agree future actions

A contract negotiation frequently involves the agreement of things yet to be done, as well as the resolution of the particular issues that come up before or during the meeting.

Using the notes taken during the meeting, the summary mentioned earlier should include a list of any such actions. This is particularly important where the meeting ends with some points unresolved. An example of this could be as follows:

Actions on the customer:

a) Produce a new draft of the contract.
b) Re-examine its needs for software modifications.
c) Check the quantity of widgets required.
d) Consult its technical people over milestone definitions.

Actions on the company:

a) See if delivery can be advanced if software unmodified.
b) Consult subcontractors over extended validities.
c) Propose additional milestones.

The aim should be to take the initiative and list the customer's actions first, pressing him to agree dates by which the actions will be complete. The negotiator can list his own actions last, avoid volunteering completion dates if it does not suit him and leave things off his list if he can get away with it. There is nothing untoward in this. It is up to each side to be alert, attentive and watchful throughout the whole process. It is perfectly legitimate to exploit and take advantage of any lack of attention to detail on the part of the other side.

The most important thing about any meeting at which people agree to take action is to make sure that advantageous actions are completed. The contract negotiator should chase his customer to make sure that the actions are done. It is not a good idea just to wait for something to happen or to wait for the date by which the actions were supposed to have been done, before making contact. In any negotiation process a golden rule is to take and keep the initiative. Keep throwing the customer a fast ball. Keep the ball in his court.

In the example above, how might the contract negotiator seize the initiative regarding his customer's actions? For action a) the negotiator might telephone the customer the next day and offer to take the action over: 'We've got the contract on our word processor as well; how about saving a little time? I'll produce the next draft and get it to you by courier by close of play today.' Not only would this speed things up but it also gives the drafting tasks to the company. Naturally this allows the language of the draft to be angled in favour of the company. For action b), perhaps there is something more that the company can do on software. Again, make a telephone call a couple of days after the meeting: 'We've had another look at the software and we think it is conclusive that no modifications are necessary. We'll fax you the details.'

Actions with the company should be taken up in a way which best suits the company. On company action b), there is a lot of difference between contacting subcontractors and saying 'Please will you extend your validity by two months', and the alternative of 'We've already told the customer that your validity probably cannot be extended. Please confirm.' On company action c), it may not be desirable to fit in additional milestones. An excuse needs to be found: 'Unfortunately our expert in this area is on a three-month walking holiday in Chile'.

The message is straightforward. There are endless opportunities to take the initiative, frustrate actions, speed them up or slow them down or manipulate the result to the best advantage of the company. This is part of the contract negotiator's responsibilities.

5 Confirm the agreement

The most crucial post-negotiation action is to have the agreement confirmed in writing. Both sides happily agree that written confirmation is urgent and important. However, it is an unwise negotiator who waits too long for the agreement to be confirmed by the customer.

Consider a meeting to negotiate the terms of a potential contract where the background is that the customer has issued a request for proposals (RFP). The company has responded to the RFP with a proposal which is reasonably attractive but requires the resolution of a number of points and the settling upon mutually acceptable terms. The company is confident of securing the order and has put the work in hand even before the meeting happens, a fact which has been brought to the customer's attention. At the beginning of the meeting the customer acknowledged the fact of this early work but said that, in the absence of a complete agreement, there could be no contract and hence any precontract work would be undertaken at the company's risk, a position which the company accepted.

At the end of the meeting all matters have been entirely resolved and in traditional manner the company entertains the customer at lunch. The parties then split up and the contract negotiator returns to his base where the work continues while he waits for the written contract confirming the agreement to arrive. After a couple of weeks he telephones to chase the customer for the documents, only to be told that the customer has decided not

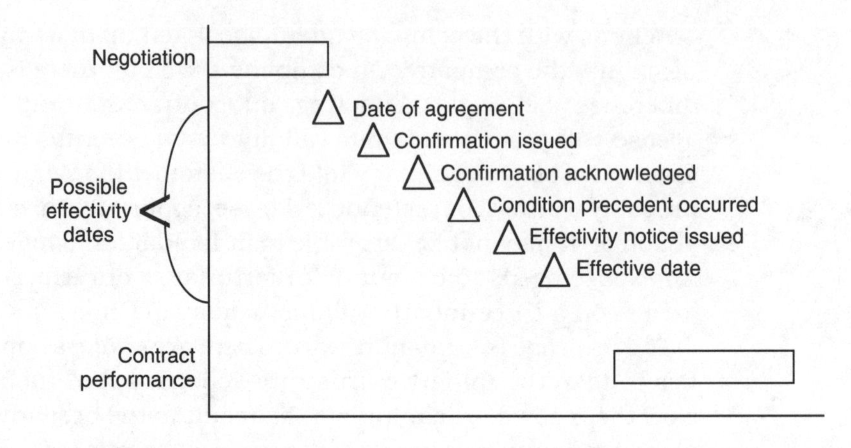

Figure 8.2: Alternative effectivity points

to proceed with the order. The company's time, work and money have been wasted. The customer thought the company understood that only a written contract would be effective. The company thought the act of agreeing created the contract. Whether or not a legal action would succeed in these circumstances is not the point. The lesson is that not only did the negotiator fail to summarise at the end of the meeting in a way which would have had the effect of establishing a mutual consent by the parties to an oral contract, but he also failed to press immediately for a written confirmation of the agreement.

Indeed, as a rule of thumb the negotiator should always make it clear what express action causes any form of agreement to be effective. Custom and practice develops whereby each side knows that there is no effectivity unless and until something specific has happened. Furthermore, a distinction needs to be made between the effective date of the agreement and the effective date of any contractual obligations which the agreement incorporates. These dates can be quite different (Figure 8.2).

The handshake at the end of the negotiation may signify an effective agreement but where a negotiation relates to the agreement of a new contract, then the effective date of the contract may be the date of the agreement. However, it may require written confirmation to be issued and/or acknowledgement. There may be a condition precedent – for example, receipt of a down payment – the non-occurrence of which would prevent the contract becoming effective. The parties may specifically agree that there is no effectivity unless and until the customer has issued an express notice to bring the contract into effect. More simply, they may agree that the contract is to become effective at some particular future date. The contract itself may include various provisions which are themselves subject to individual dates or events which activate their effectiveness. The contract that provides for a transfer of rights under licence may prescribe that such licences are not to be effective until some future date has passed or event occurred.

6 Dealing with 'unagreements'

An 'unagreement' is an agreement which forms part of the issues settled during the negotiation but which somehow, miraculously, disappears from the formal confirmation. When challenged on the omission, the other side claim there was no such agreement. Unagreements are those agreements which are deliberately unmade rather than simple failings of either memory or attention to detail on the part of the person attempting to commit the agreement in writing. These failings can be dealt with in the conventional manner. Dealing with unagreements is more problematic. Unagreements can be attributable to a variety of sources, any one or more of which the culprit can put forward to justify his action:

Incompetence	I didn't understand. I made a mistake.
Policy	It's not our policy. I didn't have the authority.
Tactics	You are mistaken. I cannot agree, but … .

Genuine incompetence is hard to forgive and forget. It is difficult to determine whether an alleged lack of understanding is a real, and therefore innocent, lack or a deliberate misunderstanding. 'I'm sorry, but if that's really what you meant I couldn't possibly have agreed.' Is that innocent or is it deliberate? It is impossible to tell. But the cause or ulterior motive of any alleged misunderstanding is immaterial. An agreement is an agreement and the negotiator should not be drawn into repeating the negotiation (which might have a different and less attractive result), nor should he be tempted to resolve how the lack of understanding arose. The agreement was made and the other side should simply but effectively be reminded of the fact. That is Rule 1.

A mistake might likewise be either real or just a convenient excuse to back away from the agreement. There is a slightly more difficult decision to make with a mistake. If it is just a ploy, then it should be dealt with dismissively. If it is real, then ostensibly Rule 1 applies. However, a measured judgement needs to be made. If the customer's negotiator has made a serious mistake (a trivial one he would have swallowed), then the individual in question is likely to suffer certain consequences from within his own organisation. These might range from dismissal, demotion or transfer through to a loss of delegated authority or simple reprimand. In any such event, if the company chooses to adhere to Rule 1 and thus exploit the mistake, there is a real danger that the relationship may be harmed at all levels. In particular, the personal relationship may suffer if the person remains in post. Thereafter he may be more difficult to deal with, he may be less responsible, less co-operative and less inclined to make decisions. He may harbour a grudge against the company or its negotiator or both. Therefore these potential disadvantages should be weighed against the benefit of exploiting the mistake ('exploit' is somewhat of an exaggeration if the company's negotiator made the agreement in good faith and in ignorance of the other side's mistake). The additional advantage of letting the person off the hook and thereby being owed a favour should not be overlooked in this calculation.

Relying on policy, whether of some specific sort or of some general sort such as delegated authority, is another approach which the customer may follow in making unagreements. It too should be met with the Rule 1 response. The contract negotiator should not be at all sympathetic to pleas for more time for the customer's negotiator to 'get approval or clearance'. Unless the customer specified at the time of the meeting that there were certain areas where he had limited or no authority, he should not hide behind this excuse afterwards.

The tactical use of unagreements is something different. Here there is a premeditated intent to mislead the other side. There may be a deliberate plan to concede a point or to give the appearance of conceding a point in order to win a concession, so as to bring the meeting to a conclusion full in the knowledge that the concession will be retracted later. Such a tactic has the effect of putting the company in an extremely difficult position in deciding whether to reopen the negotiations, thus negating progress on all other points, or simply to forget the point and live with the balance of the deal.

The stonewall 'you are mistaken' stance of the customer is a difficult barrier to overcome, particularly where the customer is protected by being at the end of a telephone rather than face to face with the aggrieved negotiator. The variation of 'I cannot agree, but ...' lines the company up to have to concede something in order for it to get the benefit of the original agreement.

No matter the source or type of unagreement, Rule 1 is the proper response. Additionally the company should consider reneging on the whole agreement. This has the advantage of calling the other side's bluff. If it is not a bluff there may be a lot of ground then to recover. A possibility is for the negotiator or his boss to attack someone in a more senior position on the customer side. This is rarely successful as the other side is bound to close ranks. If there is no other route but to concur with the customer, then it should not be forgotten that conceding the unagreement should be done in return for something else.

As with many things, prevention is better than cure. There are a number of steps that can be taken during the negotiation to preclude the emergence of possible non-agreements:

Source	**Preventive steps**
Incompetence	Check understanding, repeat agreements, summarise frequently.
Policy	Challenge/clarify hesitative agreements. Confirm delegated authority. Set terms of reference.
Tactics	Record in writing as meeting proceeds. Get both sides to sign. Take a witness. Shake hands.

All of these preventive steps are merit-worthy. Any discussion warrants the parties' time and efforts to check each other's understanding. If the other side give an agreement but seem unsure or hesitant, the negotiator can challenge this: 'Please can you repeat that. Are you sure you are able to give that agreement?' There is no point in beating about the bush. It is better to be clear straight away rather than risk having to deal with an unagreement later.

The facility that modern personal computers and word processors afford means that it is eminently practicable to record the agreement as the meeting progresses. Failing this, a manuscript summary can suffice. Whatever the medium, both sides should be happy to sign it. This can cause affront: 'You mean you can't take my word?' Trust is not the point. If certainty and thoroughness are enhanced there should be no concern or upset on either side about making and signing a written record. Having a witness along is always helpful but of limited use in resolving unagreements because people on both sides will each stick to their respective version of events. A handshake helps to cement the agreement and the relationship. Most people find it more difficult to go back on their agreement if it has been accompanied by a handshake.

7 Internal debriefs

Once the agreement is reached it is important for the contract negotiator to debrief others within his company who have a need to know the details of the negotiation. It is not sufficient for it to be assumed that others will fully comprehend the basis and nuances of the agreement just by reading the written record when it arrives.

The debrief process fulfils a number of important functions:

1. COMMUNICATES the result.
2. HIGHLIGHTS important points.
3. IDENTIFIES sensitive issues.
4. EXPLAINS how conflicts were resolved.
5. TEACHES lessons for the next time.

Without a debrief, people will put their own interpretation on the written agreement. A debrief is consistent with the doctrine of BS5750 and similar with its emphasis on communication, teamwork and total quality management. It allows others to be aware of sensitive issues which are best avoided with the customer. It allows the negotiator to convey the tenor of the agreement, the mood of the customer and the posture of the company. It is important, however, to be relatively circumspect as any overall sense of victory, or knowledge of particularly valuable customer concessions, or precedents set, should not be fed back to the customer inadvertently or imprudently.

The other essential function of the debrief is to place any actions and deadlines on others within the company where such actions were agreed during the negotiation. To follow up these actions is important not only in absolute terms but also as an aid to maintaining and developing the relationship with the customer. It is important for him to see the company acting promptly to implement the agreement and its associated actions.

8 Exploiting the agreement

Once the post-negotiation activities described in this chapter are complete, the whole process of which the actual contract negotiation meeting formed a part is at an end. However, if this whole process is considered to include the period of contract performance then things have only just begun – see *Successful Contract Administration* by Tim Boyce, Hawksmere 1992.

CHAPTER 9

The content of a contract negotiation

1 Introduction

Many books on negotiation describe the process and not the content. This book aims to do both. In particular, the first eight chapters have covered the processes relating to and underpinning the activity. Chapter 10 will consider the content in relation to the post-contract issues of variations, claims and disputes. In this chapter the content of a negotiation for a contract will be covered. That is, the purpose is not to describe how to argue and persuade the opposition to a particular position but rather to describe the content of those arguments in this specific field of contract negotiation.

Inevitably this description must be of a general nature. It would be impossible to describe in detail all of the points that are likely to come up in every sort of contract negotiation. However, it is possible to isolate (Figure 9.1) the eight features which, in practical terms, are at the heart of virtually every contract.

A distinction is made between what may be referred to as 'foreground' and 'background' issues. The foreground issues are obvious. What work is required to be done? What is the price? How and when will payment be made? When must the work be finished? The background issues are, to some extent, less

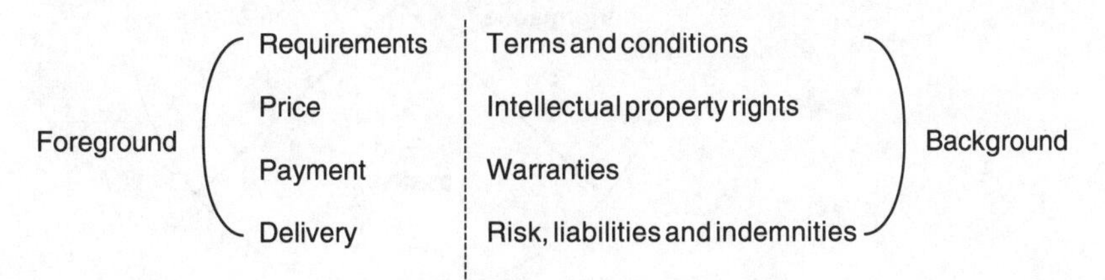

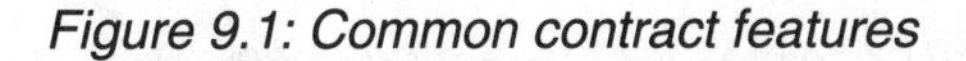
Figure 9.1: Common contract features

obvious. Terms and conditions somehow make up the rest of the contract. The obscure and difficult topic of intellectual property rights may be involved. Warranties are promises subsidiary to the main purpose and are sometimes expressed and sometimes implied in the contract. Risks, liabilities and indemnities may lurk in the agreement.

The aim in this chapter is to provide a guided tour of some of the pitfalls and customer arguments of which the contract negotiator should be wary in connection with these eight headings. As explained in Chapter 2, reader knowledge is assumed to a basic level of understanding of the principles underlying the topics.

However, before commencing on a circuit of these eight topic areas there are some general points which deserve some attention.

2 General principles

There are four general principles (Figure 9.2) which should be kept in mind when entering into the negotiation.

Taking these points, clockwise from the top, the first principle to note is the so-called 'contra preferentum' rule. This means that once the parties have concluded their agreement and committed it to writing, any ambiguity in the resultant contract document would be construed by a court against the party seeking to rely upon their interpretation of the ambiguity. This

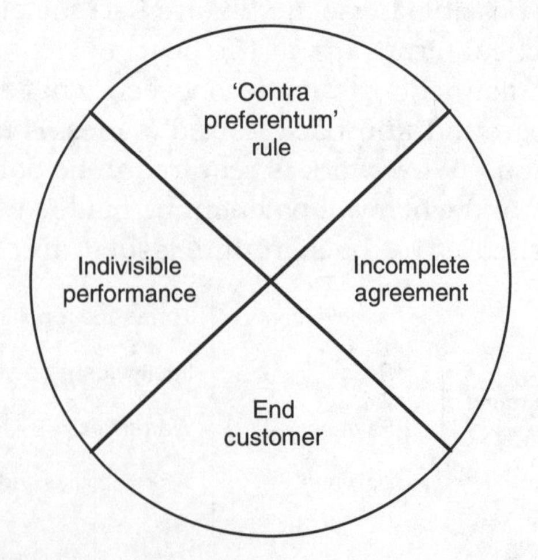

Figure 9.2: General principles for the contract negotiator

is particularly so in the case of exclusion clauses. The following examples illustrate this point. In *Wallis, Son and Wells* v. *Pratt and Haynes* in 1911, a contract for the sale of seeds contained a clause which stated that the sellers gave 'no warranty express or implied' as to the description of the seeds. The seeds did not match the description but the clause provided no defence in the ensuing legal action because of an 'ambiguity'. The failure was deemed a breach of condition and therefore not a breach of warranty, only the latter being excluded by the clause. Similarly, in 1934 in *Andrew Bros (Bournemouth) Ltd* v. *Singer and Co Ltd*, a contract for 'New Singer cars' was agreed, containing a clause which said that 'all conditions, warranties and liabilities implied by statute, common law or otherwise are excluded'. This apparently watertight exclusion failed to protect the defendants (who did not, in the event, supply all new cars) as the clause had neglected to exclude express conditions or warranties, the reference to new cars in the contract being an express condition.

However, the degree of rigour of application of the 'contra preferentum' rule may vary between different types of clauses (for example, more so to clauses which seek to exclude liability than simply to limit it) and in any event there is a willingness in the first instance to seek for the natural meaning of the clause. Further, if the contract is written by one side only (particularly those of a standard-form nature), there is a tendency to construe the clause against the drafter.

The lesson for the contract negotiator is that in committing the agreement to writing, it is as well to strive for complete clarity. If something looks as though it is ambiguous, there can be a temptation to leave it alone if a future opportunity to capitalise on the ambiguity can be foreseen. For the reasons stated, this can be a dangerous course of action. That said, the purpose of this book is to be practical and not overly legalistic. Therefore it should be said that, since most contracts and most disputes do not go to law, this is an example of where the contract negotiator must balance potential commercial advantage against knowledge of possible legal difficulties.

Turning to the completeness or otherwise of the agreement (the second general principle), reference was made in Chapter 2 to the danger of a contract being found void for uncertainty. This danger could well materialise if the parties leave too much of their contract to be agreed at some time after the main principles have been concluded and work has been put in hand. This risk is a real one but it must be said that the courts are not eager to find a business contract void for this reason, as Lord Wright was wont to point out in 1932:

> *It is clear that the parties both intended to make a contract and thought they had done so. Businessmen often record the most important agreements in crude and summary fashion; modes of expression sufficient and clear to them in the course of their business may appear to those unfamiliar with the business far from complete or precise. It is accordingly the duty of the court to construe such documents fairly and broadly, without being too astute or subtle in finding defects; but on the contrary should seek to apply the old English Law* Verba ida sunt intelligenda ut re magis valeat quam pereat. *That maxim, however does not mean that a court is to make a contract for the parties, or to go outside the words they have used, except in so far as there are appropriate implications of law, as, for instance, the implication of what is just and reasonable to be ascertained by the court as a matter of machinery where the contractual intention is clear but the contract is silent in some detail. Thus in contracts for future performance over a period the parties may not be able nor may they desire to specify many matters of detail, but leave them to be adjusted in the working out of the contract. Save for the legal implications I have mentioned such contracts might well be incomplete or uncertain; with that implication in reserve they are neither incomplete nor uncertain. As obvious illustrations I may refer to such matters as prices or times of delivery in contracts for the sale of goods or times of loading or discharging in a contract of sea carriage.*

Where, then, does the idea of incomplete contracts fit into the task of contract negotiation? Legalistically and theoretically, incomplete contracts should be avoided because of the risk of the contract proving void. However, Lord Wright's comments indicate that the risk may be small. There can be advantage in deliberately aiming for an incomplete contract, acknowledging that the legal risk is present but not significant. While all contracts set down the obligations and benefits to both sides, the preponderance of duties and liabilities usually lies with the seller. However, he can only carry these burdens if he knows about them. Therefore the advantage of the incomplete contract is that the seller can avoid many of the responsibilities that he might otherwise have under a full contract.

The objective of the contract negotiator should consequently be to look for those opportunities arising through the customer's urgency or otherwise to conclude a contract in a limited form. The scope of the work required should be as detailed as possible and set against an agreed price. If the work is poorly defined there can be unfortunate debate over what should or should not reasonably have been done within the price. It may well be that the work described is known not to fulfil the overall aim of the customer but that work to which the price relates must be clearly stated (Figure 9.3).

Thus once the work is under way, any variation to the stated scope of work automatically leads to an increase in the price (see also Chapter 10). Similarly, the limited form of contract may have resulted from a quotation from the company. The quotation should have stated the terms and conditions. If terms and conditions are absent from the limited contract, the contract negotiator can later argue that the terms and conditions as earlier stated by him are implied into the contract. Thus as the work progresses and the customer attempts to complete the missing elements of the contract, any terms and conditions which he seeks to introduce (which are bound to be less favourable to the company) can also lead to a claim by the company for a price increase or other concession.

So either the incomplete contract permits the company to avoid burdensome duties altogether or it allows a strong platform to be built for downstream negotiations. However, the incomplete contract game must be played carefully. The limited form of contract must include all the features which are important to the company, otherwise the strategy can backfire when

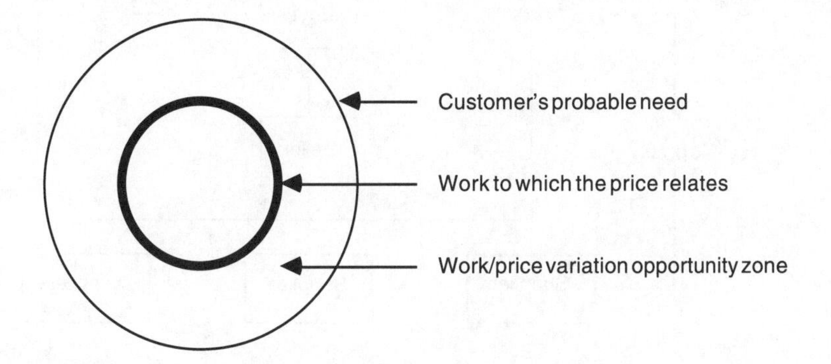

Figure 9.3: Work/price variation

the company later tries to complete the agreement as regards absent features of its interest.

The third general principle to consider is the position (Figure 9.4) of the end customer in the contractual relationship between buyer and seller.

In this diagram the company for whom the contract negotiator works is the seller. Although there can be some limited exceptions, the privity rule generally precludes there being any contractual relationship between the end customer and the seller, nor between the buyer and the seller's suppliers. The latter point will be addressed in more detail later in this chapter under the heading of risks, liabilities and indemnities. As regards the end customer, the seller is shielded from his wishes and concerns by the buyer. Or is he?

The buyer will often seek to include in the contract with the seller provisions which, while they do not make the seller liable directly *to* the end customer, aim to make the seller liable *for* performance of the contract between the buyer and the end customer. The buyer's justification for this is that he is only coming to the seller because the seller's goods or services are essential to the performance of the contract between the buyer and end customer. Logically therefore the seller should be liable for the consequences of breach of that contract. This type of justification is used equally for the contract where the buyer

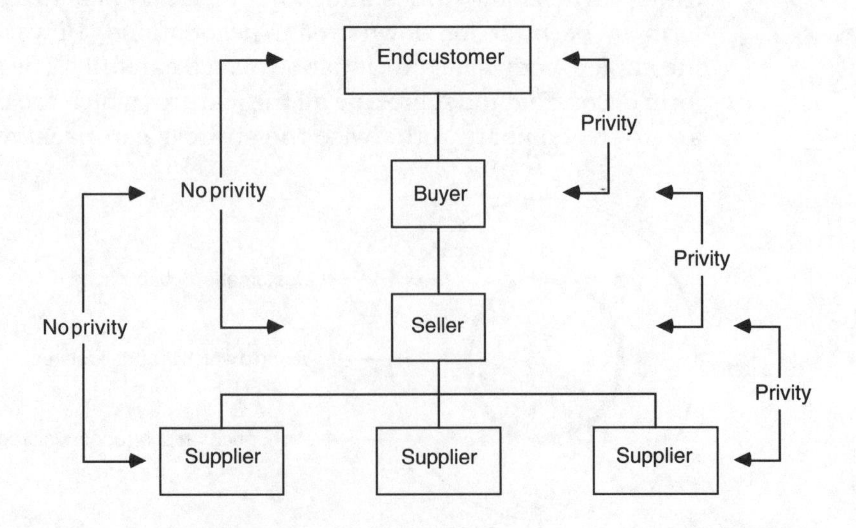

Figure 9.4: Position of end customer

intends to supply the seller's goods (eg by incorporation into his own goods) to the end customer or where the buyer intends to use the seller's goods (eg machinery, tooling, etc) for the purposes of contracts with an end customer.

The contract negotiator should be on the look-out for such proposed provisions and avoid them at all costs. The maker of horseshoe nails should not be liable for the battle that was lost. The seller should not be automatically liable for breach of a contract from which he is remote even if the breach is as a direct result of his own failure, action or inaction. Among other things, the seller may have no control or knowledge of the buyer's or end customer's use of his goods.

The buyer and seller should in their contract agree the specification and purpose of the seller's goods and there should end the seller's liability under express or implied conditions or warranties. If he is in breach, the onus should be on the buyer to prove his financial damage. Such damage might include the consequential damage to the buyer arising from his breach of the contract with the end customer but such consequential damages are subject to the reasonable foreseeability rule. Therefore the contract negotiator – and more particularly other company representatives such as marketeers and salesmen – should avoid as far as possible enquiring or learning too much of the ultimate aim of the buyer.

The fourth general principle is that of indivisibility of performance. This means that, once the contract is made, the seller is required to complete precisely all of it unless the construction or express terms of the contract permit contract performance in segments, ie on a divisible basis. Thus in normal circumstances the buyer is under no obligation to accept anything less (whether measured by quantity, quality or otherwise) than whole performance. Logically and sensibly this is correct. The risk, however, is that completion of performance of a £10m contract may depend upon the final 1 per cent of work. In Pareto law, this final 1 per cent could cost a fortune. The degree of this effect may depend upon the type of contract (Figure 9.5).

Thus in a cost-reimbursable contract the customer has a natural financial incentive to accept less than 100 per cent. In a firm-price contract, the opposite applies. In the nature of the former contract is the facility of the customer to consider the contract as divisible and to accept less than the whole. The nature of the latter contract is quite different. Therefore in firm-

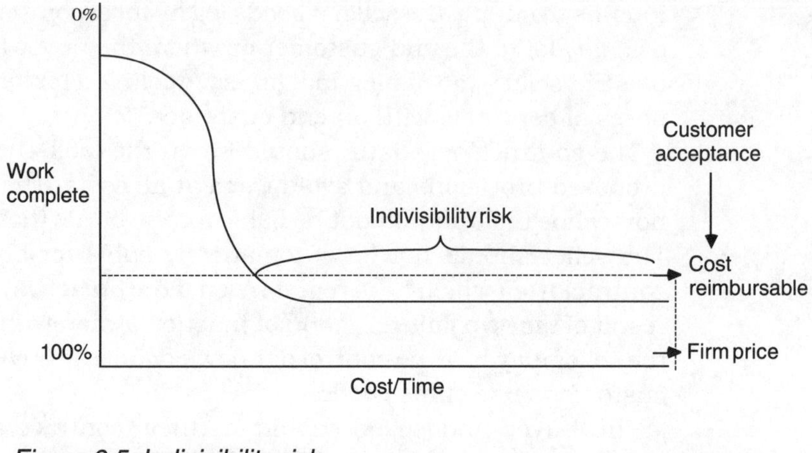

Figure 9.5: Indivisibility risk

price or similar contracts it is the construction and/or express terms which determine the degree, if any, of divisibility.

A contract which demands delivery of a number of discrete components (which the customer can independently assemble into a product) and for which specific clauses permit delivery in batches or in units, is usually construed as an indivisible contract. That is, the buyer's promise to pay is dependent upon full performance by the seller.

As a rule of thumb the contract negotiator should always seek a contract that allows divisible performance although there is a counterargument that says the probability is always very low of a customer rejecting 99 per cent for the sake of a missing 1 per cent. On this latter argument an indivisible contract affords a greater tactical advantage to the company in persuading the customer to accept a concession (see also Chapter 10) against the contract. The contract negotiator should mentally test these counterpoised arguments on a case-by-case basis.

3 The contract requirement (a foreground feature)

The expression 'contract requirement' is used to describe the work that is required to be done by the seller in performance of the contract. In most contracts the primary duty of the seller is to do the work and the primary duty of the buyer is to pay the agreed price. This is an over-simplification of most business contracts of anything other than a trivial or routine nature. It should not be forgotten that the task of the contract negotiator and the function of the contract is to fix all the duties and benefits of both buyer and seller. In contracts where the work required of the seller cannot be done without some involvement or work required of the buyer, it is very important that such involvement or work is captured in the contract as much as any duty on the seller.

With the qualifications mentioned earlier in this chapter about the possible advantages of incomplete or ambiguous agreements, the general rule is that the contract requirement and indeed any work required of the buyer should be recorded with the maximum precision, clarity and certainty. Sloppily made agreements will produce sloppy or unfortunate results.

From the seller's point of view, the single most important aspect of the contract requirement is not what is required (since presumably the company is happy to do and sell the 'what') but how it is specified. The method of specifying the contract requirement will determine the degree of risk that the company is to take on under the contract. The best way of imagining this difference between 'what' and 'how' is to consider that the customer has the basic choice of specifying what he wants or the purpose for which he wants it. If the customer adopts the former, the risk of the purchase fulfilling his purpose rests with him, although regard should be had to the Sale of Goods Act and the Supply of Goods and Services Act (see later in this chapter).

If the customer adopts the latter, the seller carries the risk that the goods meet their specified purpose. If the customer is careful to specify both the product and the purpose then the risk is ostensibly with the seller unless the contract says otherwise.

Some examples serve to illustrate these points. A customer purchasing on the strength of catalogue material, perhaps supported by product data sheets, can expect the goods to conform (eg regarding quality and description) and perform (eg level of utility and functionality) in accordance with the catalogue and data sheet information. Beyond that the customer can expect little. The reasonable assumption must be that the customer has made an assessment of available products and, having made his selection, then makes his purchase, gambling on his own judgement. In a contract for design only, the customer is entitled to reasonable skill and care from the designer but takes the risk that the design can be built, manufactured or implemented successfully. In a construct-only contract the customer similarly takes the risk that the contractor, having built to a customer-specified design, will supply something that works.

On the other hand a combined design and construct contract places the risk with the seller. A contract for the supply and installation of an air-conditioning system might require the delivery and commissioning of specified components or it may simply call for a system that refreshes the air at 1000m^3 per hour, leaving the choice of components to the seller.

The customer will always attempt to leave the maximum risk with the company. The contract negotiator should be alert to the alternative methods of defining the contract requirement and in negotiation aim to secure that form which carries the least risk to the company.

4 Price (a foreground feature)

When it comes to negotiation of price there are only two rules for the contract negotiator to follow. First, everything has a price, and second, an open mind should be kept towards the type of price that is appropriate for the contract in question. These two rules presuppose that some basics can be taken as read, such as whether the price includes VAT and other taxes, whether the currency is sterling or otherwise, and so on.

The first rule sounds so obvious as not to be worthy of mention. It is easy to list the factors to which price is directly and immediately related. Quantity, delivery schedule, delivery terms (eg the alternatives under Incoterms), batch sizes, payment arrangements (eg down payments, stage payments, payment on delivery), payment terms (eg credit period) and statement of work (eg specification, quality, volume) are all examples where only an incompetent could consider varying such factors without at least giving thought to the impact on price. However, in addition to these factors of 'scope' there are two other generic factors (Figure 9.6) which can vary the price.

The second pricing factor is the benefits that also arise to the advantage of the customer. For example, he may acquire certain intellectual property rights under the contract. These are of value although they are intangible. Finally, the contract will allocate various risks to the two parties. For example, the risk of late delivery under liquidated damages provisions or otherwise

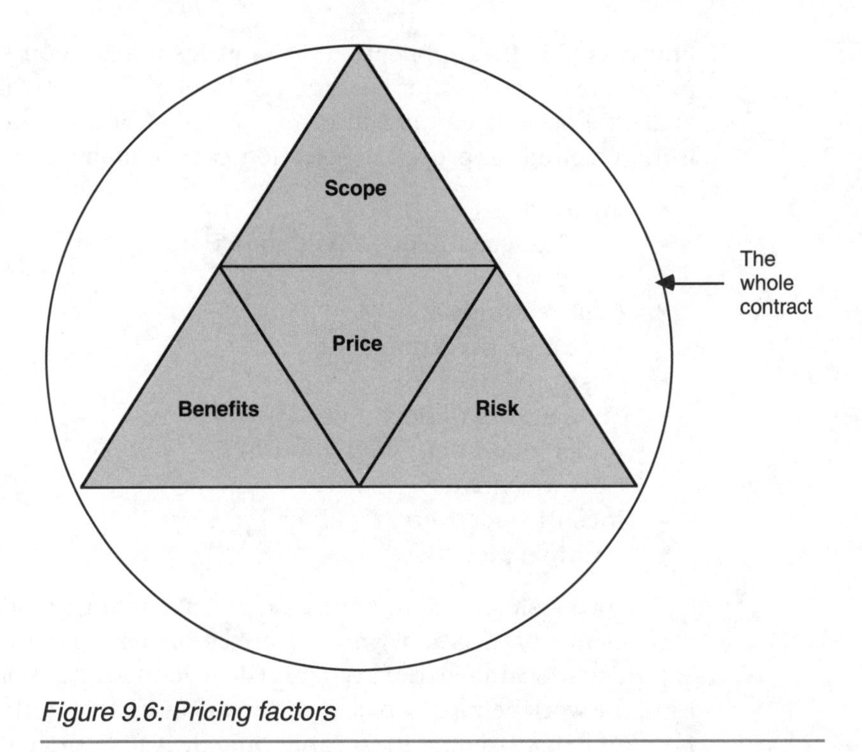

Figure 9.6: Pricing factors

may be specifically allocated to the seller.

So the factors of scope, customer benefits and company risk are all price-related. So too are benefits to the company and customer risks but these should be ignored by the contract negotiator unless and until they are raised by the customer. Scope, benefits and risks together make up the whole contract. The contract is defined by its terms and conditions. Therefore the contract negotiator should negotiate the contract as a whole. A trap to be avoided is the situation in which the customer says 'Right, that's got the price agreed, now let's sort out the terms and conditions'. To fall into this trap is to allow the customer to start on the process of securing additional benefits and diminishing his risk while the price remains unchanged. On the other hand, if the company is in the stronger position then the contract negotiator can choose to spring the trap in the reverse direction. As with so many negotiation tactics, a decision as to what is appropriate for a particular situation can only be made on a case-by-case basis.

The second rule of price negotiation is the selection of the price type. Many a deadlock can be broken, many a situation can be improved by the application of a little imagination. This is particularly true of price type. A brief run-through of the available options can remind the negotiator of the wide choice from which an appropriate selection can be made.

- Firm price
- Fixed price (subject to VOP or CPA)
- Lump sum
- Cost reimbursable
- Cost plus percentage fee
- Cost plus fixed fee
- Time and materials
- Rates (main hour/day/month)
- Cost incentive
- Incentive (delivery/technical)
- Multiple incentives

The proposing of a different type of price-fixing arrangement can resolve a situation where there is disagreement over the extent or allocation of risk. Where risk is defined as the probability of the work being completed within an agreed price, then price type and risk become inexorably linked. A firm-price contract leaves 100 per cent of such risk with the seller. A cost-reimbursable contract leaves 100 per cent with the buyer. Other forms of contract have the effect of sharing the risk.

5 Payment (a foreground feature)

There are only three objectives in negotiating the payment provisions of contract and they are to make sure that payments happen early, swiftly and automatically.

A distinction is made between earliness and swiftness. Earliness is how soon after the contract is placed that payments can be made. Swiftness is how soon after an invoice is submitted that the money is actually received. Although there are no standard definitions of these expressions, the opportunity for early payment can be realised through a variety of devices (Figure 9.7).

The paradox over interim payments is that, while the facility to draw cash from the customer as work progresses has obvious cash-flow advantages to the company, it must be borne in mind that there are also disadvantages. These are mainly that the customer will throughout the contract have a tremendous hold (by threatening to withhold payments) over the company and

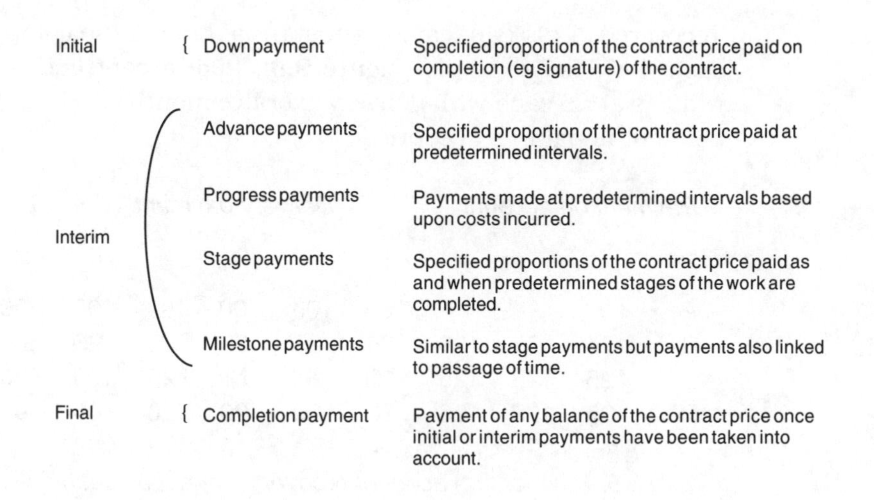

Figure 9.7: Early payment

that, if for any reason the payments are not made, the impact of the cost of financing the work in progress becomes a straight penalty on the profit and loss account. A further concern is that buyers usually expect vesting rights in contracts allowing interim payments, which gives accounting problems and restricts the commercial freedom of the company even if the payments are not actually made.

A further point to watch out for is whether the construction or language of the contract is intended to convey that payments are on account (ie on account of an anticipated 100 per cent performance) or are in settlement (ie irrecoverable) of partial completion. The former follows the indivisibility rule and favours the customer. The latter favours the company and can add weight to an argument for divisible performance.

In negotiation of an interim payment clause it is important to consider carefully how final payment will be made. A price of £10,000 could be payable in four equal instalments, paid as and when stages are achieved or dates reached. This presents no difficulty.

However, where a proportion of the price is to be payable on account and the balance as and when deliveries are made, the customer may seek to 'recover' payments on account by abatement of delivery invoice values where such abatement continues until the full value of the payments on account has been 'recovered'. This can leave a substantial hole in the company's cash flow. For example (Figure 9.8), take a contract for 100 widgets at £5 each with delivery over five months and where 75 per cent is paid on account.

	Payment on account			*Delivery payment*					*Total*
Month				1	2	3	4	5	£
A				100	100	100	100	100	500
B	125	125	125	25	25	25	25	25	500
C	125	125	125	Nil	Nil	Nil	25	100	500
D	125	125	125	20	20	20	20	45	500

Figure 9.8: Payment on account recovery: impact on cash flow

In Example A, no payments on account are made and the company invoices £100 per month (£5 x 20 widgets). In example B, the payments on account are made and the balance of the contract price is paid evenly over the delivery period (£1.25 x 20 widgets). In Example C, the customer abates delivery payments at 100 per cent until the full value (£375) of payments on account have been recovered. In Example D, the customer abates delivery payments at 80 per cent until the recovery has been made. This clearly shows the danger to the company of payment schemes that are based upon final payments being made at an abated level.

To enhance his own cash flow the customer has the incentive to prevent swift disbursement of cash to the company. A number of obstacles are erected to achieve this end. These include extended credit periods, invoice checking routines, extensive documentation requirements, rights to withhold/recover payments, pay-when-paid principles and sheer awkwardness. Overcoming these obstacles is, to a great extent, a matter for good contract administration and debtor management. However, the contract negotiator should aim to agree contract payment provisions which are clear, straightforward, automatic and as least prone as possible to the application of these obstacles.

Delivery (a foreground feature)

The single issue which should most occupy the negotiator's mind regarding delivery is the extent to which completion by a specified time or times is to be of the essence of the contract. In a business contract it must normally be assumed that time is of the essence (TOTE) unless the contract specifically says otherwise. This is the reverse of many people's normal supposition that time is not of the essence unless the contract says that it is. The latter is a common mistake. With a little thought the former is found logically to be the case. It would be unusual in a business contract for a desired delivery or completion date not to be specified. If a date is so specified, the law sees that meeting it is one of the promises made by the seller. If the promise is broken, the contract is breached. It does not need the reinforcement of an express 'time is of the essence' statement for it to be a fundamental condition of the contract, although the prudent buyer will make such a statement. Indeed many buyers' standard purchase order conditions specify that time is of the essence.

The customer's preference for a delivery date to be specified with or without the infamous tag is another typical example where the contract negotiator must weigh up the real facts before deciding where, on balance, his negotiating position (Figure 9.9) should be on the particular contract.

In other words the company and its negotiator must have a pretty good idea of whether delivery can or will be achieved on time. It is not suggested that agreement to TOTE should ever be given without a fight but only that there should be a proper evaluation of the risk. It is sensible to include in this evaluation consideration of the customer's level of friendliness. This is a dangerous thing to rely upon as it can change as quickly as and with less warning than a polar bear's mood. However, if the risk of late delivery is significant but the customer is unlikely to cancel for breach (for example, because, by the time of the breach, continuing with the contract is still the quickest route for the customer to acquire the goods) or is unlikely to claim (informally or through suit of law) damages against the company, then the negotiator can afford to agree contract terms no different to those had the risk been zero.

If dates are to be specified and TOTE is expressed or implied, the first choice for the negotiator is whether or not to opt for

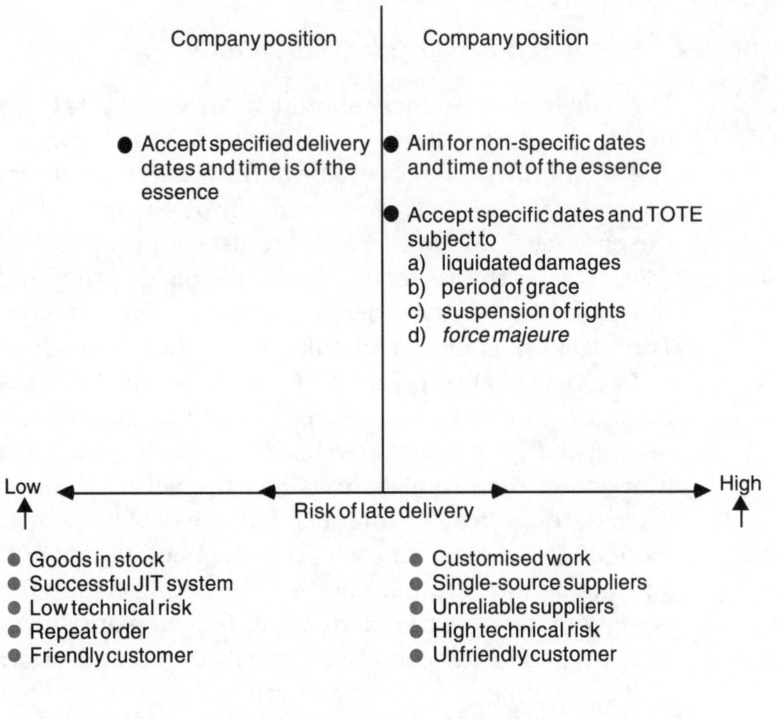

Figure 9.9: Negotiating position: risk of late delivery

liquidated damages protection. This is a further example of often misunderstood principles. It is sometimes accepted practice that buyers include liquidated damages provisions in lieu of penalty clauses (which are not enforceable in English law) and as such the seller should seek to avoid them. This is a legitimate and pragmatic commercial view, but the other interpretation should also be considered. In the event of late delivery the buyer is entitled to sue for damages. Although the burden is on him to prove such damages (ie that they have been suffered, their value and their foreseeability by the seller), the liability of the seller is unlimited. A properly drafted liquidated damages clause has the effect of limiting this liability. However, the inclusion of such a clause relieves the buyer of the burden of proof and may encourage him to press for payment of liquidated damages where he may never have contemplated ever making a claim at large against the company. Here, then, is a nicely balanced set of arguments for the negotiator to resolve in his own mind. On the one hand, a liquidated damages clause can limit liability but carries a high probability of a claim arising (see Chapter 10 for advice on resisting such a claim). On the other hand, the absence of a clause implies unlimited liability but perhaps a lower chance of a claim being made.

If a liquidated damages clause is agreed upon, the negotiator should aim to limit and define its effect in a number of ways:

a) Period of grace: to allow some degree of lateness before liquidated damages accrue.

b) Suspension of rights: liquidated damages are in lieu of all other contractual or legal rights of the buyer.

c) Application: provisions apply to the value of goods in delay (not the whole contract value).

d) Limit of liability: liquidated damages are not payable beyond a stated limit (absolute or percentage).

e) Payment: method of payment at the seller's discretion.

The first principle of liquidated damages is also worthy of mention – this is that the amount is supposed to be a reasonable pre-estimate of the level of damage likely to be suffered by the buyer as a result of the seller's lateness. This principle is supposed to apply rather than the common practice of arbitrarily selecting a maximum value of 5 per cent, 10 per cent or 15 per cent of the contract price. While the use of arbitrary amounts may of itself provide a defence to a claim (see Chapter 10), the proper alternative of a genuine pre-estimate can produce much higher values. Again, the negotiator must choose the optimum approach on a case-by-case basis.

Finally there is the question of *force majeure* provisions. For many people, liquidated damages and *force majeure* always go hand in hand. This is a useful *aide-mémoire* but also a trap. The negotiator should remember to seek *force majeure* if liquidated damages are included. This does not, however, mean that *force majeure* should not be sought in the absence of liquidated damages. Wherever there is a risk of non-performance due to circumstances beyond the company's control, then *force majeure* or similar should be sought regardless of the potential consequences (liquidated damages, damages at large, cancellation) of non-performance. The detailed provisions of a *force majeure* clause are a ripe field for negotiation as the two sides' positions are diametrically opposed, the buyer wanting the seller to be liable even for events outside the seller's control (sometimes including the acts/omissions of the buyer himself!) and the seller not wishing to be liable for anything, including his own performance!

7 Terms and conditions (a background feature)

It could be argued that a distinction between foreground and background features is a little dubious because the good contract negotiator will pay equal attention to everything about the contract. The distinction is nevertheless helpful as it reminds the negotiator not to forget those things which are not of immediate interest to the managing director. Indeed, the distinction is between foreground and background and it is not suggested that these are respectively primary and secondary matters.

The first of the background features is the terms and conditions (ts and cs) of the contract. If the contract is to include standard (ie preprinted in faint blue ink on the back of pro forma paperwork!) ts and cs, then the negotiator, being wary of the battle-of-the-forms principle, should satisfy himself either that the company's ts and cs clearly apply or that he is happy with the customer's ts and cs. Since the chances are zero of any competent negotiator finding a buyer's standard ts and cs acceptable (since they are always onerous and most uneven-handed), this is a topic with which he should concern himself closely. The customer may insist that his standard ts and cs are not negotiable but this, in practice, is not true unless the customer's bargaining position is overwhelming. Every attempt should be made to negotiate or negate the buyer's ts and cs unless it really is the case that there is not even a remote possibility of the buyer ever exercising his rights under those ts and cs.

Many business contracts are not susceptible to the simple inclusion of one side's or the other's standard ts and cs. In such cases the next most obvious choice is to settle upon an agreed set of model conditions published by one of the commercial or professional institutions. While these have great benefit in reducing drafting effort, documentation preparation time and identifying all aspects which need to be covered, their great disadvantage is that they are designed to be even-handed. This is fine if the other side have the negotiating edge, but where the company can see that it has the advantage, it is as well to open negotiations from a more extreme angle rather than to start from what is essentially a middle position.

Similarly when it is suggested that the ts and cs should be identical to those agreed for the previous contract. While there are advantages in terms of not wasting time on repeating the same old arguments, nevertheless the old contract represents a set of compromises and again, depending upon where the negotiating edge lies, opening with a compromised position is not ideal.

In the main it should be expected that the ts and cs may be those drafted especially plus a mixture perhaps of some standards and some reused from old contracts. The guiding rules must be to examine all the ts and cs profferred by the other side, to analyse them for risk, to identify omissions and to be prepared to negotiate them word by word if necessary. In this task it is beneficial to seize the initiative either by proposing the ts and cs in the first place and/or by offering to do the redrafting as discussions proceed and agreements are made. On this latter point an advantage can be gained by doing the redrafting on the spot. This takes not a little skill and nerve but it has the advantage both of allowing the negotiator to write the redraft to the company's best advantage and also of speeding up a full conclusion. If the 'modus operandi' is to agree principles and to leave the drafting to later solitude, this runs the risk of the other side changing its mind as to the principle. This is less easy for the other side to do if, not only has the principle been agreed, but also the principle has been reduced to detailed language.

8 Intellectual property rights (IPR) (a background feature)

In the world of IPR the words 'background' and 'foreground' have special meanings. Therefore in order to avoid confusion in describing IPR as a background feature it is appropriate to touch upon these special meanings. Although it will be immediately apparent that the dividing line is somewhat uncertain, foreground intellectual property (IP) can be thought of as the 'what' and background IP as the 'how'. The design of a telephone can be readily seen and as such the design is an example of foreground IP. How the telephone was manufactured may have depended upon some special skill, knowledge, process or technique. Such factors are less readily apparent and are examples

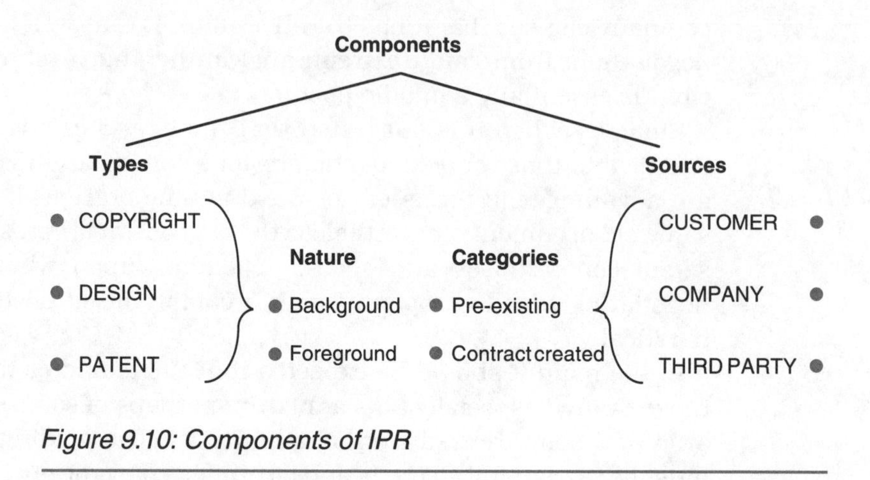

Figure 9.10: Components of IPR

of background IP. Software object or operating code is sometimes referred to as foreground material and the equivalent source code as background material.

In the general sense of the expression, IPR is usually a background feature, frequently overlooked or dealt with only superficially. Not all contracts involve IPR but perhaps more do than would be immediately expected. The obvious examples of contracts for research, design or development work are supplemented by contracts where documents (which are copyright – one form of IP) or information (which can be confidential or include valuable design or invention material – more forms of IP) are created, used or passed between the parties. Therefore the contract negotiator should always have an eye open for any IPR issues which may require to be dealt with.

IPR can appear as a daunting topic but for most practical purposes it can be analysed into a number of components (Figure 9.10) and principles (see list below).

1. All IP has an owner. No other party (with some limited exceptions in the case of the Crown) has any rights in the IP unless the owner grants him rights (or sells him the IP).
2. The creator of the IP is normally the owner – except design right which belongs to the commissioner – in the absence of contrary arrangements.
3. Rights are granted by the owner to the others by licence or by the terms of the contract.
4. Persons whose IP rights are infringed have legal remedies (primarily injunction and damages) against the infringer.

There are more types of IP and IPR than just copyright, design and patent rights. However, these are the most important types that commonly arise in business contracts and serve to illustrate the point. As has been said, a distinction can be made between background and foreground matters. The IP can only come from three sources. If it is not owned or generated by either the customer or the company, then the only other source that there can be is a third party, which expression includes the company's subcontractors or suppliers and the end customer. The picture is slightly more complicated if the ownership or generation of the IP is jointly between two or more sources. The IP is either generated under the terms of the contract or it pre-exists the contract and is brought to the table by one of the parties. Additionally the parties may bring to the table IP generated after the date of the contract but not generated under the contract.

Taking these principles in turn, there are a number of matters for the contract negotiator to consider. Regarding the first principle, it is essential to identify the owner of any IP which is being brought to the table. This allows any applicable terms or limitations to be identified. Most importantly there may be royalties, levies or fees due to the owner and arrangements must be made for the settlement of such duties. It must be clearly established whether it is the company or the customer who will make the payments.

For the second principle, the key issue is deciding who will own the IP created under the contract. If the contract is silent, then the general rule will apply. The parties have complete freedom to negotiate who will be the owner. Such negotiations will be based upon who is paying for the generation of the IP, who is best placed to exploit it and whether the IP is a derivative or adaption of something pre-existing the contract.

The third principle demands that thought is given as to what will be done with the IP once it exists. If ownership has been established and the other party needs rights in the IP, the agreed rights must be spelled out. Depending upon the nature of the IP, the range of rights (Figure 9.11) that are available for grant is quite extensive.

Whether it is the customer or company granting the rights, the question of royalties, levies and fees must be sorted out. It is also important to be explicit as to the information which the licensor will pass to the licensee under this grant. For example, the technical information which a licensee needs to modify a design

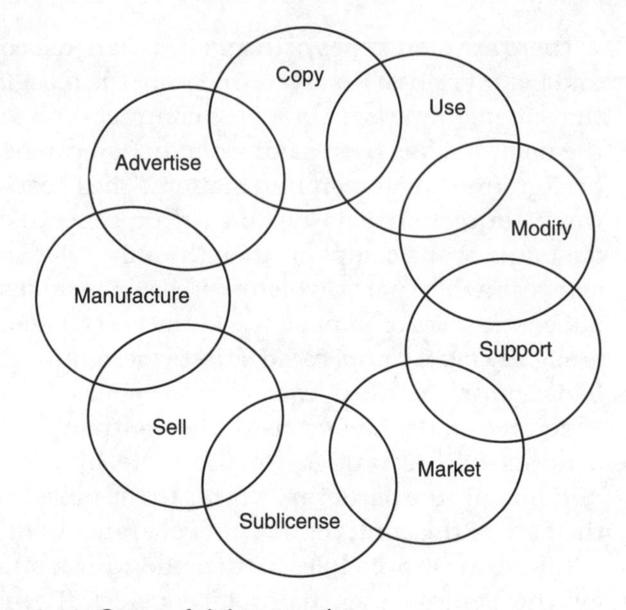

Figure 9.11: Grant of rights – options

is much greater than he would need merely to manufacture. An important right which is sometimes overlooked is the right to sublicense. For example, if the customer provides copyright work (in the form of documents of its own) to the company for the purposes of the contract, the company may well need to copy and distribute the documents to subcontractors or to allow subcontractors to make further copies. To do this without sublicence rights under the contract is to breach the customer's copyright.

The final principle introduces the idea of a penalty for IPR infringement. As between the company and the customer, agreement can be reached as to the grant of rights and terms of use of each other's IP. Not unnaturally, if either is later in breach, the other has remedies available to him. However, the concern goes wider than this. The licensee in either situation is worried that his exercise of the rights that he has obtained may leave him infringing, accidentally and unknowingly, the IPR of a remote third party. If the third party were to discover this the licensee would be vulnerable to action by the third party. Thus the licensee normally expects the licensor to indemnify him against third party action. This is logically correct but neither party is normally willing to offer indemnities of this nature because of the completely unknown size and probability of risk of third party action. In the case of the company licensing IPR to the customer, the customer will strongly argue that the risk must lie with the company because only the company knows the history and genesis of its own IPR. The contract negotiator will counterargue that, since the company has no knowledge of where or how the customer will exercise his rights, the risk should lie with the customer.

IPR is a complicated commercial and legalistic topic and it is not suggested that the contract negotiator should attempt to usurp the role of a qualified patent attorney or IP adviser, particularly in matters of statutory IP protection or serious IPR infringement. However, where it is a matter germane to the contract then he should be prepared and able to negotiate this as well as all the other features.

9 Warranties (a background feature)

A contract is made up of conditions, warranties and innominate terms. Conditions are fundamental prerequisites, breach of which entitles the injured side to damages and to cancel the contract. Warranties are subsidiary requirements, breach of which entitles the injured side to damages only, with no right to cancel. Innominate terms are those terms which may be treated as either conditions or warranties, depending upon the severity of the actual result of breach rather than the severity of the result of breach as anticipated by the parties when they made their contract.

Strictly speaking therefore, a discussion of the contract should refer to terms (ie comprising conditions, warranties and innominate terms) rather than terms and conditions which, although it is a common expression (and is used as such earlier in this chapter), is actually confusing.

The terms of a contract are either expressly stated or implied. Implied terms are terms implied by statute, by the actions of the parties or by a court of law. Statutory implied terms principally derive from the Sale of Goods Act 1989, the Supply of Goods and Services Act 1982 and the Consumer Protection Act 1987 (although this book addresses business contracts, the Consumer Protection Act imports product liability duties into such contracts). Statutory implied terms do not describe themselves as conditions or warranties and are best considered as innominate. Such implied terms include undertakings that the seller is free to sell the goods, that the buyer will accept and pay for the goods, that the goods will conform as to specified quantity and quality and that the goods will be fit for purpose and of merchantable quality.

It is expected that the contract negotiator should be familiar with these principles (the foregoing is very much a summary) but remember, from a negotiation perspective, that in non-consumer transactions the parties are free to exclude statutory implied terms provided that such exclusions are expressly stated. Some implied undertakings – eg to pay the contract price – are so fundamental that they must automatically be expressly stated in a business contract. Others, such as fitness for purpose/merchantable quality, can be argued as imposing particular duties on the seller which, because they are quite vague, imply risk and therefore cost for which allowance must be made in the price. The contract negotiator can adopt the position that the company is willing to meet the express requirements of the contract for a certain price, but if the customer seeks the additional comfort of a right to rely upon these statutory implied terms, the price must be higher. Thus the issue of excluding implied terms is brought into the mainstream of the negotiation.

From the company's viewpoint the benefit of excluding the 'fitness for purpose/merchantable quality' implied terms should not be underestimated. Regarding the scope of the company's liabilities, the aim is always for the least liability and the maximum certainty. In this sense it is better for the contract to specify the purpose or purposes to the exclusion of all others. In that construction the Sale of Goods Act merely reinforces that specified purposes must be satisfied. In the absence of a specified purpose and with no express exclusion of implied terms, the buyer can argue that the goods should meet any reasonable purpose. Even if the seller ultimately prevails, arguments over the fitness of the goods can be time consuming, lengthy and not conducive to good customer relations.

The heading of this section is warranties. While this word has a specific meaning, as already mentioned, the word 'warranty' (or sometimes 'guarantee') is also used to mean obligations regarding the goods which the seller owes to the buyer after the buyer has accepted the goods. The first point to make is that the act of acceptance forever extinguishes the buyer's right to terminate for breach. Acceptance has the effect of converting all conditions and innominate terms into warranties (using the word in its legal sense). Thus both sides to the negotiation should address themselves to the question of warranty (now and henceforth used in the ordinary sense).

From the company's position the objective is to limit the scope and extent of any warranty, and the contract negotiator should carry a mental checklist of the approaches to achieving this objective:

Aspect	*Limitation*
Period	• Length (eg 12 months, etc) • Start (eg delivery, acceptance, etc)
Coverage	• Materials • Workmanship • Design
Scope	• Define defect • Incorrect storage/maintenance/operation • Wear and tear • Defects not notified promptly • Unauthorised modifications
Buyer obligation	• Mitigate effect • Cease usage
Seller obligation	• Replace • Repair

This checklist is an example of how a little thought applied to an area of potential liability can produce a range of limitations, some or all of which might be secured in negotiation.

10 Risks, liabilities and indemnities (a background feature)

A purist might argue that it is quite wrong to categorise this topic as a background feature. Risks, liabilities and indemnities go back to the very core of a contract and yet many companies pay scant attention to these vital components.

In fact this section heading could be reduced to the single word 'risk'. It is a basic philosophy of contract law that one function of the contract is to allocate risks between the parties. With risks allocated, the ostensible liability if a risk has materialised is readily apparent. An indemnity is simply one method of trans-

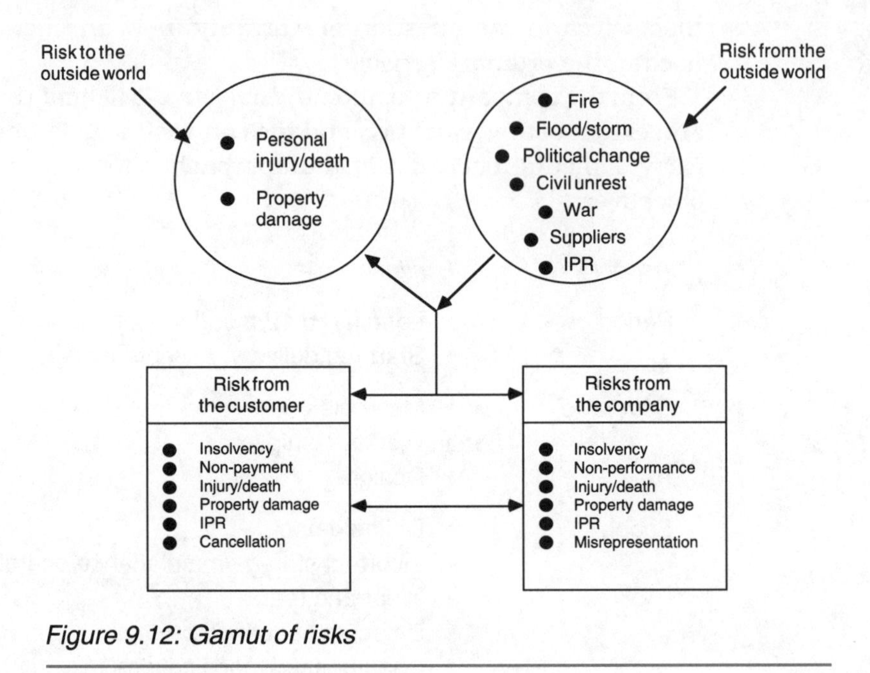

Figure 9.12: Gamut of risks

ferring a risk from the party who would seemingly carry the risk to the other party.

For example, goods may be at the seller's risk (ie in respect of loss or damage) until the buyer has accepted them, but if the buyer is in possession of the goods prior to acceptance then he may be willing to indemnify the seller against loss or damage occurring while he, the buyer, has such possession. Thus the risk is transferred from seller to buyer.

Indeed the interrelated topics of transfer of property, transfer of risk (of loss or damage), delivery, acceptance, rejection and termination for breach are one particular major area within the generic heading of risk to which the contract negotiator should pay close attention.

So the fundamental rule is that at the time of contract negotiation all risks should be identified and allocated between the parties. Before the contract is agreed the company must be assured that the price includes allowances for its risks. After the contract is placed the company should exercise positive risk management to reduce and eliminate the chances of the risks materialising. However, it is the task of the contract negotiator consciously to address the gamut of risks (Figure 9.12) in negotiation planning and where appropriate in discussion with the customer.

Seeking to avoid liability for personal injury or death is not legal. However, other acts of negligence can be excluded by contract if reasonable. *Force majeure* provisions can provide relief from risks introduced from the outside world. Letters of credit or payment bonds or guarantees can protect against insolvency or intentional non-payment. Liquidated damages limits liability for late performance. IPR indemnities allocate the risk. These are examples of where the contract negotiator should aim to include contract provisions that limit the company's exposure to risk.

CHAPTER 10

Negotiating variations, claims and disputes

1 Introduction

This book is about successful contract negotiation. In the introductory passages it was explained that the contract negotiator can expect to be involved in a whole process which includes not only the 'upfront' negotiations to secure the contract but also negotiations to resolve issues that have arisen because or out of the contract. For the most part the various philosophies, strategies, tactics and techniques proposed have not sought or needed to differentiate between a negotiation for a new contract and a negotiation to resolve a post-contract issue. A negotiation is a negotiation and the rules regarding preparation, planning, preservation of the relationship and so on all apply regardless of the purpose of the negotiation.

It is nevertheless the case that a distinction could and should be made between these two principal categories and it is the purpose of this chapter to highlight the matters which are particular to the post-contract phase. The terminology of the lawyers tends to confuse here as the strict meaning of a completed contract is that a contract has been made with executory performance (ie in the future). The layman interprets a completed contract as a contract with executed (ie finished and in the past) performance. Therefore to be clear, the expression 'post-contract phase' is used to describe the period after the contract is made. Post-contract issues can arise and/or be settled both during the period in which the work is being done and after it is finished.

2 Source of post-contract issues

Post-contract issues requiring negotiated settlements can generally be categorised between variations, claims and disputes (Figure 10.1).

'Variations' means variations to the contract to which the parties mutually and contentedly agree. This heading does not include changes which are forced upon one or both parties by circumstances beyond their control or by one party through tactics and clever manoeuvring, forcing the other to accept a change. The freedom-of-contract principle allows the parties to prescribe within the contract a right of the customer unilaterally to vary the requirements of the contract. Similarly, the contract may allow the company to vary unilaterally the work which it willl tender for performance.

Not surprisingly, it is more usual for the contract to allow the buyer the right to vary the work than it is the supplier. This is readily understood, as the motives of the two in entering into the contract are quite different. The supplier wants to do work (within reason, any work) to earn money. The buyer places the order to fulfil a specific need. If the need changes even as the work is in hand, he must have the ability to instruct the seller to vary the work so as not to be left with an unusable result.

On the other hand, if the seller can foresee circumstances in which he would have difficulty performing the work exactly and

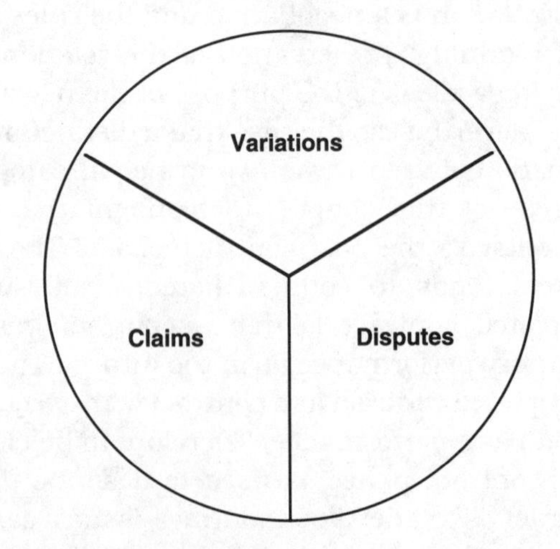

Figure 10.1: Post-contract issues

precisely according to contract, then it may be reasonable and sensible for the contract to allow him some leeway in what is acceptable. This concept is fraught with danger for both sides. The dangers will be addressed further in this chapter.

Although words such as 'unilateral' and 'instruct' have been used, the rights to which these words refer will have been embodied in the contract which the parties agreed and hence each has signalled its willingness to be bound by such arrangements to cover variations.

'Claims' means claims which the parties may make against each other in respect of a failure of some sort. Each may fail in some duty to the other party. Duties arise under the contract, under the law and under statute. The cause of the failure may be the failed party's own failure, or it may be as the result of the other party's action/inaction or as a result of some intervening external agency or circumstance.

To the extent that the parties can foresee circumstances of possible failure or other events for which one side should be entitled to a remedy at the expense of the other (for example, where the customer has a contractual right to terminate the contract for his convenience – the ultimate 'variation'), then the parties can choose to make a contractual provision or they may choose to leave the contract silent.

The advantage of a contractual provision is that, provided it properly covers the circumstance which actually arose, it is difficult for either party to dispute the contractual consequences of the circumstance. The disadvantages of contractual provisions is that, during the contract negotiations, the parties set themselves on a path of trying to imagine everything that could possibly go wrong together with all the permutations and combinations of events that might occur. While it is right and proper for the contract to provide for problems as well as success in the parties' intentions, this process can become too time consuming, costly and negative. The pragmatic negotiators take the process to a sensible level only.

The disadvantage of not having a contractual provision is that, if something happens which prompts one party to think he may have a claim against the other, then he must find some legal or statutory premise upon which to base his claim (claims which are not substantiated both on fact and upon some proper foundation will be treated with the contempt they deserve). This makes life more difficult for himself and makes rebutting the claim easier for the other side. Relying on a contractual right is usually easier than relying upon a non-contractual one. This is not to say that contractual and non-contractual claims are mutually exclusive.

The existence of a contractual right does not necessarily preclude reliance upon a general legal right, although the former may negate or condition the latter depending upon the nature of the right and the wording of the contract. In other words, whenever a claim is to be made the claimant should examine all the possible bases for claim; however, he should naturally examine the contract carefully as some contractual provisions are specifically drafted to amplify, expand, condition or negate (eg an express exclusion of the statutory right to goods of merchantable quality) non-contractual duties. A claim made against one party may be accepted without question and met in full by the other party. This is a most unlikely event. Therefore most claims will be met with a rebuttal. Such situations can quickly escalate into disputes. Once a dispute has escalated beyond the point of negotiability the parties have a number of choices. These will be covered later in this chapter.

Within the contract the parties may elect to define a class or classes of disagreements which are automatically treated as disputes for which there may be prescribed procedures for resolution. The advantage of prescribing procedures is that there is then a certain method for attempts at resolution. The disadvantage is that this then ties the hands of the parties. This may suit the side possessing the weakest negotiating strengths. The side with negotiation strength may much prefer the freedom and flexibility to settle all disputes in whatever manner seems appropriate at the time. In any event the parties would be free if it suits them both to set aside any contractual provisions for disputes and settle upon any basis (provided it is lawful) that they care to choose.

3 Variations

Variations are those changes to which the parties are happy to agree. An instruction from one side to the other to vary the contract can be referred to as a variation order. A suggested variation can be referred to as a change proposal. There are seven things to consider:

1. Non-contractual changes.
2. Contractual provisions.
3. Features subject to change.
4. Initiation of change.
5. Buyer changes.
6. Supplier changes.
7. Negotiation of change.

Variations have been defined as changes to which the parties agree under an arrangement prescribed in the contract. Such arrangements may give one or both sides a unilateral right to vary the contract. However, it should not be thought that the parties are precluded from agreeing to a change if such arrangements are absent from the contract. The parties are free to propose and agree any changes that they like. The important distinction of these non-contractual (the expression 'non-contractual' is used in the sense of something not expressly included in the contract) variations is that neither side has a unilateral right to change anything. It is sometimes thought (and customers sometimes behave) as though the customer always has an automatic right to change things. This is not the case.

In negotiating a contract which is to include express provisions for variations, it is essential that both sides aim to have a comprehensive statement of the arrangements. These should include pro forma paperwork which must be completed and authorised by the relevant party or parties in order for a change to be effective. The arrangements must set down any requirements for recording and monitoring the changes.

Serious thought should be given to deciding which of the features of the contract are to be subject to these change mechanisms. The principal features (Figure 10.2) of any contract are naturally interrelated and some must alter as a consequence of others being varied.

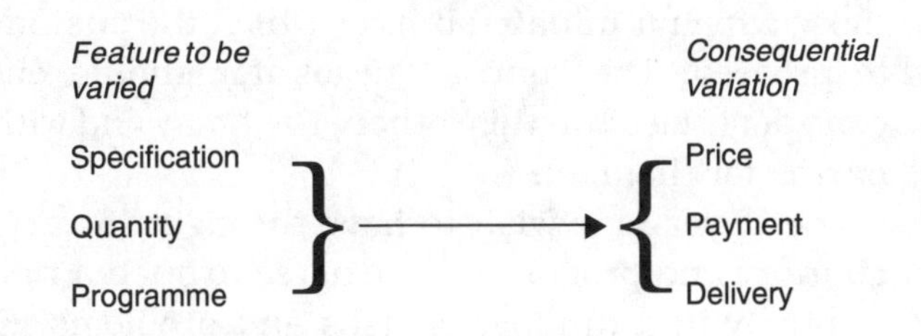

Figure 10.2: Features subject to change

In Figure 10.2 'specification' is used to mean any definition of the products or work to be supplied, including quality. 'Quantity' is used to mean any description regarding magnitude or volume of work. 'Programme' means any description regarding the time period over which the work is desired to be done. 'Price' and 'payment' are self-explanatory. 'Delivery' means any statement as to a contractual time period for performance.

Note that it is not usual and would be quite inappropriate for one side to have the unilateral right to vary other important features of the contract, such as allocation of risks and liabilities or the ownership of or rights in any intellectual property. However, other relatively minor features such as destination, mode of transport and packaging standards may well be things which are subject to the change arrangements. For these purposes such things can be considered part of the specification.

The text will return shortly to the question of which features are subject to change by customer and company and the effect of consequential changes. First though, the question of who initiates and who pays for the change ought to be considered. If there is to be a change which has a consequential cost impact then the contract should prescribe to whom the cost liability will fall. However, there can also be a significant cost involved in preparing the paperwork that describes a proposed substantial change to the contract. For example, where the technical requirements of the contract are subject to a possible major redesign, the cost of preparing detailed specifications and plans can be great. These proposal preparation costs must be allocated to one of the parties and the contract should state which party.

The parties are free to choose on this point. Perhaps one side or the other should always pay. Perhaps the customer should always pay proposal preparation costs for any change which is implemented plus those which he initiated but with which he decided not to proceed. Perhaps the company should pay for those which it initiated but for which the customer elected not to proceed. The contract negotiator should ensure that the contract is clear on this, otherwise it may end with the company paying for them all.

The buyer may wish to have the right to vary specification, quantity and programme. To agree to such a right exposes the company to a number of risks and problems. Essentially the company does not want to find itself in a position of being contractually required to do something which it physically cannot do or for commercial reasons may not want to do. For example, a customer-initiated change to reduce the quantity to 20 per cent may frustrate the company's plans to use the contract as a platform from which to expand its operations. A customer-initiated change which aims to reduce the programme by six months may simply be physically impossible for the company to achieve.

Therefore to agree to the customer having the right to demand change proposals and the right to instruct that variations are implemented, can put the company in a commercially undesirable position where even failing to put forward a detailed change proposal may be a breach of contract. The contract negotiator should be aware of these risks when negotiating the contract in the first place. Perhaps the customer's right to vary the quantity should be limited to –5 per cent +100 per cent; perhaps no right should be granted to vary the programme; perhaps variation rights should be limited to specification alone.

The best safeguard is for the contract to prescribe that a variation order is only effective once it has been fully negotiated and agreed. Thus without agreement (which can always be frustrated or delayed) the variation is ineffective. The customer will have a different objective (Figure 10.3).

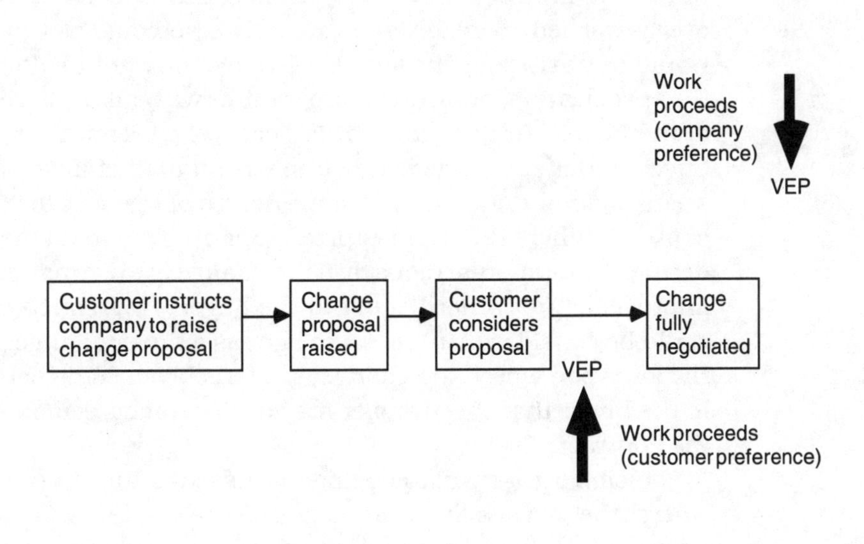

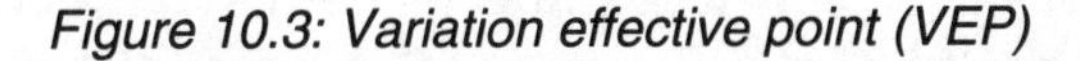
Figure 10.3: Variation effective point (VEP)

The customer would like the ability to instruct the company to proceed with the change and leave price, payment and other consequential adjustments to be sorted out later. He may wish to give such an instruction subject to some overall limit on his financial liability so that he knows in advance the maximum extent to which the price can change. In some instances, expediency may demand that the change must be implemented before all of the aspects have been negotiated. The contract negotiator should nevertheless aim to have a contract provision that states that full agreement is a prerequisite to proceeding. This does not preclude going ahead without full agreement but strengthens the company's negotiating position. Going ahead without price agreement but subject to a financial maximum leaves the company with an additional risk which should be considered carefully.

Generally, leaving the price to be agreed later does not suit the company because, if the customer has both the work and the money, the company is hardly in a good negotiating position.

Because the application to which the buyer will put the results of the contract may change during the currency of the contract, it is not unreasonable within certain sensible constraints for the buyer to have the right to vary the requirements of the contract. Provided the buyer is obliged to renegotiate the price, payment terms and time period for performance, the seller should not be overly worried. Sensibly the exact obverse could not apply. It would be absurd for the supplier to have the right to alter freely the specification, quantity or programme without the agreement of the buyer. To this extent it is perhaps misleading to talk of buyer-initiated changes and supplier-initiated changes as this seems to impute to each the same degree of freedom to vary the contract. Where the supplier proposes a change which the buyer decides to adopt – particularly if the change is to introduce some improvement or other benefit to the buyer – then such change could be considered in the same light as a buyer change. It is in the situation where the change is ostensibly of some detriment to the buyer that the supplier may desire some freedom to vary the contract.

Remember that what is being discussed is the circumstance where the parties have agreed that one side can vary the contract. Variations forced upon one or both parties – for example, late delivery due to extraneous events – are considered later under the heading of claims. So perhaps it might be reasonable in a contract for a very large quantity of items for the supplier to be allowed to deliver to within ± 5 per cent of the quantity specified and so effectively to vary the contract. On the other hand, a contract which permits the supplier to propose that deliveries are allowed to a lower specification – for example, because particular components have become more difficult to procure in the necessary time frame, or because test results have marginally deteriorated – has an implicit risk to the supplier. Of course the buyer has the freedom to accept goods to a reduced specification and, whether or not the contract prescribes it, to negotiate a price reduction or other benefit from the supplier. However, the contract negotiator should be careful about the wording both of the contract and of the change proposal. This is because, for the supplier to state that he cannot fully meet the requirements of the contract, is to expose himself to an allegation of anticipatory breach giving, 'in extremis', the buyer the right to terminate the contract: a most undesirable result of attempting to exercise a right to vary the contract!

Where a variation is to go ahead it is vital that the negotiation is built upon something solid. The solid base should be the detailed contract change proposal (CCP) (Figure 10.4).

The CCP should give comprehensive details of all the features of the contract which will be varied. It should carry signatures of both proposer and authoriser. From the company's point of view the CCP is just another form of quotation or offer of contract and it must be treated as such in terms of thoroughness of preparation and formal approval within the company. It should be clear that the customer's authorising signature signifies that the whole CCP is approved and not just that the variation in the work is to be implemented.

The validity of the CCP must be clearly stated. A distinction is necessary between price validity and what might be called technical validity. The price validity may depend upon, for example, proximity to the company's financial year end, to inflation forecasts or to the validity of supplier prices. Technical validity may depend, for example, upon the availability of capacity or of resources or upon the facility with which the change could be introduced with minimal disruption. Frequently price and technical validities do not happily coincide and so the nearer of the two should be specified.

The CCP should also specify any consequential changes to other related contracts that may be affected. This helps both sides not to forget the complete picture.

1. Contract No: A98/63
2. Description: Widget redesign
3. CCP Serial Number: 43
4. CCP Date: 28 February
5. CCP Validity: 2 months
6. CCP Description: To replace the P14 interface link with fibre-optic cable. See attached detailed explanation.
7. Effect on Price:

Item affected	From	By	To
1	£100,000	£20,000	£120,000
2	£400 each	£50 each	£450 each
3	£16,000	No change	£16,000

8. Effect on Time:
   Item 1: Completion delayed 2 months
   Item 2: Deliveries delayed 6 weeks
   Item 3: No change
9. Effect on Anything Else
   a) The following documents will be updated if the CCP is approved:
      Design Plan
      Technical Specification
      Production Drawings
   b) 600 Units delivered under contract A98/25 will require modification to ensure commonality of spares – budgetary estimate £20,000
10. Signatures
    Proposed: .... Authorised: ....

Figure 10.4: Contract change proposal

Through force of circumstance the negotiation of the price variation may be left until the contract is nearly completed or until after it is completed; such negotiations are dealt with later in this chapter under the heading of claims. If negotiations are conducted while the contract is under way, the negotiator has a number of tactics from which to choose to assist him in prosecuting the negotiations expediently and successfully:

Tactic 1: Submit the CCP at the last possible minute.
Tactic 2: Submit the CCPs in large batches.
Tactic 3: Submit excessive detail.

Tactic 1 is designed to put the customer in the position where he must approve the CCP before its technical validity time expires, thus leaving him insufficient time to interrogate adequately and thoroughly the technical justification for the change or to consider the proposed price adjustment. Tactic 2 helps to camouflage particular CCPs where the technical justification is weak or perhaps where it is not clear where liability lies, if it is a problem that the CCP intends to solve. The purpose of Tactic 3 is to overwhelm the customer with so much detail that time does not permit a proper scrutiny.

There is a fundamental question which the company must consider with regard to variations. On the one hand, variations cause disruption and delay possibly to more than just the contract to which the variations ostensibly relate. This is bad news for business. On the other hand, variations are a source of additional work, more income and improved profit opportunities. The contract which is won in fierce competition may have low margin levels, but once the contract is placed the company enjoys a captive customer and hence there is an opportunity through successful negotiation of variations to grow the contract and improve the margins.

If the nature of the business is such that the disruption of accommodating variations outweighs the possible benefits of contract growth and potential improvement of margins, the company should follow a strategy that aims to minimise or avoid change. If the obverse applies, then a conscious strategy should be followed to maximise and exploit change. The strategies can be compared (Figure 10.5).

The key point is that a decision should consciously be made to aim for either minimum or maximum change and to develop a particular strategy accordingly. If the strategy is one of maxim-

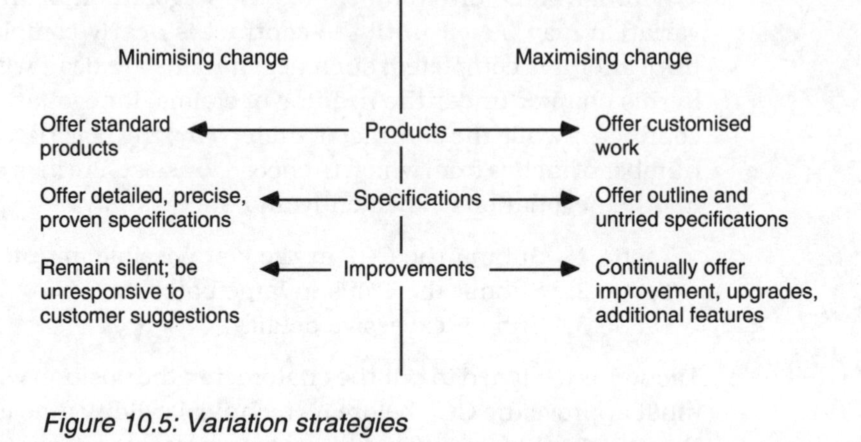

Figure 10.5: Variation strategies

ising change, a number of tactics are available to persuade the customer to proceed:

Tactic 1	Performance benefits	'Sell' the customer on the idea of real benefits to be had in the result of the contract.
Tactic 2	Frustration of purpose	Convince the customer that without the changes he will never really achieve his original purpose.
Tactic 3	Problem solving	Show the customer that there are inherent difficulties in completing the work for which variations would ease the situation.
Tactic 4	Delay	Indicate or imply that without particular variations the work is bound to finish late.
Tactic 5	Stoppage	Indicate or imply that without particular variations the work may stop altogether.

These are shown in ascending order of difficulty of execution. In particular Tactics 3, 4 and 5 must be handled very carefully so that the customer is not able to argue successfully that the company is responsible and financially liable for implementing the changes.

4 Claims

Claims resulting from the contract can be made by either party, each against the other. Each claim can be based upon a contractual, statutory or legal foundation. This part of the book will look first at claims against the company and second at claims against the customer. Finally, claims by or against third parties will be considered.

Claims against the company can be categorised under the three headings of contractual, statutory and legal:

Basis	*Examples*
• Contractual	• Liquidated damages • Price reduction for company-initiated variations • Damages following contractual termination for breach • Express warranties
• Statutory	• Implied undertakings under Sale of Goods legislation (eg merchantability) • Duties regarding product safety under Consumer Protection legislation
• Legal	• Failure in duty of care • Failure in terms implied into the contract • Damages following termination for breach

Before examining these examples in detail, the golden rules of handling a claim should be delineated:

Rule 1	Never admit a claim.
Rule 2	Rebut any claim received.
Rule 3	Make a counterclaim.
Rule 4	Muster all the defences.
Rule 5	Take legal advice.
Rule 6	Consider a financial provision.
Rule 7	Develop a negotiation plan.
Rule 8	Make a financial settlement as a last resort.
Rule 9	Only ever settle without admission or prejudice.
Rule 10	Delay.

The financial magnitude of the claim, its foundation, its substance and considerations regarding the relationship with the customer are all influences in deciding which of these rules should be adhered to on a case-by-case basis. A trivial monetary claim may be worth accepting without a fuss as the price for continued good customer relations.

Rule 1 is most important. The first hurdle for any claimant is to get the claimee to acknowledge that a claim is valid. Once the claimee has acknowledged validity of the claim, the claimant has won half the battle and all that is left is to extract a settlement. Thus when a claim is received, a written response should not say 'We are in receipt of your claim dated ...' which implies acceptance of its validity, but should say 'We are in receipt of your letter dated ...' which is a non-committal opening that leads into a rebuttal of the claim (Rule 2). In the early stages a rebuttal can be a simple statement refuting the claim. If the claim is not that seriously made, a simple rebuttal may make it go away. If it is seriously made, then revealing the defences against the claim too early can undermine the company's negotiating position.

Making a counterclaim (Rule 3) is always a good tactic. Although it is very likely to be seen by the customer as being no more than a tactic, this should not dissuade the negotiator from making such a counterclaim and, once made, he and the company must be prepared to see it through as a real opportunity. Again the choice of language and approach requires care. The company should not write to say 'We are in receipt of your letter dated 13 April and hereby make a counterclaim of ...' as this carries the implication that the customer's claim is admitted and links claim to counterclaim, which is not ideal. The counterclaim should be made not as a counterclaim 'per se' but as a claim in its own right and as such communicated separately to the customer and in a manner independent of the customer's claim.

Rule 4 says that all possible defences must be mustered. These include real, irrelevant and entirely spurious defences. There is no law in contract negotiation that demands that proper claims can only be met with sound defences. Anything that dissuades the other side from pressing its claim is legitimate (provided it is lawful – see Chapter 2). It is of no concern to the company that the customer backs down for reasons which are not legally valid, as will be seen when liquidated damages are addressed a little further on in this chapter. Thus it is a task of the contract negotiator to exercise the maximum imagination in mustering all the defences.

Taking legal advice (Rule 5) is an option which should be considered in some circumstances. While one theme of this book is that the expert contract negotiator is competent to deal with all matters which are susceptible to negotiated conclusions, it must be recognised that occasionally there will be a danger of matters escalating to the point of litigation. Where this is a possibility it is very important that no one says or does anything which may later prejudice the company's position in court. Also, while it is true that for contractual claims the company and customer negotiators are best qualified to settle issues arising under the contract, it is as well to have expert advice to hand if the customer bases his claim upon statutory or general legal reasons. Although the claim may never proceed to litigation, it is a bonus for the negotiator to know the strengths or weaknesses of the position and to utilise the legal arguments in his favour in any negotiation with the customer which may ensue.

Once a claim has been received, serious thought should be given to the prospects of the customer succeeding wholly or partially with it. If there is any possibility of money changing hands it is as well to make a prudent provision (Rule 6) in the books of account. Such a provision should ideally be made against the possibility of a claim arising wherever such a possibility can be foreseen. It is far better for the contract negotiator to seek approval to settle a claim, knowing that a provision exists, rather than to ask for the money, knowing that none has been set aside. After all, negotiation and settlement of a claim for which provision has been made presents a profit opportunity. If the claim can be settled below the level of the provision, the balance can be released to the profit and loss account.

Without reiterating the detail given in Chapter 3, it is wise to restate the principle that a negotiation plan should be developed (Rule 7) to assist in the negotiation of the claim.

Wherever the customer is looking for recompense against some failure of the company, one should not jump to the conclusion that money is the only remedy. Rule 8 says that a financial settlement should be a last resort. There are other options (Figure 10.6) which should be preferred.

1st preference	Persuade customer to drop.	Ideal
2nd preference	Offer a future favour.	↓
3rd preference	Offer alternative work.	↓
4th preference	Offer money.	Last resort

Figure 10.6: Claim tactics

If a claim is to be settled financially and by negotiation then the settlement must always be less than the amount of the claim. The customer must recognise that if he wishes to 'settle out of court', the amount must necessarily be less than his initial aspiration. However, it is usually far more preferable to offer alternative or additional goods or work rather than money, as this continues to tie the customer to the company. Even better is to offer some future favour which, in the worst case, allows for proper financial planning and provisioning, but in the best case will be forgotten or overtaken by events. Also it is possible to exaggerate the value of some benefit or favour which sits out in the future.

Rule 9 says that any settlement should only ever be made on a without-admission-or-prejudice basis. To his last breath the negotiator should deny the claim and any actual settlement should be recorded in such a way that the claim or liability is not seen to have been admitted, that no precedent has been set and that there shall be no prejudice to the company or to any future negotiations.

If all else fails, the company can always seek to delay (Rule 10) discussing the claim with the customer. As time goes by the customer may lose interest or appetite for a debate. He may be worn down by persistent rebuttal of the claim, by unhelpful and long-drawn-out discussion with the company. With a bit of luck the claim may become statute debarred.

Returning to the categories of claims against the company (p. 199), the first basis is contractual. That is, the customer can refer to a particular clause of the contract and state that in accordance with that clause he hereby makes the following claim against the company. Liquidated damages provides an example of the imagination which the contract negotiator can use to muster defences:

Defence	Legally valid
1. Customer did not actually suffer from any damage.	No
2. Clause is void because it is constructed as a penalty.	Possibly
3. Application of the clause is unfair.	No
4. The amount claimed is unreasonable.	No (subject to 2)
5. The delay was the customer's fault.	Possibly
6. The delay was somebody else's fault.	Possibly
7. The claim is improper.	No
8. The clause has been overtaken by events.	No
9. Custom and practice precludes the claim.	No

This shows nine possible defences of a claim for liquidated damages. Any one of them may persuade the customer to drop the claim and yet none is legally watertight. Defence 2 is a possibility. If the amount prescribed is obviously not a reasonable pre-estimate of the customer's likely financial damage in the event of delay, the clause may be void. Defences 5 and 6 may operate if there is an excusable delay or *force majeure* clause which relieves the company if delay is caused by circumstances beyond its control, including acts or omissions of the customer or of third parties. Nevertheless, knowledge of the weaknesses of some of the arguments should not deter the contract negotiator from deploying them. It is up to the negotiator to try anything that may dissuade the customer. It is up to the customer to look after his own interests.

Similarly with the other examples of contractual claims. If company-initiated variations (essentially to allow contract performance at a reduced or degraded quality, facility or specification) have not been resolved during the currency of the contract, they will manifest themselves as customer claims. In the extreme circumstance of the contract being terminated for breach under express conditions that also allow a claim for damage, such damages would be the subject of a claim. Goods returned under express warranties are the subject of claims, although perhaps not always recognised as such. Whatever the nature of the contractual claim the ten golden rules (p. 199) apply – with the qualification regarding customer relationships.

Naturally the ten golden rules also apply to any claim which is made on statutory or legal grounds. However, greater care is needed in these cases both for the reasons of not damaging the position in the event of litigation and because the grounds are not so obvious. Anybody can read the contract and, if the language is good, the rights and liabilities of the two sides are readily ascertainable. Statute or other law is more of a minefield. It has already been said that the injured buyer is more keen to rely upon a contractual provision than a legal right. Similarly the seller should find it easier to defeat a general claim rather than one based upon a specific condition of the contract.

Turning to the subject of company claims against the customer, these too can be categorised under the headings of contractual, statutory and legal:

Basis	*Examples*
• Contractual	• Unsettled customer-initiated changes. • Delay in payment. • Damages for breach.
• Statutory	• Implied obligations under Sale of Goods legislation (eg duty to accept delivery).
• Legal	• Infringement of intellectual property rights.

Again, sensitivity over customer relations may dictate to what extent claims are made or pressed against the customer. As before, the golden rules for making a claim should be described before these examples are examined:

Rule 1	Get the customer to admit the claim.
Rule 2	Do not give up.
Rule 3	Rebut counterclaims.
Rule 4	Muster all the arguments.

Rule 5 Take legal advice.
Rule 6 Be outrageous.
Rule 7 Develop a negotiation plan.
Rule 8 Prepare the evidence.
Rule 9 Do not forget mitigation/insurance.
Rule 10 Frustrate attempts at delay.

Not surprisingly, the majority of these rules are the exact obverse of the golden rules for defending a claim. Rules 6, 8 and 9 are different. Rule 6 is that the claim should be 'outrageous' in the sense that there is rarely the opportunity to increase the value of the claim once it has been made. Therefore the objective is to aim high in the first place. Rule 8 requires that evidence to support the claim is prepared. The lack of any evidence should not deter the contract negotiator from making his claim but where supporting evidence does exist it should be prepared and held in readiness for the negotiation. Finally, Rule 9 is a warning. In law any injured party is obliged to mitigate his loss. Normal prudence demands the taking of insurance against foreseeable risks arising. Thus the company must not automatically assume that a huge financial settlement can be extracted from the customer in circumstances where the company could have mitigated its loss or insured against the risk.

The negotiation plan for making a claim should embrace the timing of notifying and making the claim. Generally it is as well to notify the customer of a potential claim as and when the event occurs to which the claim will relate. The making of the claim in precise monetary terms can wait until the time is right. Consideration should also be given to the form of settlement desired. The customer will also prefer not to part with money and it may be that some other benefit (a new order, the dropping of some other claim) may be an acceptable conclusion.

The examples of claims against the customer are similar in character to the examples of claims against the company, and to that extent further explanation is unnecessary. However, the examples serve to demonstrate two interesting principles. First, it is often assumed that the customer's only duty is to pay the contract price. The examples show that the customer can carry many more obligations than that. Second, some duties are found in more than one category. For example, if the customer fails to pay he may well be in breach of contract, of a statutory duty and of the common law of contract. Hence the contract negotiator should not limit himself to claiming purely on a contractual basis.

Mention should be made of two particular types of claim which are sometimes referred to. These are the extra-contractual and 'ex gratia' claims. 'Extra-contractual claim' as an expression is used to describe claims which arise because of the contract but for which there is no express contractual provision. For example, an action of the customer which delays the company's performance and thereby increases its cost may not give rise to a formal contractual claim but the customer may consider it appropriate to meet such a claim. 'Ex gratia' claims are those which arise even where there is no contract. For example, a customer who puts a company to the cost of tendering for a contract and then decides not to proceed may consider it appropriate to reimburse the company's tendering costs. In both examples there is no ostensible contractual basis for claim and thus both varieties can be referred to as 'ex gratia'. However, the distinction described between an extra-contractual claim (where there is a contract) and 'ex gratia' claim (where there is no contract) is a helpful convenience.

Attention can now be given to third party claims. Third parties can be divided into those who are obvious and those who are not obvious (Figure 10.7).

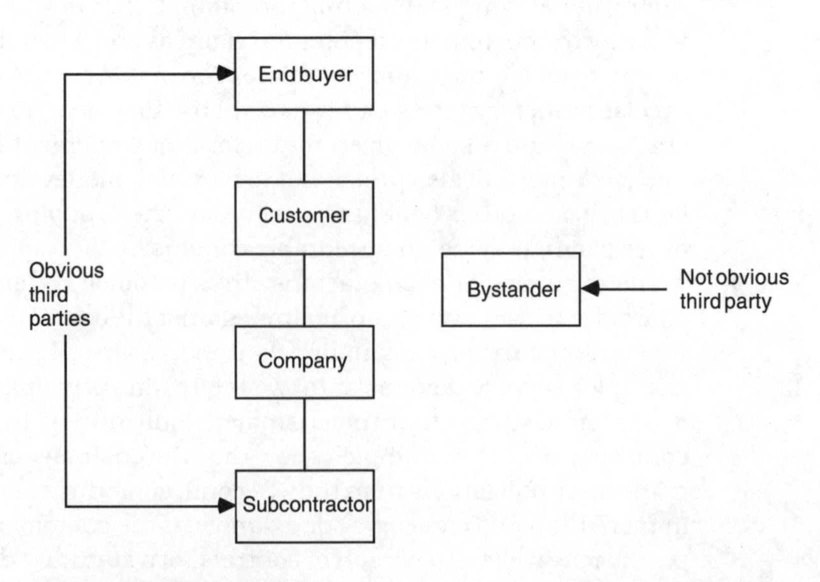

Figure 10.7: Third parties

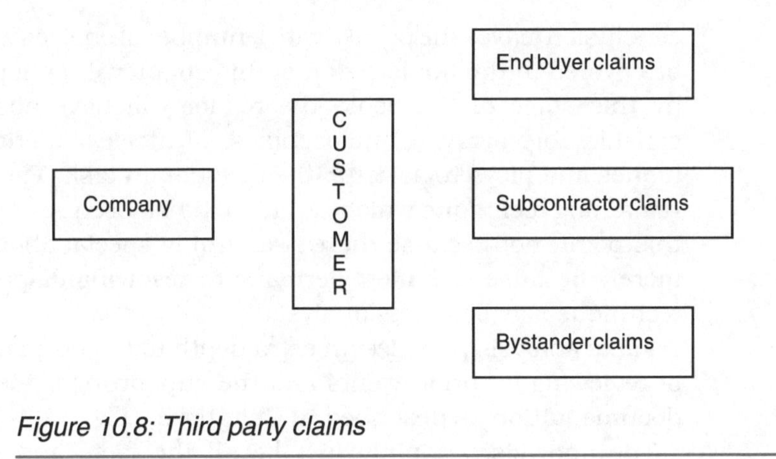

Figure 10.8: Third party claims

Generally speaking, the privity-of-contract principle excludes any obvious third parties from taking legal action against one or both of the parties to the contract. However, it is possible for the customer to argue the existence of a collateral contract between himself and a subcontractor. Fiduciary obligations can override the general principle and all third parties have a right of action in tort against any other party. It is not the purpose of this book to explore this complex field, but rather to offer practical advice to the contract negotiator, the first component of which is that the ten golden rules (p. 199) for defending a claim apply. The second component is to suggest that a decision needs to be made regarding the relative positions of company and customer to each other with regard to third party claims. It is not difficult to see the juxtaposition which the company should prefer (Figure 10.8).

The aim should be to hide behind the customer. Claims from an end buyer either directly to the company or through the customer should be bounced back to the customer. Claims from subcontractors should only ever be entertained on the condition that the subcontractor agrees that the company is liable only to the extent that the liability can be passed on to the customer. All claims from bystanders should be directed to the customer.

5 Disputes

It is the policy of most companies to settle disputes by negotiation. It is the task of the contract negotiator to execute the policy. Failure to negotiate at all or failure to take the negotiation to a conclusion leaves the parties with a number of choices which will be covered in the final section of this chapter. It is hoped that, by this stage of the book, the reader will have absorbed a considerable array of philosophies, strategies, tactics, techniques and ploys to assist in the negotiation task. There is one remaining technique which can help. It has been reserved until this point, not because there is anything special about it, but merely because it is most germane to resolving disputes. The technique is called facts analysis.

Facts analysis provides an extra depth to the normal process of reviewing all prior events and the supporting evidence and documentation as described in Chapter 5.

The analysis is simply to take all the facts and critically examine them to see if, on balance, particular facts support one side's position better than the other. This sounds obvious, but in practice and in the heat of the moment it is all too easy to jump to the conclusion that a particular event or piece of correspondence supports the company's case when in fact it has or could have completely the opposite effect. One approach is to rehearse the negotiation with one of the negotiation team – or just a negotiation-experienced colleague – taking the part of the customer and arguing the customer's position from the same set of facts.

This facts analysis provides an objective assessment of the benefits of citing particular facts and of the order in which it is best to use them.

6 Mediation, conciliation, assisted dispute resolution (ADR), arbitration and litigation

This book has aimed to assist in learning the skills of contract negotiation. It is appropriate to touch briefly upon the options available if negotiation is not preferred or if negotiation fails. There are five options (Figure 10.9).

In mediation the mediator is not allowed to suggest solutions but merely looks for common ground and encourages the parties to carry on talking. In conciliation the conciliator is allowed to act as a catalyst bringing the two sides together and proposing compromises. Assisted dispute resolution (ADR) brings the parties together and acts out their cases following legal principles but allowing the parties to arrive at their own solution. Arbitration has the benefit, as with the previous three options,

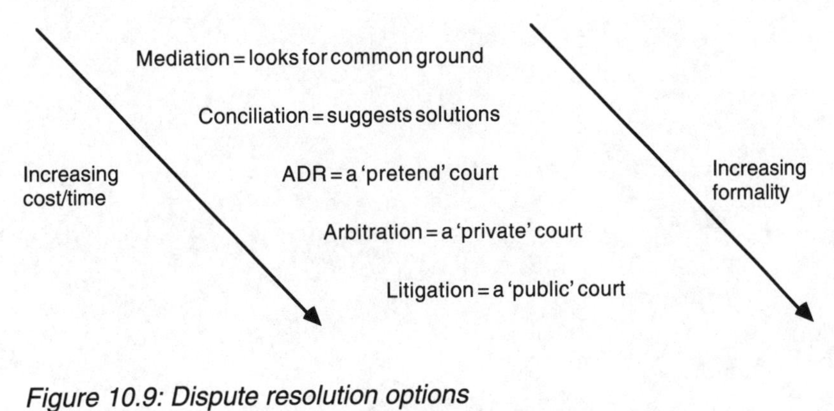

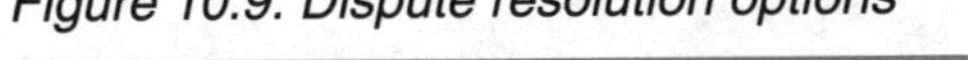

Figure 10.9: Dispute resolution options

that the outcome is kept private; it too follows a legal process but the result determined by the arbitrators is binding upon both parties. The final step into litigation has the same effect but of course the result is in the public domain which may not suit the interests of the parties.

Afterword

I would like to conclude this book with a few words on two important aspects of negotiation to which I have given little attention within the text.

In developing the text and the associated diagrams I have intentionally set out to provide an analysis of contract negotiation that goes into some considerable depth. This I believe to be warranted on the basis that the subject is intrinsically worthy of detailed examination, but also because I have found some books superficial in their treatment of an activity which can be underestimated in terms of its importance to commercial success.

However, the depth of treatment given here can appear perhaps to create two disadvantages in so far as the reader is concerned. The first of these is that an impression may have been given that there is a daunting weight of analysis to be done for every negotiation and that only a Shakespearian actor could possibly remember the lines and achieve the performance necessary to get the deal done. This is not the case. For the novice negotiator, learning just one or two of the ploys will make a difference. For the more advanced negotiator the extra depth will provide an additional dimension to his skill. However, there is one factor which will inevitably be more beneficial than any book: experience. The more experience is gained, the more natural and effective the negotiator becomes.

As experience is gained, the re-reading of this book will focus and crystallise the processes and interactions that negotiation involves within the reader's mind. Thus equipped, the individual's ability during a negotiation to stand back and say 'How am I doing? Where are they coming from? Where am I on my plan? What is my next tactic? How do I counter their next move?', etc, is much enhanced.

The second impression that may have been created is that the seriousness of purpose in negotiation and the weight of analysis condemns negotiation to the most serious-minded type of person. Without detracting for a second from the importance of successful contract negotiation, I must say that from the individual's perspective a main objective must be to have some fun. Negotiation has the excitement of the chase, conflict and conquest. There is the theatrical fun of role playing and emotion. There is the intellectual challenge equivalent to grand master chess. He who is not excited by the prospect of a negotiation will not achieve the best result. He who is fearful of the prospect will fail.

So for those who have gained something from this work, the final message is to learn by experience and to take negotiation seriously but have fun.